MENZIES
AT WAR

ANNE HENDERSON is deputy director of the Sydney Institute, which she has operated with her husband, Gerard Henderson, a well-known political commentator, since 1989. She also edits the *Sydney Papers Online* and co-edits the *Sydney Institute Quarterly*. Anne Henderson is the author of *From All Corners: Six Migrant Stories* (1993), *Educating Johannah: A Year in Year 12* (1995), *Mary MacKillop's Sisters: A Life Unveiled* (1997), *Getting Even: Women MPs on Life, Power and Politics* (1999), *The Killing of Sister Irene McCormack* (2002) and *An Angel in The Court: The Life of Major Joyce Harmer* (2005). Among her essays of note are 'Dad's wake' in *Fathers: In Writing* (1997) and the biographical chapter on Prime Minister Joseph Lyons for *Australian Prime Ministers* edited by Michelle Grattan (2000) and the United Kingdom's *New Dictionary of National Biography*. She was a contributing editor with Ross Fitzgerald of *Partners* (1999). In 2008 she published *Enid Lyons: Leading Lady to a Nation,* and in 2011 *Joseph Lyons: The People's Prime Minister.*

MENZIES AT WAR

ANNE HENDERSON

NEWSOUTH

A NewSouth book

Published by
NewSouth Publishing
University of New South Wales Press Ltd
University of New South Wales
Sydney NSW 2052
AUSTRALIA
newsouthpublishing.com

National Library of Australia Cataloguing-in-Publication entry
        Author: Henderson, Anne, 1949– author.
        Title: Menzies at war/Anne Henderson.
        ISBN: 9781742233796 (paperback)
             9781742246987 (ePDF)
             9781742241791 (ePub/Kindle)
        Notes: Includes index.
        Subjects: Menzies, Robert, Sir, 1894–1978.
             Prime ministers – Australia – Biography.
             Politicians — Australia – Biography.
             Australia – Politics and government – 20th century.
        Dewey Number: 994.04092

Design Josephine Pajor-Markus
Cover design Josephine Pajor-Markus
Fron cover image Robert Menzies gives a victory salute. c. 1954, Fairfax
FXJ98734.
Back cover image Mr Menzies in England, 1941-03. Mr Menzies and
Mr Winston Churchill at No. 10. Australian War Memorial 006414.
Printer Griffin

Produced with the assistance of Kooyong 200 Club

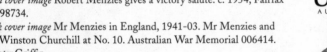

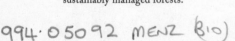

Contents

Foreword

Robert Menzies remains the giant of Australian politics. Even those who challenge the principles he espoused, and oppose the goals he pursued, concede that he was a giant though they wish he had been toppled. He was prime minister longer than any of the nation's leaders before or after. When he stepped down in 1966, he had led the Commonwealth of Australia for almost one-third of its history.

He had sustained or presided over a period of remarkable prosperity and national growth. Though he is now seen as British 'to the bootstraps', he was also a nationalist, and it was in his last year that East Asia suddenly replaced Britain as our main trading partner. He is widely seen as vigorously anti-Labor in his ideology, but he usually stood near the middle of the political compass; and even some of Labor's prized landmarks – the vigorous postwar immigration and the Snowy Mountains Scheme – were to gain infinitely more financial support from Menzies than from his Labor predecessors. The big influx of Italian, Greek and central European migrants happened largely during his reign. Though he was firmly protestant, a nonconformist moreover, he is said to have saved the Catholic schools from steep decline. In many areas of national life, especially higher education, he began to change the nation. Like nearly all leaders he had his serious setbacks and personal regrets, but his success is beyond real dispute.

And yet Menzies' first term in power, from 1939 to 1941, was not a foretaste of his later success. He was finally defeated by his own coalition colleagues in Canberra rather than by Labor. He was entitled to feel disillusioned, for he had devoted his mental talents, speaking skills and sheer energy to the nation's needs. Though he was only forty-six, he now heard the emphatic predictions that his political career was over. He refused to accept them. This is the theme of Anne Henderson's book, and through her research we gain a deeper understanding of the man and a detailed knowledge of the politics of those years so perilous for Australia. For many readers it will be an eye-opening book.

The death of JA Lyons had initially thrust Menzies into power in April 1939, only months before Hitler invaded Poland. Power, however, could easily slip from Menzies' hands. His own United Australia Party lacked a majority in the federal parliament and had to rely totally on the support of the Country Party, whose traditional leader Earle Page was now an opponent, almost a hater, of Menzies. France surrendered in the face of Hitler's swift invasion. And so, Australia and Canada (minor nations when weighed on the military scales) were Britain's two main allies at a time when it was fighting for its life.

Even in that crisis, a big minority of Australians did not fully support the war against Hitler. Sections of the Labor Party were hesitant or apathetic, though not its leader John Curtin. Several powerful trade unions even strenuously opposed Australia's participation in the war strenuously being fought in Europe, and sometimes disrupted the war effort. Petrol rationing, which was vital for the nation's defences, was opposed by some business groups. In March 1940, Menzies' party formed a working coalition with the Country Party, but their combined majority was sliced after the federal election that year.

In Europe and North Africa and the Atlantic Ocean, Hitler's successes continued. Menzies feared that Japan would seize its opportunity to enter the war, and so he had to divide Australia's overseas army into two – one defending the approaches to Egypt and the Suez Canal, and the other defending Malaya and the naval base at Singapore. By making exhausting air travel in the hope of

persuading Winston Churchill that Singapore must be strengthened, Menzies almost exhausted himself: at times he was 'desperately homesick'. While he strengthened the nation militarily more
than is now realised, he was on the verge of political humiliation
at home.

How Menzies finally fell in 1941, defeated by his own colleagues rather than by the electors, is lucidly analysed in this book.
How he emerged, bruised but determined, and eventually won the
federal election of 1949, brings Anne Henderson's narrative to its
close.

'Bob' Menzies had gained from adversity. He learnt new skills
in dealing with people, and improved those natural talents he
held in abundance. He learnt especially to oil the frail and noisy
machinery of a coalition, thus making the Liberal–Country Party
Coalition from 1949 onwards one of the most successful and dura-
ble in the history of modern democracy. Above all, he had remade
himself and his ideology – and that goes far to explaining his ultimate triumph.

Geoffrey Blainey

Introduction
The Menzies history wars

No figure has dominated Australia's political history like Sir Robert Menzies. His lengthy second term as prime minister alone qualifies him as one whose record is unlikely to be broken any time soon. Yet this record was not achieved easily. His development as a leader was a feat of endurance over time, albeit too often glossed over by historians. The man who emerged, for a second time, in 1949 as Australia's new prime minister had been years in the moulding. And these early years of professional growth and trial are crucial to an understanding of the man and leader Robert Menzies became, a man too often diminished in his early years as a party leader by the turbulence of the times and dysfunction in political parties on both sides. In the 1930s, Robert Menzies came to high office just as Australia's federal government was emerging gingerly as the true centre of power in a fledgling federation suffering the consequences of global depression and world war.

Scholars of the left, whose numbers in Australia dominate mainstream political history writing, have often sought to cut down in size such a conservative tall poppy as Robert Menzies, viewing him as remote, 'un-Australian' and ineffectual. His motives have been questioned, and his lack of radical vision derided. For all that, the legacy of Robert Menzies is increasingly being revisited; even political rivals have begun to concede that his judgment and strength of commitment to a harmonious, safe and prosperous Australia were ahead of their time. This applies to his first term as prime minister between April 1939 and August 1941, as well as his record-breaking period in the Lodge from December 1949 until January 1966.

The story that follows looks back on the trials and strengths of Robert Menzies in the years 1939–49, when he was variously prime minister, ordinary MP, leader of the opposition and founder of a new political party – the Liberal Party of Australia – which would take government and hold it through the 1950s and 1960s. It also examines the making of a leader for whom policy direction and a sense of mission were fundamental ingredients of leadership. And it lays to rest a number of myths about Menzies created by popular theory and misconceptions used to explain his opposition to communism.

Following Robert Menzies' first term as prime minister, the derogatory phrase 'You'll never win with Menzies' was often muttered in non-Labor circles. Yet within a decade it was evident that Labor could not defeat Menzies. And the seeds of this success were sown in the years immediately following Menzies' defeat in 1941.

History, it is sometimes said, is no more than the stories we tell ourselves. While true for folk history, this should not describe the work of the professional historian, who produces an ongoing historical record using all available evidence, understood within its known context. Yet with the advent of the docudrama and movie reincarnations of historical action and heroes, there is a temptation to imagine the past and surmise outside the context of the historical period, or to retell our past as entertainment, in a keenness to attract larger audiences, more book sales and the like.

Take Australia's Robert Menzies, a larger than life historical figure – erudite barrister turned politician, leader of an earlier Australia when white Anglo values ruled an ancient Pacific continent and the British Empire ruled the waves. Menzies represented the values of the Australian middle classes of his day in many respects. His success as a professional was hard won, his family life traditional and secure, his political leanings conservative and lacking the reformist's zeal, his moderation topped only by his own sense of superiority among his peers.

To political rivals and opponents, Menzies was a constant irritant. Labor and his United Australia Party/Country Party parliamentary colleagues had both toppled him in 1941, only to see him rise again and become Australia's longest serving prime minister over a period of sixteen years, a record not readily surpassed. To the storytellers, popular historians and scriptwriters, Menzies is also a problem. Where are the dramatics, the colour to spark a contest lively enough for television? Gough Whitlam delivered in spades in this regard, a prime minister in turbulent times eventually sacked by his governor-general, and a colossus who divided a nation. With Menzies, however, there is stable government, albeit in an era of smaller wars and international skirmishes, alongside loyalty to Australia's British head of state and two decades of prosperity – the gripping docudrama does not easily flow from here.

In part, imaginative and sweeping modern judgments of Menzies, endowing him with aloofness, grand ambition and ego, and flaws such as a paranoia over communism, come with a view that rejects the success of Menzies and the Liberal Party against Labor over two decades. In keeping Labor from office, they say, he robbed Australia of a Labor prime minister for twenty-three years, from December 1949 to December 1972. As opinion, it is also a protest against the Liberal Party's approach to foreign policy, which Menzies came to stand for.

Robert Menzies, as Australia's longest serving prime minister, never queried the importance of Australia's alliance with Britain and the United States, and he unashamedly supported US opposition to communism throughout the Cold War. For his critics, however, Menzies came to represent the status quo of the 1950s against the 'people power' of the Vietnam era. Pushed especially at universities, this view soon saw successive authors with a left-wing or Labor perspective writing essays, books and screenplays where Robert Menzies was drawn as Anglophile rather than Australian. All such writings forgot that the majority of Australians in the 1950s and 1960s accepted their Menzies governments precisely because he represented what they saw as the Australia of their day.

The first Menzies Government (April 1939 – August 1941), whose work the war historian Paul Hasluck judged to be 'considerable' and 'a major factor in Australian survival under Japanese threat',[1] has also been downgraded by some popular historians in their acclaim for the Curtin and Chifley Labor governments that followed. In fact, during the two years of the first Menzies Government, Curtin and Menzies worked up a reasonable partnership, in spite of failing to form a national government. Both led very divided political groupings, Labor racked by the continuing split in its NSW branch and Menzies' colleagues divided by personal bitterness and personality clashes. The balm that United Australia Party (UAP) leader Joe Lyons had brought to the querulous party and its Country Party colleagues had disappeared with his death.

Taking over as prime minister in April 1939, Menzies very soon found himself not only leading an unwilling nation towards a second global conflict in the space of just two decades but also at the helm of a fractious political team that at times publicly aired its dissent with his management. As Hasluck has described it, 'in concentrating on the first he [Menzies] had not made progress with the second'.[2] With all the impatience of a younger leader, it was Menzies' tendency to look at the national interest and global security while expecting that his colleagues would rise to the unity required for national needs in a time of peril.

What is not considered in the assessment of Robert Menzies as an Anglophile rather than an Australian is that he was in fact ahead of his time as an internationalist. From his first years in federal politics, Menzies seized opportunities to explore Australia's relations with Europe and the United States by making visits overseas – in much the same way younger MPs do nearly a century later. Significantly, Menzies began this travel when the voyage took weeks by sea and the time away from Australia could be many months. On his first trip, he and his wife Pattie accompanied Prime Minister Joseph Lyons and his wife Enid to London for King George V's Silver Jubilee. Although Joe Lyons was Australia's first prime minister to make use of regular air travel within Australia, his trip by sea to Europe and the United States in 1935 spanned five months and set the pace for future Australian prime ministers while abroad. Such trips took in daily meetings and briefings, along with opportunities to address dinners and lunches, and engage face to face with the leaders and businesses upon whom Australia depended for foreign trade and security. Lyons and Menzies brought Australia closer to its international partnerships. In 1941, Menzies was facilitating that process, in a more urgent way, at a time of real national danger.

By contrast, Labor lacked such global experience and often seemed locked in a class-conflict mentality, hanging onto arguments about national defence using isolationist rhetoric – some of which appealed to a nation yet to feel the full force of the threat of invasion or the impact of the carnage in Europe on their own country's international relations. On his return from Europe and the United States in May 1941, Menzies despaired that he would have to 'play politics' once again while, as he saw it, Australia's security and more important world-shattering matters deserved his prime ministerial attention. Britain was at Germany's mercy, and the Empire, in which Australia was a key player, was likewise threatened. A German defeat of Britain would immediately affect the Empire's dominions and their relationships across the globe. But Menzies had underestimated the domestic political game as part of the democratic process. Within months, that game would have defeated him.

Menzies' preoccupation with Westminster in 1941 has since been misconstrued in the Australian record. Historian David Day, in *Menzies and Churchill at War: A Controversial New Account of the 1941 Struggle for Power*,[3] spends some 250 pages developing a thesis that Menzies' ultimate ambition in 1941 was to topple Churchill and become prime minister of Great Britain. More than a decade later, this thesis was repeated, to the exclusion of all other historical interpretations based on concrete evidence, in the television documentary *Menzies and Churchill at War*, made by 360 Degree Films in association with ABC TV, with the financial assistance of Screen Australia and Film Victoria.[4] It aired on ABC TV on 30 October 2008.[5]

As myth-making goes, both David Day and 360 Degree Films have scored well. They have certainly had wide exposure in Australia, but their thesis about Robert Menzies and Winston Churchill owes much to commentator imagination and little to the historical evidence. Several names of alternatives to Churchill were bandied about in the first half of 1941 among the chattering circles of London, political operatives, some MPs who found Churchill's authoritarian ways hard to bear, and others in high places who had never fully accepted his leadership from May 1940. During Menzies' lengthy UK visit from February to May 1941, with his attendance at the War Cabinet and prominence as a dominion premier supporting Churchill, the name Robert Menzies was passed around by some of Churchill's opponents for a brief while as that of a leader who might be used to influence, even challenge, Churchill. Menzies' rallying calls for Empire loyalty captured the attention of the UK press at a time when British forces were failing in Greece and the Middle East, a manoeuvre

Churchill had forced on General Archibald Wavell, then commanding in North Africa. For all the interest of some in the press elite and occasional suggestions of Menzies' potential at the top, however, in his own diary entries while in London he mocked such gossip. His mission was to temper Churchill's dominance of the War Cabinet in order to convince him the Pacific dominions needed strengthened defences. The Day/Screen Australia/360 Degree Films thesis shows little understanding of what was involved in the appointment of a British prime minister, both in 1941 and for years beyond, or in the appointment of a Conservative leader – or of Churchill's standing with his nation at the time.

Interviewed in 2013 at the House of Lords, the Conservative Lord Carrington was startled by the absurdity of the suggestion that Robert Menzies thought he might be able to topple Winston Churchill to become the UK prime minister in 1941:

> It's the most unlikely story I've ever heard. I don't think there's an element, not even a grain, of truth in it. In those days, Churchill was dominant ... there was never any doubt whatever that he was going to survive. That's the most absurd story I've heard for a very long time.[6]

Peter Carington,[7] whose distinguished career included portfolios in Margaret Thatcher's governments, took his seat in the House of Lords in 1939 and was the UK High Commissioner to Australia from 1956 to 1959. He knew Menzies – and Churchill – well.

There was never a political ambition in Robert Menzies that sought to topple Winston Churchill as prime minister of Britain. From all the evidence Day has produced, the same evidence Menzies' biographer Allan Martin also examined and found wanting, it is clear that Menzies' moment in the sun while visiting the

United Kingdom in 1941 was that of a leading dominion prime minister taking his British connections to heart. Lady Astor, as Heather Henderson (née Menzies) has said, may have offered Menzies 'all her sapphires'[8] if he would stay in England, but this did not mean such a group intended that he replace Churchill – or that Menzies ever thought of it. The erudite, tall and broad-shouldered Australian prime minister met with a heady broth of attention while abroad, but in London it came from a small elite who used him to poke at Churchill's bulldog approach to leadership at War Cabinet meetings. As a dominion prime minister, Menzies did not owe his political position to any favours from the UK prime minister. Moreover, the public support of an Australian prime minister was invaluable at the time to Britain, where national nerve was under siege from air bombardment by Germany, an onslaught made all the more effective with supporting action on fronts in northern Europe and North Africa from Italy and the Soviet Union. Invasion of the United Kingdom was a real possibility, and the threat only abated after 22 June 1941, when Germany invaded the Soviet Union and tore up the Nazi–Soviet Pact.

Robert Gordon Menzies looms large in the Australian story. His unbroken sixteen-year record as Australian prime minister alone magnifies his presence in the history time lines. His administration after 1949 took a nation from the initial stages of postwar recovery through to the prosperous mid-1960s, when social revolution and a new style of conflict in South-East Asia began to refashion global relations for the coming decades.

Yet history has not so readily recorded the other Robert Menzies: a man of stature and professional success but a man at war within himself to some extent, pushing forward in the ways his talents took him but, after August 1941, seemingly unable to accomplish his ultimate dream. In his memoir *Afternoon Light*, written decades after his demise as prime minister in 1941, something of this ambivalence or tussle of spirit comes through. He could acknowledge that he had misjudged his abilities to carry his colleagues with him, that his trip abroad in the early months of 1941 had taken him too long away from home, that he had handled colleagues badly and that he had relinquished the leadership rather than held firm and stared down both government malcontents and opposition hardheads. But, as Menzies himself put it upon reflection much later, he 'was in a very exacerbated state of mind'. In his own words, the shame to his pride, the shock of the bitterness, hit him hard:

> I had been weighed in the balance and found wanting. And
> yet I felt that I had done a great deal. I had not spared myself;
> I had worked seven days a week for at least twelve hours a
> day. This was, perhaps, an error, for it so absorbed my mind
> that I soon appeared to be aloof from my supporters in
> Parliament and to be lacking in human relations. But when
> the blow fell, it was like the stroke of doom; everything was at
> an end.[9]

The enigma that Menzies presented over years left a vacuum, one that academics seeking a modern and psychological understanding of power could fill. Menzies was the product of a different time, an Edwardian era when private lives were very separate from public performance. He did not reveal his private relations to the public – and any testimony of his private feelings regarding his public actions was offered only very carefully, and in hindsight. Long after Menzies' death in 1978, historians remained bereft of private insights into this highly public figure in the Australian political landscape. Such a lack of personal information around a national icon allowed the stereotypes to multiply. It also invited academics such as Judith Brett to speculate as to what might fill the gaps in our knowledge.

In 1992, Brett published a study of Menzies using an examination of the language he had used in a series of radio broadcasts in 1942–43. Brett's study, *Robert Menzies' Forgotten People*,[10] offered an imaginative approach to psychoanalysis, based on a non-psychologist's reading of Freud's Oedipus complex and using the psychobiographical interpretation fashionable at the time. Read now, the book comes across as suggestive rather than authoritative or empirical. Brett admits in her introduction to the new edition of *Robert Menzies' Forgotten People* that work for her doctoral thesis on Austrian poet Hugo von Hofmannsthal was the forerunner of her theory on Menzies:

> I now see that my PhD on Hofmannsthal was a rehearsal
> for my work on Menzies. Both take a central text and use it
> as a pivot; both develop their arguments from detailed close
> readings; and both ponder the interplay between private
> meanings and publicly available forms for their expression.

Menzies' biographer Allan Martin took great exception to what he saw as the dogmatism of this school of political sociology, fostered by Alan Davies (1924–87) at Melbourne University, and its effect on political biography. In a letter to author Gerard Henderson in August 1997, Martin opined that Brett's interpretations of Menzies, 'being theory driven and not evidence based, *are* often simply impertinent'.[11]

Brett's conclusions about the private Menzies are heavily theoretical – at no stage did she seek to interview members of the Menzies family or significant others who might have spent time with Menzies in private. Since then, Menzies' daughter, Heather Henderson, has published a memoir of her parents and a volume of her father's letters written to her over a twenty-year period (1955–75) while she was abroad as a diplomat's wife.[12] These have opened a window on the private Robert Menzies – and his relations with his family. Much of the Brett thesis on Menzies now fails to hold up. The Menzies tribe was close and loyal – Menzies' parents operated as no 'Oedipus' muddle in their son's life but were, rather, a key to his success.

The same is true of the outdated treatment by left-leaning Australian historians of Menzies' opposition to the Communist Party of Australia (CPA). Chief among these has been Stuart Macintyre, who as a young academic was a member of the CPA. In various works, Macintyre has dismissed Menzies as politically intolerant due to what he characterises as an irrational fear of the communist menace. This was a view popularised during the anti–Vietnam War protest period of the late 1960s, when Macintyre was an undergraduate at Melbourne University. It was a time of popular leftist flowering, in 1972 witnessing the installation of a Labor government, headed by Gough Whitlam, after the more than two decades of conservative government under Menzies and his short-term successors Harold Holt, John Gorton and William McMahon. Hunger for fresh ideas had exploded among the Australian public with the election of a Labor government after so long, but it was all to end dramatically, with popular support, three years later. Yet the academy of the left rode on in the universities, painting the Menzies' years as a reactionary Australian era headed by an Anglophile. For Macintyre, Menzies' opposition to communism in these years was a 'preoccupation', with the idea of a 'threat from without ... linked to the danger within'.[13] In other words, Menzies suffered from a conspiracy mentality, or fear of a bogeyman.

Judith Brett took up this thesis, seeing Menzies' support for the views of civil libertarian John Stuart Mill as contradicting his use of Lady Macbeth as a metaphor for the work of the CPA. For Brett, Menzies' interest in the covert nature of Lady Macbeth, and thus all women, is part of an internal conflict given his adherence to Mill's philosophies. Brett links this belief to her analysis of Menzies' anti-communist stance when, as attorney-general in 1934, he attempted to prohibit communist Egon Kisch from entering Australia. Kisch was not only a communist who had lied about his Communist Party affiliations to gain his visa, but was also one of the most important communist agents in the Comintern (the Third International).[14] Brett makes a similar point about Menzies' attempt to ban the Communist Party of Australia by constitutional amendment in 1951. As Brett sees it, 'here was the kernel of personal resonance which he used to reorient his argument from a firm commitment to civil liberties to a determination to ban the Communist Party'.

As more recently published evidence has shown, however, there is nothing inconsistent in Menzies' support for the civil libertarian arguments of John Stuart Mill while opposing the intrigues of the CPA. Menzies was one of a majority of his time who believed that the covert operations of the CPA endangered the stability and freedoms ensured under Australia's parliamentary democracy. Mark Aarons' *The Family File*,[15] with its revelations about the intrigues of the CPA – of which Aarons' parents were long-time operatives – supports Menzies' view. Former Labor premier of New South Wales and former federal foreign minister Bob Carr, speaking to the Sydney Institute in 2011, agreed with Aarons:

> The CPA was a Stalinist party in that it was taking money
> from Moscow … In the 1940s, the CPA was embedded in
> Soviet espionage activities in Australia. From Mark Aarons
> and other sources we now know that those activities were
> significant. There were communist spies in the Department
> of Foreign Affairs in Canberra. They were getting material
> to the KGB representative in Sydney in his guise as a TASS
> [Telegraphic Agency of the Soviet Union] agent … This is a
> very important part of Australian history because it represents

a vindication of the Petrov Commission. It suggests that Menzies, perhaps against all his instincts, was not an opportunist. In fact, he was more right than wrong in what he said about Soviet espionage in Australia.[16]

Menzies needed no paranoia to be convinced of the covert nature of CPA operations. His analogy of the CPA with Lady Macbeth was quite appropriate for his generation. That the metaphorical figure using a covert attack was a woman is also not surprising, either for the era in which Shakespeare conceived *Macbeth* or the era in which Menzies used it.

In the months following his resignation as prime minister in late August 1941, Menzies swayed between relief at his release from the burdens of office and despair that his life at the top had come to so little. The evidence suggests that his removal from a position at the centre of the war effort left some in official positions dismayed. Representations to Whitehall, from both Australia's Governor-General Lord Gowrie and the UK High Commissioner Sir Ronald Cross, for Menzies to be offered a British Government posting or even seat in the House of Commons came to nothing. Australia's most prominent statesman had plummeted.

At some point after these rejections from both Churchill and the Dominions Office, however, Menzies began to mull over his options. For the first time in his career, he had been forced back to personal fundamentals and political beliefs. Then, in early 1942, the voice of Menzies was once more being heard, as he scripted and presented his views of the world as a series of radio broadcasts in which he began to outline a few basic political principles. These were to forge a new non-Labor philosophy of sorts. Just over a year later, at the August 1943 federal election and after disastrous results for the UAP and its many splinter groups, Menzies won back the leadership of his party, which was by then a disillusioned collection of MPs seeking fresh direction.

Within a year of regaining the helm of the UAP, Menzies was leading the newly formed Liberal Party of Australia. Although it would take another five years in opposition before Robert and Pattie Menzies returned to live in Canberra's Lodge, this time saw the earlier Menzies largely transformed. Between leaving the prime minister's residence and returning to it, Menzies would shed much of his younger man's hubris in his dealings with colleagues. He would master some of the political skills by which his predecessor Joe Lyons had triumphed – easy communication and empathy with voters – and catch a wave of popular resentment at the attempt by the Chifley Government to extend wartime controls still further by nationalising Australia's banks. Nevertheless, not even Menzies' could have imagined the success that lay ahead.

But those sixteen years of uninterrupted Menzies Government – from December 1949 to January 1966 – have overshadowed the most important years of his political blooding: the years of struggle and evolution, the years that would be the making of the record-breaking prime minister he became. With this book, the gaps can now be filled – not with imaginative interpretations but with glimpses of the private man behind the very prominent figure he presented in the Australian and British political landscape.

1

Nadir

The enemy says that British overseas countries just take their orders from London, and that we have been 'ordered to fight' ... We are not fighting to anybody's orders except our own ... It had never occurred to me that we were not independent in relation to our own affairs. It had never occurred to me that London gave instructions to Canberra.

– Robert Menzies[1]

It happened after dinner at a meeting of Cabinet colleagues reconvened at 8.30 pm on 26 August 1941, in Parliament House, Canberra. Australia's Prime Minister Robert Menzies had been home to the Lodge for dinner with his wife, Pattie. The Lodge, just a short drive from Parliament House, in its fledgling national capital, stood like a modest country manor house in the midst of paddocks where sheep grazed. Once dinner was over, to ensure a private discussion, Menzies and his wife had set off to chew the rag over his future, walking along marked tracks beyond the manicured gardens of the house. Together they discussed his position. He told her how he had met his Cabinet colleagues that afternoon. The government was awaiting a decision from the Labor opposition on yet another invitation from Menzies for it to accept positions in a national government. In the event of a refusal, Menzies had asked his Cabinet colleagues for frank assessments of his leadership. Clearly, party fortunes were at a low ebb. His colleagues' responses had been a harsh reality check.

By the time the Menzies couple had ended their walk that evening, they were in agreement that he should resign as prime minister of Australia. It was a firm decision, albeit one that would hurt deeply in the process; the press reported two weeks later 'Mrs Menzies tearfully leaves home' after she made a small, lonely figure, weeping quietly as her train pulled out of Canberra. Their dream was in tatters – and in so short a time. But, in the paddocks that evening, the Menzies' couple were fixed in their intentions. When Menzies returned to Parliament House, it was to inform his Cabinet colleagues of his decision.

Menzies wrote a personal record of the events surrounding his resignation a few days later, which is reproduced as the Appendix to this book.[2] It is a unique document; none like it has been penned by any other Australian leader. In his account, Menzies recalled how he had snatched one last small act of revenge on those he saw as disloyal colleagues. Telling the meeting that the afternoon's discussion had 'shown that I have forfeited the confidence of a majority of my colleagues', he had, for just a moment, left them wondering what he would do. With all the timing of the polished barrister he was, Menzies savoured the silence, then reminded the meeting that 'the normal procedure in such a case' would be for him to ask for the resignations of those who had declared against him. His words had an instant effect, one that he noted was 'almost ludicrous'. So he let the words sink in for another length of time, the faces before him a screen of apprehension. Then, just as the silence became leaden, he added that while this was normal procedure in a time of peace he did not propose 'to adopt it in time of war'. In his view it would 'completely split the Ministerial parties and ensure a Labour [sic] administration for a long time'.

So it was that Robert Menzies announced, to the twelve ministers who were able to attend, that his intention was to resign. Two days later, at a UAP meeting, Menzies informed his remaining party colleagues of this decision. In spite of months of intense division and criticism of his leadership from coalition ranks, the announcement left confusion, even upset. Arthur Coles, the independent from Victoria who had only just joined the UAP, announced he was resigning from the party and left the room. Yet, as Menzies noted, there was 'no real attempt to discourage me from the indicated course'. It was too late for that. Menzies' resignation was formally announced on 29 August 1941.

The departure of Robert Menzies as UAP prime minister at this time seems completely out of character when placed beside the achievements of Sir Robert Menzies, hero and founder of the Liberal Party, as recalled half a century later. Here was this erudite and talented figure, making a sad, even tragic, early exit from the calling that would so dominate his life. Shortly after his resignation, in a personal cable on 8 September 1941 to the British prime minister, Winston Churchill, Menzies conveyed his fragile frame of mind:

> I greatly appreciate your personal cable No 446 and warmly reciprocate your expressions of goodwill. My own mind is much disturbed as I feel that the political future so far as I am concerned is extremely uncertain and that from now on my war contribution will be of an unsatisfying kind. Still, as you say, one must be comforted by the recollection of duty attempted.[3]

It was a consolation prize of sorts, but the comfort Churchill had passed on to Menzies would have come as a further blow to the proud man's sagging self-esteem. It would be some months before any new thinking or direction became clear to him. For many who supported Menzies at the time, it seemed as if he had simply thrown in the towel by resigning. And there would be a lengthy period of regret – in Menzies' own words to 'bleed awhile' – that he was forced from the limelight of a glamorous life on the public stage, both at home and abroad.

From the time of his entry into federal politics in 1934, in just seven years, Menzies had made four lengthy visits to Britain and Europe, on two occasions travelling via Washington and Canada on his way home. On the first trip, accompanying Prime Minister Joseph Lyons and his wife Enid in 1935, Menzies paid the fares for himself and his wife Pattie – as both an opportunity and an investment towards future political success. For his generation, Antipodean Robert Menzies was indeed a global player.

Menzies' resignation as Australian prime minister in August 1941 was a personal train crash. In London on a visit lasting many weeks between late February and the first week of May 1941, this striking political figure from afar had made an impact among leading Westminster names, only to return home and quickly lose command of the numbers in his governing coalition. Menzies' morale, so high in London, Washington and Ottawa, was very soon spent after he climbed from the seaplane that brought him into Sydney from New Zealand on Empire Day – Saturday 24 May.

Within weeks of his homecoming, Menzies' sense of purpose about the war and his role in Australia's war effort had collapsed under the criticism from colleagues and opponents that his efforts abroad showed a lack of concern for home defence in the face of a Japanese army rapidly advancing south through China. And those who opposed him could be found as much on his own side as on the opposition benches. Robert Menzies had, suddenly, many a character flaw to deal with.

Nevertheless, on finding himself in a marginal role under the prime ministership of Country Party leader Arthur (Artie)

Fadden after 29 August, and still more removed from the action when a Labor government took power on 7 October 1941, Menzies' tendency was not to walk away from politics. He sought instead, after weeks of mulling things over with a few close associates, to return to that political ambience he had found so warm and welcoming in the early months of 1941.

Robert Menzies by this stage had reached a point, albeit one that would prove to be wishful thinking, where he was ready to leave Australia to become a British MP. While, decades later, this might suggest a lack of patriotism, in Menzies' view he was part of a British world order. And, if sanctioned by both Australian and UK prime ministers (Menzies believed this was possible), that a move between the two Westminster systems was entirely appropriate for a Commonwealth leader. Menzies had returned from abroad in 1941 as strong in his commitment to saving Britain as he believed Britain should be in its commitment to the defence of Australia.

Communications, in October 1941 on behalf of Menzies, by Australia's governor-general, Lord Gowrie, and by the UK high commissioner, Sir Ronald Cross, in February 1942, reveal that for some months after his resignation as prime minister, Menzies harboured feelings of despair at his increasing lack of influence over government policy. Cables from Gowrie and Cross to the Dominions Office indicate that Menzies ached for a nod from Winston Churchill, a nod that would allow him to move into British politics by joining the House of Commons.[4] As prime minister, Menzies had believed he could make his best contribution by arguing Australia's case with Churchill, face to face. Menzies had standing among key players at Whitehall. Only towards the end of his 1941 visit did he come to accept what others had told him – that Churchill could not be easily swayed from his fixed view that saving England was the priority before all else, and that above all the Empire dominions existed to save

England. It was not an equal partnership. Soon after arriving in London, Menzies had come to realise that Britain, and Churchill in particular, had entirely Atlantic and Mediterranean perspectives – what might happen in South-East Asia, or more seriously to Australia and New Zealand, paled in comparison to the dangers to be faced in Europe and Britain itself. Seen from Whitehall, the United Kingdom's remote dominions in the South Pacific had the security of distance. Appeasement of Japan, for Churchill at that time, seemed possible. As historian Geoffrey Blainey put it in an interview in 2013, 'It is understandable, isn't it? Somebody's going to be dropped'.[5]

For well over a year, from the fall of France in late June 1940, Britain stood alone except for the assistance of its dominions. In the United States there was no public empathy for Britain's predicament, and Americans, like many Australians, felt that another war in Europe was not for them. Campaigning for the 1940 presidential election, Franklin D Roosevelt went so far as to tell a crowd, 'I've said this before, I'll say it again and again and again, your boys are not going into any foreign wars'.[6] Not until the passage of the 'Lend-Lease' legislation in the United States on 11 March 1941 could the US president authorise materiel aid to Britain for the war effort. As late as 21 March that same year, the *Sydney Morning Herald* reported President Roosevelt's media statement that the United States would not be involved directly in the European war for 'a year or more'. In this situation, Australia's support for Britain was significant – in the numbers of men sent, pilots trained and the early success of Australian forces in the North African campaigns. For a small while, Australia looked like the one lucky omen for Churchill's embattled isle.

Back in Australia, Menzies had refused to see it that way. On 8 August 1941, as Churchill and Roosevelt were about to conduct a historic rendezvous to draw up the Atlantic Charter aboard USS *Augusta* in Placentia Bay, Newfoundland, Menzies cabled

Churchill urging him to include the 'Far Eastern position' in the deliberations, saying: 'I do not think there is any doubt that firm and unequivocal attitude by the United States is the one thing that will deter Japan from continuing on a course leading to war'. Stressing the importance of the 'Far East' to Churchill as much as he could, Menzies argued that for Japan to enter the war or even threaten to force Britain into a wider conflict would mean 'a naval problem of the gravest character'. South-East Asia, Menzies assured Churchill, was not 'a remote, incidental matter but something crucial and intimate' to Britain. Moreover, Menzies was adamant that only 'precision and firmness are the real antidote to Japan', although in his own discussions with Roosevelt he had found the president not so precise.[7]

At this juncture of the war effort, Australia and the Pacific were a concern but not a priority when viewed from London and even Washington. On 12 August, after the meeting between Churchill and Roosevelt on USS *Augusta*, Australia's high commissioner in London, Stanley Melbourne Bruce, conveyed to Menzies decisions made between the two great leaders of the Atlantic about Japan and its territorial advance beyond China. Roosevelt had committed to negotiating 'the neutralisation of Indo-China and Thailand under joint guarantee of the United States, Japan and Britain'. On return to Washington, Bruce reported, Roosevelt would hand the Japanese ambassador a statement that conveyed the United States' determination to 'take counter measures even though these might lead to war' in the event of Japan ignoring such a neutral zone.[8] On 21 August, Australia's newspapers reported that the United States had developed a policy of 'containment' regarding Japan, and was using the new British alliance with the Soviet Union to put added pressure on the Japanese. As events would unfold, such threats made no difference to the advance of Japan or to the United States' entry into the fighting – not, at least, until the Japanese bombed the

US naval base at Pearl Harbor on 7 December 1941 with the loss not only of US navy battleships but also more than 2400 American lives.

Menzies' calls for Washington and London to focus on Pacific defence at the Newfoundland meeting resulted in disappointing failure. Diplomatic efforts to 'contain' Japan proved futile and, even as the Western leaders conferred on board USS *Augusta*, Japan's army continued its moves south and took Cambodia. This renewed Japanese threat resonated with Australia's leaders. Suggestions came from both the press and inside the government that Menzies should return to Britain to push for urgent support from London. Labor leader John Curtin backed the proposal that Menzies return to London in August 1941, but other Labor members of the Advisory War Council (AWC) objected and it was opposed. As historian Paul Hasluck noted, this decision of the AWC meant 'domestic political issues had been introduced into the examination of the Far Eastern situation ... in retrospect a lost opportunity for pressing the interests of Australia'.[9] When the Labor opposition refused to agree to Menzies going to London, a crisis of confidence within the government parties followed, a crisis that saw Menzies resign.

A move to the House of Commons for Menzies after August 1941 would never happen. One's personal sense of importance rarely imprints itself on other dominant players, unless they have something to gain from it. Australia's governor-general, Lord Gowrie, might well write to Secretary of State for Dominion Affairs Viscount Cranborne on 10 October 1941 that 'it is evident that Menzies' remarkable gifts cannot fully be utilised here' and that this appeared to be a 'deplorable waste of valuable material' at such times.[10] Lord Gowrie might well suggest to Viscount Cranborne that if a 'seat could be found for [Menzies] in the House of Commons if he went home' to 'render useful service' and that if an 'invitation to stand could emanate from

[Cranborne's] political organisation', it would indeed facilitate Menzies' 'severance from Australian politics'.[11] Sir Ronald Cross might well also argue, a few months later, that Menzies was wasted as a member of Australia's AWC under a Curtin Labor Government, given the council only advised on 'such matters as the government chooses'. Cross could also argue that Menzies would be of more value in the House of Commons, which 'has better appreciation of debating power' and that Menzies believed Curtin 'would be agreeable'.[12] Such influential pleading on Menzies' behalf would fall on deaf ears.

Churchill was running a War Cabinet that he ruled and dominated only through the popularity he evoked from an embattled but feisty population. He had no wish for the distraction of a personally popular former dominion leader who continued to remind him, and others in Britain, that the Mother Country – its back to the wall and barely surviving invasion – also had responsibilities to defend a distant Commonwealth member, itself under threat of invasion from an Asian neighbour, a dominion still in February 1942 providing thousands of much-needed troops for Britain's European campaigns.

The requests on Menzies' behalf were rebuffed not only by Churchill but by each secretary for dominion affairs, Viscount Cranborne and Clement Attlee, in turn. Reporting back on 13 October 1941, Viscount Cranborne was the bearer of high praise for Menzies' well-regarded talents, which he cutely turned back on Menzies as talents needed at home. Through that same dominion secretary, Churchill also conveyed his belief that 'it would be unwise of Menzies to leave Australia at the present time' as, although not in office, 'he will occupy a unique position in the politics of the Commonwealth'. And, as if to emphasise the denial with further balm, Churchill added, 'With his outstanding abilities and experience, he will be able to speak in the Australian parliament with a voice of combined authority and independence which no one else could command'.[13] These words could well have cracked Menzies' spirit for all time.

In the letters from Governor-General Lord Gowrie and UK High Commissioner Ronald Cross to the Dominions Office in London, it is evident that Menzies sought service in London as a way to stay in the action of the war, and hold a position of influence around government. In time, Churchill was prepared to accommodate him away from London. Just before the fall of Singapore, through Churchill's emissary to South-East Asia, Duff Cooper, who visited Australia, Menzies was offered a post as UK minister of state in South-East Asia. Menzies indicated he would be happy to accept, but Singapore fell to the Japanese and nothing came of it.

In hindsight, Menzies wrote that his fall from office made him even more determined to pursue his political ambitions all over again. Whether this was something that came to him only after he realised his chances of a post from London were non-existent is unclear. But a fight within him developed. Would opportunity knock to allow him to go abroad and serve as a diplomat or minister, or was there a future of significance for him in faraway Australia where Labor ruled so successfully under Curtin in a time of war? Quite a few people, Menzies recalled in his memoirs, were ready to 'write my political obituary'. As he remembered it:

> True for years there were observers who would say to my
> party and my friends, 'You'll never win with Menzies!' But
> when such slogans reached my ears, I treated them as a great
> challenge. My unspoken response was that of the small boy –
> 'I'll show them!'[14]

Yet nothing was certain in early 1942, when another opportunity to serve overseas appeared to come Menzies' way. Richard

Casey, Australia's minister (ambassador) to the United States, was suddenly made Churchill's minister of state in Cairo, leaving the Australian post in Washington vacant. Prime Minister John Curtin advised Menzies that Churchill had suggested appointing Menzies to Washington, an idea Menzies was ready to accept. As Menzies also predicted, however, the Labor Cabinet recoiled when they found that Churchill was sending instructions to the Australian Government. They would send their own man – not one chosen by a British prime minister. So prominent legal figure Owen Dixon went to Washington instead, and Menzies turned his attention to a life in politics at home. It was a choice forced upon him but one that would prove, as he himself would later write, to be a great turning point in his life.[15]

Those months of malaise after losing his prime ministership in 1941 were Robert Menzies' darkest time, a test of character in the extreme. There was no certainty that he would work through such a public blow to his ego and come out the other side, content to start all over again for the top job. Yet by moving beyond it, the seasoned and refashioned political figure that emerged to lead the Liberal Party of Australia into government in December 1949 became an icon in Australian history. How this turning point came to be is the story of the first Menzies Government – and its failure.

2

The clan and its legacy

My father's mother, Kate Sampson, was of Cornish descent. Her father was a miner and helped to form the Australian Miners' Union, but her brother, Sydney, was non-Labor and represented Wimmera in the federal parliament for thirteen years. My father's father, James Menzies, was of Scottish descent. He became a shire councillor, then shire president, then Member for Lowan in the Victorian parliament. Thus, with both sides of politics represented in the family, politics was well and truly in my father's blood.

– Heather Henderson[1]

Robert Menzies, father of the Liberal Party of Australia, was an elected member of Australian parliaments for a total of thirty-eight years. But what is often forgotten is that for sixteen years Menzies was not a Liberal Party MP. And, for most of his early years in parliament, from 1931 to 1944, Menzies belonged to the United Australia Party (UAP). It was an organisation Menzies devised with some of his Nationalist Party colleagues, along with a handful of business associates including Keith Murdoch and a small group of breakaway Laborites, headed by former Labor premier of Tasmania and former federal Labor acting treasurer Joseph Lyons. It was thus a pragmatic answer for the non-Labor side of politics in desperate financial times. In a matter of weeks, from April to May 1931, these men and a handful of women moulded the rapidly multiplying citizens groups into a functioning political party, spearheaded by a majority of federal Nationalist MPs.

Making his political mark had appeared to be a seamless run for Robert Menzies, who came from nondescript beginnings, a matter of glittering prizes for the lad from the bush. In fact, the root of the Menzies story is a universal one for many ordinary Australians – the spirit of making a go of things as life turns difficult. For James and Kate Menzies and their three children, the hard times came as a result of James's ill health and the precarious financial times of the early 1890s. James had been making 'good money' in Ballarat as a coach and machine decorator but the effect on his nervous disposition of the hours of work required brought him to the verge of a nervous breakdown. The 1890s were years of an evolving banking crisis, which tested business confidence just as Victoria began to suffer loss of population as its boom years gave way to better opportunities in Western Australia and New South Wales.[2] Facing the challenge, the Menzies family relocated to the north-western Victorian town of Jeparit, where they opened a general store with what Robert Menzies later described as 'no qualifications except courage, character, and a will to succeed'.[3] Just a year after Australia's banking collapses came to a head, and with the full repercussions of financial loss about to usher in a depression, in a dry and dusty Mallee settlement at the end of the railway system, on 20 December 1894, James and Kate Menzies welcomed their fourth child – a boy they named Robert Gordon.

As growing-up stories go, Robert Menzies' history is quintessentially that of an Australian of his time, albeit from diligent Methodist–Presbyterian stock. Menzies himself recalled the harshness of the natural backdrop his parents survived. The heat, the dust storms, the burning scrub as it was cleared for farm-ing, the frugality in a community where locals struggled to make money against the odds, the drought of 1902 that turned grass-land to soil lying 'burnt, and pale brown, and vacant'.[4] But he also recalled the expanse of Lake Hindmarsh before the drought, where he and his siblings went fishing and swimming. And he remembered the Government of Victoria coming to wheat farm-ers' aid with cash advances for seed wheat, and the bumper har-vest that followed the drought years, bringing to the boy a new consciousness of 'that mystical giver of all good things, "the Gov-ernment", and only second to ourselves'.[5] Amid their troubles, however, James and Kate Menzies refused to allow isolation in the small country town of Jeparit to prevent their offspring from gaining a good education. In primary years, this was found at the local one-teacher government school in Jeparit under the watch-ful eye of 'Daddy Livingston', as the children called their school-master Mr Livingston.

When Les, Isobel (Belle), Frank and Robert Menzies reached their late-primary years they were sent in turn to Ballarat, the boys attending Humffray Street State School and Belle going to Queen's College. In turn, Grandma Menzies took in her grand-children as boarders so they remained in family care, albeit away from their parents. Discipline in each of the homes the Menzies children inhabited was paramount – not that it seemed to inhibit their bursts of insubordination. Menzies' daughter Heather Henderson relates how, in Jeparit, her uncles and aunt had taken apart their mother's new sewing machine – a possession much treasured and vital in isolated Jeparit – out of curiosity. In their distress at not being able to put it back together, the children had thrown the parts into a drain in the road. As Heather Hen-derson writes, 'The punishment doesn't bear thinking about'. In Ballarat, Grandma Menzies would mete out punishments that involved learning long passages of the Bible – of which Heather comments, 'I assume Bob was quite a naughty boy because he acquired an extensive knowledge of the Bible'. As with most children of that era, the Menzies kids lived in the shadow of the 'strap', both at home and at school.

While historian Judith Brett has seen in James Menzies, with his irascible and hard parental rule, a particularly negative influence on Robert Menzies, this must be viewed in the context of the time. Most children grew in sternly disciplined environments in those days. And, as Bob Menzies grew and achieved academic success, he challenged his father's authority in new ways – by argument and smart rejoinders – at a time when fathers were expected to be afforded respect. The Menzies–Sampson family collective was a broad church – and included not a few significant achievers for regional Victoria. In Ballarat, Bob would visit his Sampson grandfather, who offered the boy a chance to air his views on politics whether the old man agreed with his arguments or not. The family's collection of books was traditional rather than broad, but a love of reading became Menzies' weakness through the influence of both his parents – so much so that he was chastised for burning his candle into the night when living with his grandmother. Bob's Uncle Sydney Sampson had owned the *Jeparit Leader* and, even after he had sold it, Bob Menzies aged nine would help after school with the newspaper's preparation. Further widening of the family horizons came in 1911, when James Menzies was elected to the Victorian Legislative Assembly for the electorate of Lowan and the family moved to Melbourne. James Menzies would hold the seat until 1920.

So it was that the aspiring young Bob Menzies developed an experience of public life and a confidence in his intellectual abilities, along with a sense that his father, for all his importance, was also fallible. A recollection from a family friend, Dorothy Blair, of an incident at the Menzies family dinner table in January 1914 captures this not-so-unusual tension between father and young adult son. Robert Menzies at the time was a university student. At the dinner table an argument arose that Dorothy Blair described as something akin to 'Bob Menzies against the rest', and Kate Menzies had suggested to those who had finished eating that they might vacate the room. That evening, James Menzies apologised for his 'bumptious son Bob's precocity'.[6]

To some extent, loyalty to Bob Menzies' image and a lack of publicly available personal history from the Menzies clan has drawn a veil over much of the variety of lives and personalities that lived within it. The idea that this hardworking and seemingly settled group represented any sort of elite in the Australian character is far from the truth. It was an irritant for Judith Brett that Menzies' memoir writing did not disclose more, but this was simply the character of the man – and others of his generation. Irish-born Melbourne archbishop Daniel Mannix left very few personal papers on his death. Paul Hasluck once described, in a personal letter to biographer Allan Martin, Menzies' tendency to build 'a fence around what he regarded as his private property' adding that 'he opened the gate to very few people'.[7] From the perspective of decades later in a modern world where the famous and not so famous regularly expose much of their private lives, the more nineteenth-century preference for keeping one's private life from public view can seem somewhat mystifying. As more of the personal has come to light, it has become clear that the Menzies family contained the headstrong alongside the conventional.

As a boy, Frank Menzies reprimanded his younger brother, telling him he had a very bad temper and he needed to control it.[8] Some of Menzies' early hubris can be traced back to a growing ego. Then there was Bob's sister Belle, another headstrong member of the family. As Heather Henderson has recorded, Belle fell in love with George Green, a soldier, during the First World War. Warned not to marry George by her father, Belle was more determined than ever. Two days before George was to leave for overseas service, they married with a special licence and Belle was cut off by her parents. The story excited her great-nieces in the telling much later, but for Belle, who was reconciled with her parents after the war, there were years of deprivation as the young couple made a go of things in makeshift accommodation on a soldier settlement in the Murray River region of Mildura and Red Cliffs. Belle and George did well in time, but Belle's story of rearing her small children in tent-like conditions is far from the Bob Menzies image at the Lodge in Canberra. For all that, Bob and Belle were always very close.

Bob's brother Syd, who was ten years younger, was the only Menzies sibling who managed to get away with giving cheek to James Menzies. Over the years, Syd and Bob shared martinis on special 'drop-ins' when Menzies was home in Melbourne. Syd wasn't one to bother with the fuss of politics, and this was no doubt a good antidote for his very political brother. If Kevin Perkins' sources are to be believed, on the night Bob Menzies decided to resign as prime minister, asked by his father James whether Bob should step down, Syd is supposed to have said words to this effect, 'Of course he should. He's been there long enough. Is that all you asked me here for? In that case I'm going. Cheerio'.[9]

For aspirational parents the world over, giving children a head start also means giving them their heads, whether into the wind or not. Bob Menzies had proved to be the bright one in a bright family. His mother Kate was said to dote on him, although her indulgence should be put in context. Her granddaughter Heather recalls her being a stern force.[10] From Humffray Street State School, Bob Menzies had gone on by way of scholarships first to Ballarat's Grenville College, then to Melbourne's Wesley College and Melbourne University, from which he emerged by 1918 not only with a fistful of prizes but also an LLM. The way up was unchallenged for this bright mind. He read with legal heavyweight Owen Dixon and, in 1920 at the age of twenty-five, was advocate in the landmark Amalgamated Society of Engineers case before the High Court and won. The same year, Menzies married Pattie Maie Leckie, the daughter of prominent business-man and politician John Leckie, and in 1928 took his seat in the Victorian Legislative Council with the help of his good friend and fellow Nationalist MP Wilfrid Kent Hughes.

As political paths go, Menzies had a dream run. Moving to the Victorian lower house before a year was up, it was only a matter of time before he was an active leader of the increas-ingly popular Young Nationalists and, due to his friendship with stockbroker Staniforth Ricketson, became involved with the Labor government's acting federal treasurer, Joseph Lyons, who was facing a credit crisis for a massive loan conversion.[11] The connection Menzies made with Lyons during the November–December 1931 conversion campaign set in place a relationship that would develop through to the formation of the UAP six months later, after Lyons and a handful of Labor members left the Labor Party.

This would lead in time to the landslide victory of the UAP in December 1931 and seven years of Lyons Government. On 15 September 1934, Menzies won the UAP blue-ribbon seat of Kooyong at the federal election, sharing the day's win with his father-in-law John Leckie who, after a seat in the Victorian par-liament from 1913 and two years as the federal member for Indi (1917–19), had won a Victorian UAP Senate seat. As John Leck-ie's daughter, Pattie Menzies was the perfect partner for her politi-cally ambitious husband. Menzies was in an elated mood with the win – he had been given an assurance from Lyons that he would, in time, take over as leader of the federal parliamentary UAP.

The fairy tale, however, was to hit bumps when Menzies found the UAP preferred to leave Lyons as prime minister even as his health failed after the 1937 election. Menzies walked the political stage as a fine mind and competent political strategist but he failed to convince his colleagues that he had the same attraction for ordinary voters at a time of financial downturn. Frustrated with both policy and direction, and impatient for greater influence, Menzies resigned from the Lyons Cabinet in March 1939, only to see Lyons die in office just weeks later.

So the fairy tale took off again when Menzies became UAP leader and prime minister on 26 April. By now he had been in parliamentary politics for just over a decade. He was 44 years old, a master at political speech making, with a barrister's killer manner in the House. He was attractive to the eye, a bulky but impressive figure in an age that did not require makeovers for bushy eyebrows or a lighter build for television appearances. His voice was strong and deep and lacking in pretension, educated, but without the haughtiness of any attempt at an English aristocratic accent. In spite of this, Menzies' accession to the leadership of the UAP and role of prime minister did not occur without attracting acrimony and distrust. He won the party ballot for leader by only a handful of votes. He had stood out as a leader but had not brought colleagues with him in a significant way. To understand how this could be, it is pertinent to take a closer look at Menzies' personality and the Menzies family itself.

Robert Menzies: enigma

Menzies' rise within the UAP was not only rapid but was made with distinction. And yet, just weeks before Joe Lyons collapsed and died from heart disease largely exacerbated by the exhaustion of leading both his coalition and the nation, Menzies had resigned from the Cabinet. This had come after months of intrigue and inner-circle jostling for the chance to succeed Lyons, who had been unwell and was seeking a way to retire. Within government ranks, Menzies stood out as a leading public voice, but he could not overcome a suspicion among many of his colleagues that he was unpopular with the electorate and lacked the skills to unite their own very troubled and divided ranks. Some of this was undoubtedly due to Menzies' young man's hubris and lack of a personal touch with colleagues. But it also had a lot to do with his tendency to take advice from his close family circle and a handful of non-parliamentary associates in Melbourne rather than from any faction among parliamentary colleagues. At the same time, the presence of his influential father-in-law, Jack Leckie, in the Senate led some of his rivals in the party room to believe Menzies had an unfair advantage via upper house support within the UAP.

One of the distracting theses in any understanding of Menzies has been Judith Brett's belief that the Menzies mystique – and thus his aloofness with colleagues – can be summed up in unresolved family conflict. Brett's analysis of Robert Menzies relies on various biographies, many using comments from assorted siblings and rivals, and colleagues who had published memoirs, along with the occasional document on the public record. Brett concluded that much of the Oedipal complex applied to Menzies. His love for his gentle mother and assumed resentment of his overbearing father she saw as evidence of a son metaphorically killing his father and marrying his mother. Brett judges Menzies' loyalty to the British Empire and Queen, and relations with powerful men in this context, writing:

> The family romance is designed in part to drive a wedge
> between mother and father and it assigns them different roles.
> My main interest is in the way Menzies' relationship with his
> father played itself out in his relations with other men … It
> is not too fanciful to suggest that Menzies' feelings for his
> mother were the basis of his later deep attachments to Queen
> Elizabeth II and the Queen Mother.[12]

In other words, Robert Menzies resented his father James and went on to replace him by looking up to more powerful men ('his childhood awe of his father lived on in his life-long pre-occupation with great men').[13] This view of Menzies, with his putative resentment of his father, whom he replaced with powerful men as his mentors; and his dismissive view of women, even suspicion of women, due to his mother's purported betrayal of him as his protector, makes him an enigmatic figure with patriarchal hang-ups.

Brett's reliance on Kevin Perkins' biography of Menzies and Allan Dawes' unpublished work on Menzies,[14] however, leaves open the possibility that some of her evidence is not sustainable. Former Menzies colleague (also a journalistic colleague of John Curtin) and respected war historian Paul Hasluck regarded much of the Perkins' biography of Menzies to be 'a poor piece of journalism in hard covers' with 'no study of source material to give a body of verified fact and no understanding of the man or of the political situations in which he moved'.[15] Overall, Hasluck regarded the Perkins biography as a put-up job strongly supported by Perkins' friend Bill McCall, a knockabout type of UAP MP from Sydney who harboured a strong enmity for Menzies. The (undocumented) hearsay and gossip upon which Perkins relied left Hasluck believing it to be 'an unworthy book' and 'in the larger sense ... an untrue one'.[16] In these same notes, Hasluck also referred to Allan Dawes as 'a bloated, and frequently sozzled journalist' who was 'notorious' for self-inflated yarns. In other words, much of what Dawes claimed had often little respect for reality.[17]

Since the publication of Menzies' letters to his daughter, Heather, and the release of other family letters and papers, it is now obvious that Menzies was not at all distanced from his family. In fact, he was quite the reverse. His close attachments to the Menzies clan gave him a support base that was both strongly encouraging of his success and well versed in political experience.

In his appearance of self-sufficiency as a public figure, one with impeccable political contacts and networks, Menzies could come across to colleagues who had barely their personal experience for political background as having an untouchable air. Many took this for smug self-satisfaction. That, combined with his legal and bar training – which encouraged him to see the world as an intellectual duel – and his erudite mind, did much to distance Menzies from the ordinary, easygoing Australian ambience. His most acid denigrator during his prime ministership between April 1939 and August 1941 was UAP colleague Bill McCall. McCall had been schooled at Sydney Grammar but was forced to leave at sixteen to help support his family after his father died.

For most who knew Menzies, he was explained not by the unconscious mind theorised by Brett but the mind of which they were very conscious. The young lawyer Robert Menzies, called to the bar in 1918, had quickly secured rooms at Selborne Chambers, in Chancery Lane, Melbourne, just before the burgeoning in numbers of barristers joining the Victorian bar following the end of the First World War. Accepted as a bright star among legal graduates, Menzies was instantly at home in this club-like atmosphere of chambers, where a crowd of learned males swapped banter and quips, along with smart-alec comebacks. The lawyers were housed in inadequate space in rooms on two levels that opened onto a long gallery where silks and clever younger minds alike exchanged opinions and reports of the day in the open.[18] It was a milieu, following a prize-winning time at university, to help preserve in Menzies much of his outward confidence and impatience with slow thinkers.

Menzies' legal contemporary Percy Joske often saw Menzies at close quarters. Like Paul Hasluck, Joske came to a view that it was more than vanity in Menzies that accounted for his sharpness with opponents and abrasiveness in his quick backhanders and put-downs. While Hasluck considered much of Menzies' inflated behaviour a cover for shyness, Joske also felt that a certain amount of inferiority complex was responsible:

> It has been a matter for discussion on various occasions
> whether an inferiority complex accounted in large measure for
> Menzies' thrusting himself forward on all occasions and for
> his habit of denigrating rivals. Possibly an inferiority complex
> exists to some degree in each individual. In the case of
> Menzies there was certainly a fierce determination to succeed,
> which made him cause offence to others, often thereby doing
> himself harm.[19]

Both Hasluck and Joske recognised the actor in Menzies – something all first-rate barristers and politicians need to be. This also covered Menzies' lack of ease in social networking, where pressing the flesh too often means leaving oneself open to spontaneous warmth. Professor Geoffrey Blainey, while an academic at Melbourne University, spent many occasions at formal events where Robert Menzies played a leading role, yet he could not recall ever having had a conversation with the man, even though he had observed that among Menzies' books donated to Melbourne University as the Robert Menzies Collection there were quite a number of his own.

In the 1950s, Blainey's Labor-leaning father, a Methodist minister, had been asked to preach at an anniversary celebration for Jeparit's Methodist church, where James Menzies, although a Presbyterian, had been a stalwart member and Bible teacher. Robert Menzies attended the occasion and sat in the front row of the church, yet he did not speak to the Reverend SC Blainey on the day. Years later, when Reverend Blainey was introduced to Menzies at a function, Menzies could recall how good Clifford Blainey's preaching had been at Jeparit. The prime minister had observed it on the day and yet not made his feelings known or even engaged with the minister. In recalling it years later as a way of making conversation, Menzies' belated praise left a warm glow with the Reverend Blainey, but it also suggests that Menzies MP was a very formal networker.[20] This sort of public formality, the need to have something in common to discuss, can often provide a safety net for those who find small talk difficult, for the personality who would prefer to mix with the familiar rather than make connections at a host of political gatherings.

Menzies was not a natural people networker of the Bob Hawke or Joseph Lyons variety. His connections with people were all too often conducted on the basis of information and common experience, and therefore he could appear aloof. In Percy Joske's recollection, even as a brash fifteen-year-old new boy at Wesley College, Menzies threw himself at others immediately, boldly talking of where he was from and all manner of matters, even those he was wrong about, so that 'within a week' he knew most of the 500 boys at the school.[21] But it was a case of throwing himself at others rather than winning their friendship.

Menzies' way into politics lacked the grassroots thrust of most aspiring politicians – the way up of his father James, for example, the storekeeper who won the seat of Lowan in the Wimmera, or of his mother's brother, Sydney Sampson, editor of the Warracknabeal newspaper and a federal MP from 1906 to 1919. Robert Menzies' political rise came via a position of note in a profession of top minds. The good connections he had gained as a university high achiever, editor of the *Melbourne University Magazine*, president of the student representative council and a notable debater, and then as an up-and-coming barrister at Selborne Chambers, had delivered, after one false start, a seat in the upper house of the Victorian parliament. This was followed by a relatively safe seat in the lower house and then, in quick succession, the offer of the blue-ribbon federal seat of Kooyong where little could shake him. Only at the 1937 federal election did Menzies ever suffer any shock at the electoral count, and even then he still had an absolute majority of 1500 votes.

Like all successful public figures who lead nations or large followings, Robert Menzies was observed by many over time. In any life, a cocktail of experiences and people leave their mark on personality, and one's genes and temperament also play their part. Menzies himself, and others who knew him, believed he took more of his personality from his mother's Sampson side – the Cornish not the Scottish side – and yet it was as a Scot that Menzies so often identified his ethnic inheritance. As he told his audience in Ulster on 3 April 1941: 'First I am an Australian; second, I am the descendant of a Scot; and third, I am in Northern Ireland'.[22] The Scots influence was strong among the elite of Melbourne's business and legal circles, and this may have facilitated Menzies' rapid assimilation into Nationalist Party ranks.

Even so, while Menzies' political sensitivities were strongly aligned with non-Labor, a great deal of his early appreciation of the play and nuance of politics came from the grandfather he loved to spend time with – old John Sampson, who had been president of the miners' union in Creswick and who had what Menzies recalled as 'the divine facility of not talking down to children'.[23] Then there was James Menzies, who left his son with not only sharp memories of severe chastisements but also an ability to curb a hot temper in public. Joske writes of Menzies' boast that he was the only Victorian barrister never to have had a row with one particularly irascible judge, recalling that Menzies said the judge reminded him of his father and 'knowing the signs of rising tide, I was able to avoid it welling over'.[24]

There is little evidence that Robert Menzies, any more than other sons, spurned his father's authority. All adults readjust their relationship with their parents. Many grow quite distant from their early influences. This cannot be said of Robert Menzies, for whom the family conference often determined decisions. A family conference set in place the resolution that Robert Menzies would not join his two older brothers, Frank and Les, to enlist for action in the First World War.[25] The decision left Menzies with a burden he would have to carry for the rest of his life – the stigma of having stayed at home while others went to their graves defending the Empire – and it was not a decision he felt he could share in public. So the stigma hung about him, to be pulled out at political meetings by his opponents, and eventually by his Country Party colleague Sir Earle Page in federal parliament in April 1939, after Menzies won the leadership of the UAP. Even then, Menzies refused to make public the real reason he had not joined up, saying, 'Those questions relate to a man's intimate, personal and family affairs'.[26]

Like any large family, the Menzies family was a diverse mixture of the ordinary and extraordinary. On the Sampson side alone, Kate Menzies was one of thirteen half-siblings and siblings. Pattie Menzies told author Ronald Seth that their wedding was a 'large quiet one' because 'my husband's family was a very big one, and though most of the guests were members of the family, there seemed to be hundreds of them'.[27] The Menzies–Sampson collective was something of a tribe, and like all tribes had its tensions and rivalries but remained together. Writing to his enlisted son Ken on 18 February 1943, Menzies gave away something of the nature of this tribal unity:

All the rest of the family are well. As you can imagine, last weekend and the weekend before I was inundated with good family advice from Father and Mother, Frank and the rest of them. Thank Heaven, they are never entirely obdurate because, though when I arrive on Saturday morning I usually find that they all disagree with me – by Monday night, when I am leaving for Canberra again, they seem to be satisfied that

I wasn't wrong after all. You must not take this as a proof of my persuasiveness but of their willingness.[28]

Menzies kept in close contact with his parents and siblings throughout his life. In the week he made his momentous decision in 1941 to quit as prime minister, Menzies was photographed for the press with his father by his side as he arrived back in Melbourne from Canberra on 23 August and again on 30 August. His father remained among his mentors and supporters. Heather Henderson told her audience at the Sydney Institute on 23 October 2013 that while she had found her grandparents somewhat old and austere, her father was devoted to them always.

At home in Melbourne, especially during his years in opposition, Menzies often dropped by his younger brother Syd's house. 'Whenever I am in Melbourne on Saturday', he wrote to Ken on 5 June 1945, 'I usually end up my walk by calling on Syd and drinking what he calls a "Southerly Buster" '.[29] His older brother Frank was a strong supporter, and offered special strength following Menzies' resignation as party leader in 1941. Frank Menzies could also offer cautionary advice, such as that delicately tendered in a long letter on 5 May 1942:

> Of your capacity – mental, physical and spiritual I have
> no doubt – for making this acknowledgement I refer more
> particularly to your deep-down innate qualities of mind and
> soul. They have required some tempering as with the rest of
> us but few have shown the same patience and good temper in
> much less rigorous testing.[30]

The Menzies family was both fan club and nurturer. Advice, in the quieter political years from late 1941, came with hope that their talented family member would once more fulfil his destiny as a political leader. In his letter, Frank went on to point out gently the value of collegiality: 'Cultivate particularly your political fellows – by words of praise when they can be spared. I have been conscious lately of the value of the attitude declared by a friend as that of the old AIF: "We learnt to appreciate men, not to criticise them"'. As he wrote this, Frank also pushed his brother to remain resolute, to find a way back as leader of the UAP:

> The leadership of the Opposition will follow. I am persuaded, when the call comes to assume a vital role as Opposition, Fadden must fade as real leadership is demanded … a day is not distant when the 'backbone' of which you have spoken so eloquently and so movingly will stir and the nervous system will become re-invigorated to deal with the ever rising tide of politics and knavish tricks.

Menzies' parents remained close to their children and attended events at high points in Menzies' career. They were present as he appeared for the first time in a case before the High Court, which he won. This impressed James Menzies, who opined later to his wife, 'It seems that I've underestimated Bob'.[31] It was a tale Menzies enjoyed telling. They were also present in Canberra on 3 May 1939 as their son made his first appearance as prime minister in the House of Representatives. Father and mother were important as loyal supporters in Menzies' public life – as are any parents proud of their children.

Letters Menzies wrote to his son Ken, in the war years and beyond, hold snippets of family reflection. Menzies had a warm regard for his own father James, and had long since shelved any resentment at his father's disapproval. In fact, for Menzies the seasoned politician, his father was something of a family treasure who had become fondly amusing in his idiosyncrasies. Menzies had much fun relating to Ken, on 2 September 1943, the scene created by James Menzies' efforts at a Kooyong polling station during the federal election:

> He got to the booth at 8 am as usual and was on how-to-vote card duty all day. Syd went across during the day, but was very soon ordered off as a nincompoop! The old man was performing his usual stunt of taking Labor tickets out of the hands of people and tearing them up and dropping them over the fence, and using honeyed words as he pressed my own ticket into more or less reluctant hands! … Unfortunately, one result of the day's exertions is that Father is now in bed with a heavy cold, but even in a recumbent position he can still reconstruct the political world to his own complete satisfaction.[32]

And it was not to any adopted great male mentor that Menzies turned as he weighed up his most momentous decision in politics in August 1941. During the hours he contemplated resigning as prime minister, from the dream he had harboured as a schoolboy, the dejected Menzies rang his father for advice. James Menzies shared the moment with the assembled family, who listened in and gave their various opinions of what Bob should do. James and his son were a close team. It made the son strong and ambitious, and set the bar high. In public leadership, however, Menzies had been forced to face for the first time a test he would fail. His close family ties had not prepared him for that.

3

Last days of appeasement

Churchill's outlook on foreign policy and defence has
been given a retrospective consistency that the facts hardly
warrant. He referred in 1933 to Mussolini as 'the greatest
law giver among living men' and as 'the Roman genius'.
In 1935 he wrote a piece on Hitler which gave him, if not
the benefit of the doubt, at least the possibility. As late
as 1937, he thought that Hitler might yet do good for
Germany.

– Robert Blake[1]

War was to haunt the first Menzies Government, and also its
prime minister. As the last months of the Lyons years played out
in 1938 and the first months of 1939, the UAP split into personal
factions over the government's approach to rearmament and
conscription, the Munich agreement with Hitler over Czechoslovakia, and the introduction of a national insurance scheme.
Ministers resigned while Prime Minister Joseph Lyons held
strong in public as his failing health became increasingly plain in
private. His death on 7 April 1939, Good Friday, came suddenly
all the same. He had collapsed on the way to the Easter Show
in Sydney and barely regained consciousness over most of the
two days he lay in St Vincent's Hospital. As the first Australian

prime minister to die in office – and one so loved by ordinary people – his death was a dramatic moment for a nation. The mourning was immense, onlookers many deep along the streets of Sydney as his coffin passed to the quay from where it was to go by destroyer to his home state of Tasmania for burial.

Nature had decided what the UAP could not – there would be a fresh start and direction for a party that had moved beyond the financial crisis that prompted its formation in 1932. Depression had given way to the more chilling dangers of another world war, and the question of the party leadership would now have to be resolved. Lyons had gone. He could no longer be asked to hang in at the helm to bandage over party differences. The party now had to decide for itself. The last months of the Lyons Government had been weeks of tension, described bluntly by Dick Casey's wife, Maie, in a letter to her friend Hilda Abbott at the end of 1938: 'Politics here have been ghastly for the last six months. Dick has been struggling along preserving his sanity ... Bob [Menzies] is going about disgruntled and moaning because he isn't PM and daily threatens to resign. What one needs is a little more team spirit'.[2]

Menzies was elected leader of the UAP on 18 April, *The Age* reporting the following day that he would 'probably' be prime minister by 'tomorrow evening'. The outcome had been close – Menzies had won by just four votes against the ageing and irascible Billy Hughes. In fact, the victory was achieved against strong opposition from the NSW section of the party, which had tried to swing the NSW members' votes by arguing state issues in the party room.[3] An attempt had also been made before the vote to get NSW premier Bertram Stevens to move to federal politics so as to become leader – his supporters finally threw their weight behind Hughes in the hope he would keep the seat warm for Stevens.[4] It was not a resounding start for Menzies, and he had yet to convince Country Party leader and acting prime minister Earle Page that it was in the interests of his party to continue in coalition with the UAP to retain government.

Earle Page, whose bitterness towards Menzies was common knowledge, had also tried to convince Australia's high commissioner in London, former prime minister Stanley Bruce, to offer himself as a national leader.[5] The move was full of backroom high drama and a number of lengthy telephone calls to Los Angeles where Bruce, returning to London from Australia, could be reached briefly on his way home via Washington and San Francisco. Page's moves were supported by UAP heavyweight Dick Casey, who stood for the leadership position himself when Bruce eventually declined. Paul Hasluck, in notes he made about Kevin Perkins' biography of Menzies, writes of Bruce telling him that while Page had approached him to put his name forward, he said he would do so only with the 'assurance that a significant majority of both the United Australia Party and the Country Party wanted him and that the two parties would work in coalition under him. He did not want to be caught up in Page's own manoeuvres'.[6] The account by Page in his memoir *Truant Surgeon* confirms that he was obsessed with keeping Menzies out of the top job. But his resentment over Menzies' resignation from the Lyons ministry in March and his suggestion that this had pushed Lyons to his death was not matched by Lyons' actual reaction to the Menzies resignation. Enid Lyons recorded that her husband had not resented Menzies going, despite wishing it had not happened. Lyons told his wife that he believed Menzies had shown a basic integrity in resigning over his disagreement with policy.[7]

Hasluck believed Perkins had misunderstood Bruce's position; quite possibly so had Page. In his interview, Bruce told Hasluck he had never suggested to Page that he would be happy to lead a national government. Indeed, reading the transcripts of Page's conversations with Bruce (taken down by a stenographer at Page's instruction), it is obvious that Bruce was somewhat unsure of what exactly he was being asked to do.[8] Moreover, Page himself had a very poor idea of what might be possible – his plan was strangely makeshift and ignored the realities of party feeling and constitutional possibilities. In the transcripts, Bruce's signature aloofness comes through and he sounds nothing like a man who wanted to return to Australia and lead a nation – he had a US president to meet in Washington, a Trade Fair to attend in San Francisco, and the only concession he would make was to stay on the west coast for a day or so until Page could sort out if Bruce would be 'asked' to return to Australia (by whom it was not clear) to become a non-party prime minister

In the hope of pushing Menzies aside, Page continued to favour the formation of a government of all parties. Soon enough, opposition leader John Curtin publicly rejected any notion of a national government on the grounds that, 'If there could be anything worse than a government consisting of two parties it would be a government consisting of three parties'.[9] All three parties continued to shake with internal divisions. As Gavin Souter has observed, 'In the confused period immediately ahead, from 1939 to 1941, parliament could have produced something worse than a government of three parties, namely a government of three disunited parties'.[10] It had been a circus, out of which Menzies assumed a shaky mantle at the head of the not-so-very-united UAP.

Menzies was now leader of his party but had lost the UAP its coalition partner – Earle Page had declared the Country Party would not maintain a coalition with the UAP while Menzies was its leader. Page announced in the House, on 20 April, that 'it is beyond question that the change in leadership of the United Australia party has resulted in a change in the relationship of the two parties composing the Government'.[11] He followed this with an outburst that rocked the House. Helen Page, Earle Pages' daughter-in-law, typed the speech and in 1979 she wrote to Ken Menzies about it:

> I happened to be Sir Earle Page's secretary in April 1939 and typed the fateful speech for the eighth or ninth time, taking the paragraph in and out many times. Everybody involved at the centre like Lady Page, Tom Paterson, myself, advised against this, knowing that it would reflect more on himself for using it than your father. But Archie Cameron, who was a very militaristic Highland non-gentleman with very authoritative urges, kept on at him until he persuaded him … he was such a strong willed man, but he regretted it for the rest of his life.[12]

The tragic paragraph, which gave listeners an embarrassing jolt, took just a few minutes. Page had three indictments to make against the new UAP leader Menzies: twenty-four days earlier he had resigned from the Lyons ministry over the domestic matter of national insurance, just as the world moved through a series of crises most likely to end in war; twenty-four weeks earlier Menzies had made a disloyal speech on the UAP leadership; and twenty-four years earlier Menzies had refused to fight for his country in the First World War. As Page saw it, Menzies was not fit to lead a nation facing a global war. He was not the leader Australia needed. The House was in uproar at such a shabby, even outrageous, outburst. Andrew Tink has recorded that Page himself had an ambivalent service record in the Great War and, personal spite and malice aside, was hardly in a position to judge the worth of others' contributions.[13]

The speech ensured Page would soon lose the leadership of the Country Party, and it opened a large gash in coalition unity that would hover around Menzies' leadership of the UAP. The enmity between the two men would not be easily overcome for years, their differences arising as much from personality as policy settings. Menzies had distrusted Page for more than a decade and made much fun of him in private after their time together for trade talks in London in 1936. And Page could never quite match Menzies in superior put-downs, which meant he left himself open to reprisal following his bitter parliamentary attack on Menzies. In all this, like old warriors in the field, neither man gained ground – Menzies needed unity but could not match Joe Lyons in the diplomatic relations required for coalition; Page needed the respect of his colleagues and had lost it, despite retaining his hold on the leadership for another few months.

Four days after his speech to parliament, Page faced a testy meeting of the NSW Country Party's Central Council, at which he defended and rationalised his words to the House. In spite of much debate at the meeting, colleagues endorsed Page's decision not to form a coalition with the Menzies' Government and only to support a national government 'under a leader who would be acceptable to all parties prepared to co-operate'. But as Country/National Party historian Paul Davey has concluded, 'Page was in an untenable position', and after the declaration of war in September 'his leadership was finished'.[14]

While he remained acting prime minister after the death of Lyons, however, Page could determine the sitting dates of parliament until his successor had been sworn in. So he made sure Menzies would wait. On 20 April, when Page had announced in the House that he would hand in his commission to the governor-general that afternoon, he also announced that there would be a two-week parliamentary recess to enable the new government to choose a ministry. The Country Party would not be part of that ministry. In yet another ploy, Page hoped Governor-General Lord Gowrie might be persuaded that without the Country Party, the UAP would not be strong enough to form a government. Instead, Page's attack on Menzies resulted in Artie Fadden and three of his Country Party colleagues dissociating themselves from the party. In the political turmoil, Lord Gowrie handed the government to Menzies, asking him how long he thought it would last. Menzies' tongue-in-cheek reply was six weeks.[15] In September, a few months later, Page was replaced as Country Party leader by Archie Cameron, which seemed to heal the party's rift. Menzies was nevertheless unable to attract the Country Party to rejoin the coalition, as both Page and Cameron insisted they should have the right to advise on ministerial positions given to their party members, something Menzies refused to allow.

Empire or isolation

The First World War still threw a long shadow over the world; the 1919 Treaty of Versailles had brokered a peace that left unresolved many territorial ambitions and imposed heavy penalties on Germany. At the same time, new agents of change had been released in the rise of Soviet communism, with its ideological crusade to overthrow capitalism and create an international Soviet republic. The old arguments of capital versus labour had morphed into battles between left and right, between fascism and communism. In Australia, as in other democracies, the growing influence of followers of the Comintern and the spread of international socialism was felt keenly at Labor Party conferences and trade union meetings. This complicated party aspirations and, at times, hampered Labor in its ability to forge a foreign policy clear of ideological baggage.

Paul Hasluck gives a comprehensive analysis of Labor's dilemma over its international priorities in *The Government and the People, 1939–1941*. By 1938, Labor's defence policy had boiled down to one of isolationist homeland defence, opposed to Australia's involvement in what might be termed 'other people's wars'. Writing for the *Australian Worker* after the Munich crisis,

Labor leader John Curtin opined: 'Australia must keep out of the quarrels of Europe and not dissipate its resources, thereby exposing this country to far worse dangers'. He followed this up with an article on 'collective security' in the same magazine in November 1938, writing, 'As an ideal, collective security is admirable. But as a practical policy in a world based upon imperialism ... it is a highly dangerous idea'.[16] This was one step beyond appeasement. With the Munich agreement, leaders such as Chamberlain, Lyons and Menzies were desperate to make extreme, albeit futile efforts to broker a peace deal with Hitler in an attempt to stem his advance – a policy now derided as 'appeasement'. Australia's then opposition went one step further, however. By its isolationist approach to international collective security, Labor embraced a policy that left Hitler to do what he might – it was not Australia's affair.

It says much about the dominant issue of 1939 that within a week of the Menzies Government coming to office, a day was set aside for parliament to discuss the international situation. On 9 May, Minister for External Affairs Sir Henry Gullett opened the House debate saying, 'The time has come when Australia should show a keener interest, and play a larger part, in discussions and consultations upon foreign affairs, and especially, as my right honorable leader (Mr. Menzies) has already said, in the affairs of the Pacific'.[17] Telegraphic communications would also ensure that correspondence from Australia's contacts around the world would be received 'immediately', and this 'diplomatic service' would include dispatches to and from Whitehall and 'from consuls and agents spread not only throughout Europe and parts of Asia but also over many countries even further afield'. Collective security would be a key component of the new Menzies Government.

Gullett's speech, however, underlined the delicate and dangerous game the Western powers had entered. Appeasement still governed what passed for policy in confronting the increasing territorial expansion in central and eastern Europe by Germany, which had long since disregarded the constraints of the Versailles peace agreement. Gullett referred to the intensified negotiations between Hitler and Britain and France during 1938, after Germany's annexation (*Anschluss*) of Austria, as 'all these recorded conversations and consultations between the defensive nations', which had come about because of 'an ardent, almost a pathetic, desire and prayer for peace'. He did not believe this was in any sense out of a fear of 'the Fuhrer of Germany or the Duce of Italy and their vast armed legions and various hideous engines of destruction' but a 'fear of modern war'.

This was the generation that had so recently participated in the carnage of the First World War, a generation that faced with horror any suggestion that war might happen again. In graphic ways, this was also the generation reminded of the outcomes of war – the tens of thousands of maimed husbands and fathers who had returned and the tens of thousands who had not, so that acres of white crosses had filled new military graveyards across northern France and Belgium, graveyards that Australians visited throughout the 1920s and 1930s, from leaders such as Joseph Lyons to relatives who could afford the sea voyage to Europe. The fear of 'actual war', Gullett believed, was 'the strongest factor working for peace'. It would be this conviction that undermined any realistic assessment of Hitler's intentions and character on the part of the British Government and its Allies over the next four months.

Sir Alexander Cadogan, UK permanent under-secretary at the Foreign Office, recorded the view from Whitehall in his diary entries for 1938–39. In October 1938, after Munich and before *Kristallnacht*, he mused, 'We must cut our losses in central and eastern Europe – let Germany, if she can, find there her "lebensraum", and establish herself, if she can, as a powerful economic unit'.[18] Historian Ian Kershaw argues that 'it is easy to see in retrospect' how misguided were judgments of Hitler by Britain but 'less easy at the time to grasp the enormity of what Hitler meant'.[19] In the early years of the Third Reich, this meant the Nazi regime could use its 'initial position of international vulnerability and isolation to forge one of formidable strength'.[20]

Such sentiment and its tendency to evaluate Germany's Nazi leader in similar terms to previously known dictators could not envisage the horrific reality that would be the Third Reich's 1940s Europe. This explains both Menzies' and Curtin's rationalisation of German totalitarianism as a matter only for the German people. As John Curtin explained to parliament on 9 May 1939,

> [Germans] learn that democratic systems do not necessarily
> mean work and food and decent living standards, and,
> therefore, they are warranted, not in contrasting the speeches
> of leaders of other countries ... but in measuring up how far
> the form of political system that they have accepted yields
> to them a more satisfactory internal social standing than does
> the democratic system.[21]

While Curtin argued that such a system of government was unacceptable to the people of democracies such as Australia and the United Kingdom, he suggested that the system of government chosen by the German people was a matter for them and not something Australia or the British Empire had any justification for opposing.[22] As Cadogan's diary entry suggested back in October 1938, the hope was that Hitler might find his 'red line' somewhere in continental Europe, and in a way that would not involve the United Kingdom.

As Henry Gullett made clear in his speech to the House on 9 May, however, that red line was already moving to the west of Europe. 'It is disclosing no secret to say', Gullett told the House, 'that in very recent months, even weeks, there has been profound concern for Holland, Switzerland, Belgium and even Denmark'. For all that, Gullett believed there was still hope that war, for Australia and the United Kingdom, might be avoided. Japan was a signatory to the anti-communist pact with Germany, but why should it prefer new friends such as Germany to 'far older friends throughout the British Empire'? He added, 'Why should Japan enter upon a war – I do not suggest that it will, and the latest news from Japan declares that it will not – which would be of incalculable proportions and dangers to it in the Pacific?'

When Gullett looked to Europe, he could not believe Mussolini would want to be dragged, by Germany, into a crippling war either. As for Hitler, he had broken the Versailles conditions, taken Austria and Czechoslovakia and persecuted the Jewish population – most obviously in the horrors of *Kristallnacht* on the nights of 9–10 November 1938. But Hitler had also restored the German economy and spirit, which led Gullett to ask: 'Will Hitler, now that it is made plain to him that bloodless mobilisation, demonstration and intrigue, will no longer win him enlarged dominion, pause and consolidate his Germany, and give to it early prosperity and riches by relieving it of the crushing burden of armaments?' There were no answers to Gullett's rhetorical question – only hope.

Labor's appeasement and home defence

Labor leader John Curtin, in responding to Gullett, confirmed his party's support for enhanced diplomatic involvement as a way to avert war, but also pointed out that Labor was opposed to any involvement in war by Australian troops without the sanction of a parliamentary vote. He also gave voice to Labor's pacifist suspicions about warmongering, which suggested that Curtin, as much as any other, favoured appeasement:

The efforts of the British Government in its negotiations
for peace were to some extent made difficult by the partisan
activities of those who are more concerned, as it were,
with fighting Hitler than with establishing peace. There is
unquestionably in the world a class that has a vested interest
in war and war-making, and the propagandist activities
which are employed in the interests of this exploiting and
ruthless class, which is international in character, have made
difficulties for all governments, including, I believe, the
governments of dictators.[23]

Curtin placed his faith in Australian public opinion to the extent
of believing that no action should be taken without first consulting that opinion. Paul Hasluck makes it clear that public opinion
in Australia during 1939

was still concerned almost solely with home defence in the
sense of resistance to a Japanese invasion and the protection
of Australia against raids or blockade ... The common
thought seemed to be that Australia would have enough to do
to keep herself alive while someone else won the war.[24]

On the question of the Axis powers, and Germany in particular,
Labor continued to see capitalism as the ultimate evil, so that
a degree of moral equivalence prevailed in much of its evaluation of any culpability for the deteriorating situation in Europe.
John Curtin reminded the House that 'the leaders of those countries [Germany, Japan, Italy] would probably blame happenings
antecedent to the present situation, for which the democracies
will frankly admit that they have a degree of responsibility'.[25]
For Curtin, the voices of the Australian people should be heard
throughout the world, those voices of a democratic nation, voices
that could influence the aspirations of dictators such as Hitler

and Mussolini far more than the leaders of Britain or France in their negotiations with those dictators. As strongly as any, Curtin wanted peace through negotiation. He also opposed war as an instrument of change within totalitarian nations: 'No war, even in Europe, should be a war fought either to defend or to create political systems against other political systems'.[26]

In the debate in the House of Representatives on 9 May, Curtin was followed by Labor's Maurice Blackburn, who added his support for appeasement, along with naivety of judgment, wilful or otherwise, on the totalitarian forces of Europe, saying:

The only sure way to peace is for the people of the British races to negotiate with the German people to-day, and to show a willingness to meet them on such terms that everybody will be able to live in security … The alignment of democracies against totalitarian states does not worry the hungry man. He can be just as hungry, unhappy, and miserable in London or Paris as in Berlin or Rome, or, for that matter, in Melbourne or Sydney; the system of government he lives under is not, to him, the all-important consideration. No great difference exists between democracies and totalitarian states … There is no great difference between Mr. Chamberlain and Herr Hitler.[27]

It took Labor's Frank Brennan to voice what many on his side of the House and beyond the parliament were thinking. The years of financial downturn had left a long shadow; the aggression of a European dictator towards countries many Australians had barely heard of – what John Curtin referred to as 'remote parts of the world'[28] – did not especially resonate. After sneering at 'this little, marooned, helpless, minority-Government', Brennan, a Labor-heartland heavy, summed it up as he saw it: 'And so we are spending the greater part of to-day's sitting on matters which really have very little concern at all with Australia, not-withstanding the fact that there are many pressing and urgent matters awaiting attention that do intimately affect the people of this country'.[29]

War: yes and no

The new Menzies Government was technically a minority government. At the time, the Victorian Country Party Government was supported by state Labor MPs. Federally, however, the non-Labor parties had established a working coalition, both informally and formally, over almost two decades. Page had now taken his party out of the ministry but there was little likelihood of federal Country Party MPs siding with Labor on any significant issues. Soon after taking office, Menzies also shelved the national insurance scheme that had so troubled the Country Party with its costs to business, taking another point of contention among non-Labor MPs out of play. And, while the overriding concern was international instability and the possibility of war, all parties had no disagreement with the option, while it worked, of appeasing potential aggressors in the hope war would not eventuate. As Menzies told the House on 9 May, in reply to other speakers: 'I am concerned with whether we can, as a civilized nation in a civilized world, stand for any method of rectifying grievances only by armed threats'.[30]

The world of the 1930s had relied on the presence of the newly formed League of Nations to police global tensions, especially those among the great powers. By 1938, however, the league as a peace body was increasingly finding its efforts to preserve relations between many of its members, and non-league nations such as Germany, less and less effective. Hitler had taken Germany out of the league in 1933; in 1936 he had remilitarised the Rhineland, and in 1938 he had annexed Austria. Meanwhile, under Mussolini, Italy had invaded and acquired Abyssinia (now Ethiopia), a member of the league. In addition, Germany's massive rearmament after 1934 was against all terms of its peace settlement under the agreement at Versailles. The hastily negotiated Munich agreement between Britain and Hitler on 29 September 1938 had lasted just a few weeks, after which Hitler had taken the Sudetenland. By the end of March 1939, Hitler had invaded and taken control of Czechoslovakia. The league remained powerless to stop any of this. As Hitler moved, the overwhelming impulse of the leaders of the United Kingdom, France, the United States and the British dominions was to work for negotiated settlements between disputing nations, all in the potential shadow of another global Armageddon.

The new Menzies Government had its first test of strength with its legislation to create a Department of Supply and the National Registration Bill – a project begun but by no means completed by the Lyons Government. The legislation once passed would set up a manpower survey conducted by census of all males aged eighteen to sixty-four and establish a National Register Board to oversee the allocation of manpower. Labor opposed the bill on the grounds that it meant industrial conscription and would be a forerunner to military conscription. As late as 25 May, news reports suggested that the vote was uncertain and would be close. Former minister for Customs Thomas White and UAP member Bill McCall moved amendments to the legislation.[31] On 31 May the government had to apply the guillotine to shut down the debate, during which Country Party leader Earle Page had told the House he 'was prepared to support certain portions of Mr Forde's [Labor] amendment'.[32] The bill was passed by thirty-seven votes to twenty-six with no defections from the Country Party, despite that party's earlier opposition to parts of the bill. In news reports, the Country Party was accused of delaying the legislation. Soon after the bill was passed, in mid-June, parliament rose and did not assemble again until 6 September, by which time war had been declared.

Robert Menzies had become prime minister of a country with both unsettled party leaderships and unsettled feelings about national goals. For a decade, economic hardship had governed the lives of most citizens. Australia had recovered from the Great Depression better than most – real GDP growth in the United States between 1929 and 1940 was only 1.6 per cent, while in Australia over the same period it was around 16.6 per cent.[33] But as Australians slowly returned to more settled financial times, the uncertainty of their international security bedevilled expectations. In spite of aggressive provocations by both Germany and Japan, negotiated settlement with both countries continued to occupy the minds of key players at Whitehall, up to and beyond the declaration of war in September. Throughout 1939, the new Menzies Government worked towards opening diplomatic missions in both Tokyo and Washington DC.

In the House, during the debate on international relations on 9 May, Menzies reminded members of the 'patience' with which the United Kingdom had handled the aggression of the European dictators – 'two years of forbearance in dealing with the affairs of Europe'[34] – and that Australia's sea routes and trade would not be 'unmolested' should a European war break out. Then there was the problem of Japan in the Pacific. In Whitehall, Foreign Secretary Lord Halifax had reacted very slowly, prevaricating with growing apprehension, to the murder in April of a Japanese agent by two Chinese in the British concession of Tientsin (now Tianjin), less than 160 kilometres south-east of Beijing.[35] The city was well inside the zone gained by the Japanese in 1937 but the British refused to hand over the two Chinese. Finally, the Japanese blockaded the city and all but starved it to force it to surrender.

The eventual handover of the accused Chinese and some fancy diplomacy by the British ambassador, Sir Robert Craigie, in Tokyo saved Britain from hostilities with Japan, but the whole affair emphasised how weakened the British were in the region and how overstretched was their global naval capacity. As historian David Dilks put it,

> Australia and New Zealand had been assured on a number
> of occasions since 1937 that a battle fleet would be sent
> to Singapore in the event of serious trouble with Japan,
> regardless of the European situation. On 20 March 1939,
> Australians were told that this undertaking no longer held
> good, a painful fact which the Tientsin crisis confirmed.[36]

Doubt within Australia over whether Britain could be relied on in the event of Australia being attacked by the Japanese was of growing concern. This gave strength to Labor's arguments that, whatever military divisions Australia might raise and equip, home defence was of paramount importance. And if negotiating or talking could push the idea of armed conflict further from the nation's shores, well and good. When, in July, Menzies headed off to meet and greet voters in South Australia and Western Australia, he confronted criticism that his government was planning for all-out militarisation. He defended his government, arguing that Labor was scaremongering over industrial conscription and propagandising about a 'chaotic' parliament. He could point to a successful parliamentary session – starting just six days after the ministry had been sworn in. The prime minister had the confidence of his team, and government was rolling along with an up-beat productivity.

But even as Menzies spoke to meetings and answered press questions, Earle Page was addressing the electoral council in his own electorate of Cowper and attacking Menzies in much the same vogue as his bitter parliamentary address: 'The national leader must have courage, judgement and loyalty. Mr Menzies does not possess these qualities which are needed to fit him to be the leader of the country in these times of international crisis'.[37] Menzies replied, when asked, that he had become 'accustomed' to personal attacks from the leader of the Country Party, which he assumed were supported by all members of that party except its four rebels – Fadden, Oliver Badman, Bernard Corser and Tom Collins.[38]

Before the Imperial Conference in London in 1937, the Lyons Government had made an assessment of Australia's defence options. The Department of External Affairs under Lieutenant Colonel William Hodgson had prepared a memorandum titled 'The foreign situation, March 1937'. This document outlined Australian defence realities plainly. Paul Hasluck noted of such advice: 'A *rapprochement* with Japan appears to have been the core of Australian views on a Far Eastern policy at this stage … the danger of attack from Japan was considered so great in some quarters that the hope for an agreement was, in part, a hope of gaining time'.[39]

The memorandum pulled no punches in evaluating Australia's need to know Britain's intentions in the third of its major commitments – the defence of its possessions in the Far East. Questions in the document ranged widely – for example, was the maintenance of the integrity of the Netherlands East Indies (now Indonesia) vital to the security of Singapore and the scheme of defence of Empire interests that hinged on this base?[40] There were also many questions relating to the construction and fortification of the British naval base at Singapore, which was finally completed, at great cost, by mid-1939 but was never fully equipped, a situation that would preoccupy the Australian Government over the next two years. And as Earl Beatty, a former UK MP and the son of a former first sea lord, opined in a letter to London's *Daily Telegraph* on 27 June 1939, 'Singapore would be of little value without a strong battle squadron being placed there'.[41]

A decade of depression and debt, with high unemployment levels following the credit crisis of 1929–32 and the fallout from the 1929 stock market collapse, had focused governments in western Europe, North America and Australia on domestic needs and world markets for most of the 1930s. With the decisions of the 1934 Ottawa Conference, imperial preference was to govern markets and trade between the dominions and Britain. But Australia had interpreted these guidelines broadly, leading to considerable unease between the United Kingdom and Australia throughout the 1930s over Australia's trade with countries such as Japan and the United States. By 1939, Australia's trade with the United States in the development of an aircraft industry would intensify this unease as the competition for war supplies and industrial production sped up.[42]

In the latter half of the 1930s, Britain and Australia began increasing defence budgets – albeit from a low base. Given the constrictions on budgets in the 1930s, however, Andrew Ross believes 'from an economic perspective, the basic philosophy of Australian defence preparations was bold and sensible, the emphasis being placed on technology and productive power rather than increasing greatly the size of the standing Armed Services'.[43] Meanwhile, the 'dictator countries', as they were often described – Germany, Italy and Japan – had rallied their populations to heightened nationalism through government investment in rapid industrial growth and rearmament on a massive scale.

Going to war

With appeasement, as Western leaders delivered messages of peace through negotiation in the hope of averting war, citizens were falsely becalmed even while war seemed imminent. On 28 May 1939, 60 000 Catholics rallied at the Exhibition Building in Melbourne to remember, as *The Argus* reported, 'the other

60,000 Australians who had died in the Great War', describing how the great mass of people had 'prayed that the world might never again have to seek recourse to war'.[44] Prime minister for just a month, Robert Menzies addressed the rally, joined by Country Party Victorian premier Albert Dunstan, Labor MLA Bert Cremean, Melbourne's Archbishop Daniel Mannix, other Victorian bishops and a young BA Santamaria. The meeting marked the end of a crusade for world peace initiated by the Pope. Similar meetings were held across Australia. The Melbourne gathering carried a resolution, to be sent to British prime minister Neville Chamberlain, urging that international problems be faced by 'arbitration and friendly discussion' alongside the 'abandonment of the armaments race'.[45]

The words of Robert Menzies, in a cable to Neville Chamberlain on 18 August, as Hitler advanced on Poland and just a fortnight before war was eventually declared, captured the conundrum appeasement had become:

> My Government has noted with deep interest the report
> of peace moves for the settlement of various European
> questions ... In particular we consider that efforts should be
> made to ensure that Poland adopts a reasonable and restrained
> attitude and that no nation should ignore real efforts at
> settlement because of false notions of prestige ... Nevertheless
> I strongly hold the view that pressure upon Poland should not
> be carried to a point which might awaken in Hitler's mind
> any thoughts that the Anglo-French guarantee to Poland in
> the event of aggression was in the least doubtful of fulfilment.
> That would in my view certainly lead to German aggression
> and war.[46]

The message of concern was for Australia and Britain – with Poland expected to be a lot more reasonable. Mark Aarons has reminded his readers that Menzies privately conceded to Bruce, after war had been declared, 'nobody really cares a damn about Poland'.[47] Little wonder *Argus* cartoonist Mick Armstrong, on 29 August 1939, pictured the situation as a huge and nasty German elephant yelling, 'Who are you shovin'?' while squeezing Poland in the guise of a frightened woman against a large tree trunk.[48] For two months, the British had tried to coax Russia onto their side, while their efforts to win a peaceful settlement with Hitler had gone as far as secretly offering Germany a large loan. Instead, on 23 August, Germany's principal ideological opponent – the Soviet Union – signed the Molotov–Ribbentrop Non-aggression Pact, ensuring Germany an easy route to the conquest of Poland.

Following the Nazi–Soviet Pact, on 24 August, the *Canberra Times* reported that 'German Nazis, who are revelling in the shock to Britain, France and Poland, are optimistic about peace, assuming that Britain and France will withdraw their guarantees to Poland, which obviously could not protect itself'. That was the German game plan, but the appeasers at Whitehall continued their hopes that negotiation might still prevail. So the efforts of a year before, which led to the Munich agreement, began again. All the while, as the *Canberra Times* reported two days later, the House of Commons passed emergency powers ten times more extensive than those of 1914. Leaders hoped for peace while they prepared for war. British and French embassies in Berlin were already destroying confidential papers while piles of travel luggage crowded the halls of their embassies and consulates. British newspaper correspondents, stationed in Berlin, had all left for Copenhagen. Troops were being mobilised in Belgium and the Netherlands; the French borders were being militarily strengthened, with recently graduated French cadets commissioned as sublieutenants; and the defences of Malta were now manned. At the same time, in what would soon become a tragic swan song, Polish reservists marched through Warsaw singing patriotic songs and shouting 'Long live a free Poland'.

Britain finally declared war on Germany on 3 September. Behind the scenes – as the governments of Britain's dominions waited for guidance – every last effort was made to avert Germany's determination to take Poland. Even as low-flying German aircraft dropped bombs on Polish towns and citizens in the open over twenty-four hours, Britain wavered. The Cadogan diaries chart the last moments while hope for appeasement hung on:

> Drove in car to F[oreign] O[ffice] about 9.30. No news.
> Dahlerus rang up 10.50 to say German reply on its way. Only
> hope was to ask Goering to fly over. I said 'Rats'. I went over
> to H[alifax] at 11 to PM. 11.10 still no news. PM due to
> broadcast at 11.15. 11.12 definite message from Berlin that
> no reply received so PM let fly at 11.15. Very good.[49]

As word came through to Australia of Whitehall's grave announcement, at first in short-wave radio news and then by a cable sent to the Navy Office in Melbourne and passed on to the prime minister, Australia also declared war. On Friday 25 August, Menzies had told Australians to remain calm. Headlines in the press emphasised the deteriorating situation – Germany would not be influenced by appeals to reason, but those appeals still went on. Such was the urgency of conciliation, Menzies had begun to echo Curtin in his reference to German grievances over Versailles, although this was something he could not believe justified war:

> It may very well be Germany still has some grievances which
> would be all the better ventilated ... [but] the British and
> French Governments have given a pledge to Poland ...
> [and] those pledges will be honoured. ... We in Australia
> are involved because the destruction or defeat of Great
> Britain would be the destruction or defeat of the British

Empire, and would leave us with a precarious tenure of our independence.[50]

It would be a last hurrah for serious appeasement. With the declaration of war came British resolve ('Mr Chamberlain cheered. Speech in the Commons. The destruction of Hitlerism. "I hope I may see the day"' were the headlines in the *Sydney Morning Herald*).[51] And, for a few weeks, there would be unity of purpose for the yet very divided Australian parliamentary parties.

But nobody wanted war. Menzies referred to his declaration on 3 September as his 'melancholy duty'; Curtin told parliament on 6 September that it was 'a most grievous calamity' and 'a grievous day in the history of Australia'. And still many hoped a ceasefire had a chance, wishing, as Curtin told the House 'even now, while the guns are still blazing, [to] sit down to discover whether, after all, right cannot triumph without being backed by might'.[52]

War for Australia in September 1939 was not a unifier for long. Although recruitment proved popular and the Second AIF quickly formed, dispute with Labor soon arose over the dispatch of troops to the European campaigns on the one hand, and on the other arguments from critics, such as the *Sydney Morning Herald*'s editorial on 14 September, that the Menzies Government was not getting its military capacities together quickly enough. By the end of September, Menzies was publicly answering his critics:

We have come into this war, I believe, sick at heart at the tragedy of it all. There has been no hysteria, no flag-waving – only determination and the will to preserve a cool and strong morale. We do not yet know what our responsibility will be in our own territory.[53]

He went on to add that Australia did 'not yet know who our enemies may be'. Menzies had quite a few enemies in his own parliament, and not all of these sat on the opposition benches.

Australia's prime minister required a strong sense of duty and perseverance to survive by the end of 1939. The tensions of leading a country at war, a war Menzies' generation on both sides of parliament had invested so many words and so much emotion in resisting over half a decade, had considerably complicated the job. Writing to his son Ken on 6 December, Robert Menzies expressed not just weariness but somewhat conflicting emotions, concluding: 'The only piece of fatherly advice I can think of at the moment is that it is much better to be a good lawyer or even a good agricultural expert than an indifferent Prime Minister'.[54]

The Menzies Government had lasted a good bit longer than the six weeks Robert Menzies had predicted to the governor-general in April. But the complicated power plays at the end of the 1930s, both within parties and between, along with a fluid public sentiment about war and its implications for Australia, had made the job of prime minister one of messy diplomacy at many levels – and diplomacy had not been an obvious quality in Robert Menzies to that point. His fatherly advice to young Ken also suggested that he recognised his leadership was about to be tested. In an ominous collage, *The Argus* would report photos of Melbourne's New Year's Eve party celebrations alongside headlines of Hitler's New Year's message with its attack on Britain and the 'Jewish capitalistic world'. On page three, the Japanese offensive against China was reported as having reached a new intensity. Whatever Menzies' deep misgivings and earlier support for appeasement, as 1940 dawned, Australia's prime minister had no choice but to accept that he had become a war leader.

4

Collective insecurity

Following the split in the Labour Party after the conscription
issue in 1916–17, it adopted a pacifist outlook, unrealistically
divorced from the trend and dangers of the international
situation. It led to their constant opposition to an effective
Defence Policy between the wars ... The pre-war Defence
program of the Lyons and Menzies Governments and
the preparation of precautionary plans for an emergency
established a basis for expansion in war by the Menzies
Government. Had this pre-war policy not been carried out,
the magnitude of the Menzies Government's war effort
would never have been achieved, and the legacy of the Curtin
Government in 1941 would have been very poor indeed.

– Frederick Shedden[1]

By 1940, Australia's part in the war was a divided operation.
While general feelings were opposed to another global slaughter, half a million Australians lined Sydney's streets on Thursday
5 January to watch and cheer the 6000 Anzacs ready for deployment in the Middle East. Eight military bands played to the long
stretch of crowds bordering Elizabeth Street from Oxford Street
all the way to the Town Hall, where Governor-General Lord
Gowrie took the salute – joined by Brigadier General Thomas

Blamey, general officer commanding the Second AIF, and nine generals who had served in the First World War. *The Argus* reported that one digger on the corner of Park and Elizabeth streets had noted that this was a different send-off from 1914, with 'more tears than cheers'. Apprehension shadowed feelings, but the music boosted spirits with 'Roll out the Barrel'. The song that brought the keenest response was 'Hang out Your Washing on the Siegfried Line'. Antipathy towards a German enemy was not far below the surface this time either.

Patriotism, local and for the Empire, ruled Australians as it did other Empire citizens in January 1940. Don Bradman had just scored his thirty-fourth first-class double century in Melbourne, playing for South Australia against Victoria, but his efforts reminded locals that he was Australia's hero in battles for the Ashes. The striking cartoon in *The Argus* on 2 January of Hitler and Goering, wearing Nazi uniforms and heavy boots, snapping umbrellas as they jumped on a large book open at a page labelled '1940 HATES' opposite a map of Western Europe, hit its mark. These crazed autocrats with their mania for domination were the enemy. The same day, an article in *The Argus* by Nazi defector Dr Hermann Rauschning illustrated Hitler's contempt for the United States, his confidence the United States would never go to war while its millions of unemployed were 'on the brink of revolution' and his belief that only Germany could save it from chaos. While all this sounded like the delusions of a maniac, the sinister ambitions were obvious. Rauschning had listened to conversations at Hitler's apartment that chilled him: 'I was amazed to hear that Hitler was reaching out to the Pacific. Above all, he was interested in the former great German Island empire embracing the Dutch possessions and the whole of New Guinea'.

Some left-leaning historians have looked back with the advantage of considerable hindsight on the early years of

Australia's experience of the Second World War and concluded that it all might have been approached more nobly or avoided altogether but for apathy and a reluctance to stand up to dictators of the right more readily and much earlier. Stuart Macintyre, for example, has emphasised that 'Australians then and now interpret their initial experience of the Second World War as a betrayal'.[2]

The Macintyre thesis – with its analysis that Australia relied too heavily on Britain's assurances over Singapore (what Macintyre labels 'a lethal form of defence on the cheap') and had fallen into war 'automatically' as an ally of Britain – has sharply coloured historical treatment of the first Menzies Government. As Macintyre tells it, Australia ignored Britain's indifference to its dominions' dangers in the Pacific, to its own detriment. Macintyre dismisses the Menzies Government's contribution to the war effort in a paragraph, concluding, 'He "couldn't lead a flock of homing pigeons", declared the ageing warhorse, Billy Hughes. The government fell in August 1941'.[3] After this, Macintyre moves with ease to the Curtin years, where victory is assured by the entry of the United States into the Pacific War after the bombing of Pearl Harbor, for Macintyre a moment of maturity in Anglophile Australia as it leant away from mother England. Ironically, Macintyre would later view this same US alliance in the postwar Menzies years as an impediment to an independent foreign policy.

Such recording of the Australian story has a lot to do with a dismissive attitude of both historians and political players to the achievements of the Lyons governments (1932–39).[4] It is a flawed history that focuses on personalities and hero figures of various administrations. To that extent, the fixation on Labor heroes John Curtin, Ben Chifley and, much later, Gough Whitlam has not helped the Menzies legacy. But history is a continuum, and the Lyons years were significant not just because they pulled Australia out of financial disaster more quickly than most other Western nations, but also because of the international relations forged during these years and the domestic industrial base that was developed.

Australia's first mission to Washington was opened in February 1940 by Menzies' choice for the job, Dick Casey, but the idea of this mission had evolved steadily from discussions between Prime Minister Lyons and President Roosevelt at the White House in July 1935. Lyons' wish to open a mission in Washington had not been backed by Cabinet until 1939 and then he had died. Similarly, ideas about a Pacific peace alliance with the United States had also dated to that same meeting between Lyons and Roosevelt.[5] The acceptance of an increased role for Australia's defence and foreign policy after 1941 owed much to both Lyons and Menzies. Similarly, as Defence Department chief (under both Menzies and Curtin) Frederick Shedden wrote:

> The military results of Curtin's miraculous conversion
> through responsibility when he came to power, and the
> measures he took at great personal political risk to have the
> Defence platform of the Labor Party amended, could not
> have been immediately effective but for the foundations laid
> by the Defence Programs of the preceding United Australia
> Party Governments. Curtin generously acknowledged the
> inheritance he had received.[6]

Frederick Shedden was one of the most effective architects of Australia's wartime administration. Nicknamed 'the pocket Hankey', Shedden was known for his assiduous remodelling of public service organisation learnt from the expertise of Whitehall's Sir Maurice Hankey, after having dealt with Hankey while executive affairs officer in London in 1932–33. It was Hankey who revolutionised the UK public service as a support staff for the enhanced role of Westminster prime ministers after Versailles.[7] Maurice

Hankey would have recognised the embodiment of many of his reforms in the fictional figure of Sir Humphrey Appleby in BBC TV's *Yes Minister*. Under Shedden's guidance, from 1935 Australia's Council of Defence was revamped to include both ministers and chiefs of the defence staff, while a War Cabinet was set up immediately war was declared and a highly efficient secretariat installed. It was Shedden's organisational skills, learnt from the Hankey model, and his ability to ignore the limelight, that made him a most successful bureaucrat, underpinning administrations from conservative to social democrat.[8] His knowledge of the workings of administrations was assiduous.

By January 1940, Australia had introduced compulsory military training for able-bodied, unmarried men aged twenty-one, and *The Argus*, on 2 January, announced that of the 1300 men first called up a 'high percentage' had passed. Just 8 per cent had been rejected. Meanwhile, the RAAF was advertising for 'more than 2000 fitters, 250 cooks and large numbers of flight mechanics and flight riggers' all to be employed before June.[9] The war call-up was being heard, but the ambivalence of the public spirit in some quarters was also reflected in tensions within the governing parties.

Archie Cameron's Country Party

It was an election year and the Menzies Government suffered its first reality check at the Corio by-election for Dick Casey's seat on 2 March. With an almost 11 per cent swing, Labor's candidate John Dedman scored an easy win. This added to the loss of UAP seats since the 1937 election – Joe Lyons' seat of Wilmot had also been lost to Labor in the by-election following Lyons' death. Serious talks with the Country Party were needed. Fred Shedden noted that on the Monday after the election loss in Corio, the Country Party had privately demanded Menzies' resignation.[10]

Correspondence shows that Menzies had exchanged thoughts

on a coalition with the Country Party from late in 1939 – ever since its new leader, Archie Cameron, had been unable to accept Menzies' terms for a coalition in September 1939. Cameron was a volatile and unpredictable personality with a tendency to commit unpolished and emotive thoughts to official communications, regardless of who might read them. His lack of professional manners startled Menzies. His attempt to get Menzies to meet his party halfway over ministerial positions lacked effect and, within weeks, Cameron was attempting to bully Menzies with intemperate stories of the prime minister's unpopularity across the countryside.

On 19 October 1939, Cameron had written at length to Menzies, a letter that Menzies in reply called 'astonishing'. Menzies denounced Cameron's claims in the letter as 'an extraordinary collection of false and/or misleading statements and distorted comments'.[11] Among the accusations against the government were complaints that the minister of defence had declared the National Register legislation 'worthless'; that after the declaration of war state authorities had not been able to get in touch with the prime minister about how to deal with 'aliens' (there was much strong feeling in Cameron's complaints against 'aliens'); that a delay in deciding on a second AIF had dampened the 'war spirit', and the AIF had not reached 20 000 men after six weeks 'at war'; that Menzies had not done nearly enough to market Australia's wheat crop; that 'the Australian lamb producer is being sacrificed to the greed of certain interest'; and that complaints had been made about banks calling up overdrafts.[12] The letter was a summation of grievances – many unjustified or simply misrepresentations from unhappy farmers – but Cameron made no attempt to dignify the complaints or offer them to the prime minister in any constructive way.

On 20 January, after a visit to Western Australia and in apparent frustration egged on by hostile Western Australian Country

Party members, Cameron sent Menzies a telegram outlining his belief that the feeling in the west was hostile to Menzies personally. Cameron's meetings had been in York, Narrogin and Katanning, where some voters told him the Menzies Government was the 'worst administration in history'. Menzies' response was to caution Cameron about such indiscreet methods of communication. Cameron followed this up on 29 January with a letter to Menzies in which he listed the complaints of wool and wheat farmers and then repeated scuttlebutt regarding Menzies' ownership of shares in particular manufacturing industries, and a false suggestion by some critics that 'you held shares in your wife's name'. Cameron added that one person had told him that there were 'four plagues in Western Australia – Rabbits, Foxes, Federation and Menzies'.[13] The letter was raw with discontent and more in the nature of an alienated constituent. By February, Cameron had compiled a list of what he regarded as the missed opportunities to discuss coalition possibilities.[14]

At the heart of such strong feelings against the UAP among many country constituents was the problem of wheat sales. War had interrupted the steady flow of exports along sea lanes, with consequent shipping shortages, and wheat prices fluctuated, often below farmers' expectations. The Australian Wheat Board had been set up in 1939 and become the sole seller and exporter of wheat for the Australian producer. Farmers were thus both protected and at the mercy of government deals, the prices underpinned by the government's 'deficiency payments'.[15] As John 'Jack' McEwen put it later when reflecting on the politics of the Menzies Government in 1939: 'The Country Party could have combined with the Labor Party to defeat the government on the floor of the House. It was quite clear that the fate of the government depended on its attitude to wheat'.[16]

On 21 November 1939, as Menzies delayed his decision to commit troops to overseas service, both Country Party and

Labor members in the House attacked the UAP for the price it had offered farmers for their wheat. Dick Casey, in London for talks with the UK Government over the purchase of British aircraft and sales of Australian wheat, received a cable from Menzies that same day pointing out, somewhat caustically, that the British could find shipping for troops and a naval convoy but not for shipments of wheat.[17] Casey was pressed to do more. With assurances from the British at this time that it would not leave Australia without adequate defences, and with New Zealand committing troops overseas without consulting Australia, the War Cabinet decided on 28 November to deploy troops for the Middle East. But as word came that Whitehall had gone ahead of the Australian Government advice with plans for the embarkation, Menzies retorted in a cable to Casey, 'It has been in this matter a quite perceptible disposition to treat Australia as a Colony'.[18] It was a spat too far. And whether it was a result of Menzies' ire or Casey's tact is not revealed, but in January Britain agreed to buy a substantial amount of Australia's wheat crop and processed flour through 1940. Historian David Horner has noted, 'Britain did not need this quantity of wheat and much of it never arrived',[19] but Menzies had eased one of the problems besetting his relations with Australia's rural constituents.

Minority government also had its problems. Being on the cross benches still rankled with the Country Party, but Cameron's approach was hardly likely to move Menzies. Cameron's belligerence did not recommend loyalty or Cabinet discretion, and his letter had falsely accused Menzies of personal improprieties, yet neither did Menzies try any sort of seduction before this became apparent. In a belated reply to Cameron's October 1939 letter, in February 1940, Menzies began calmly. He had, he said, just drafted a letter regarding ways the two parties could cooperate. As he had done so, an accusatory telegram, then a further letter, had arrived from Cameron. In response, off came the prime ministerial gloves. Menzies described Cameron's accusations as 'a farrago of injurious gossip … intended to wound'. If Cameron thought this was a tactic likely to push better terms for a governing coalition, he had better think again: 'I can assure you that I am prepared to fight out any of these issues at any time, but you will permit me to say that your telegram and your letter are of a character of which I have no previous experience'. In conclusion, Menzies accused Cameron of behaviour that was entirely counterproductive: 'The Cabinet relationship is one which requires a great deal of mutual confidence and mutual respect. In the face of your communications, can I believe that effective Cabinet co-operation between us is possible?'[20]

The Corio by-election, however, changed things – faster than even the press could have imagined – and Menzies grasped the urgency of coalition with the Country Party. His tactics needed to change. On 7 March, the *Sydney Morning Herald* predicted that talks between Menzies and Cameron were unlikely to succeed unless Menzies was replaced as UAP leader. That would not happen. Menzies would outplay his Country Party colleagues. The correspondence between Menzies and Cameron not only reflected Cameron's hostility but also that the Country Party was suffering ministerial starvation beyond its comfort levels. There might be bluster from Cameron and leaks from party meetings that various divisions in the party preferred not only a new UAP leader but also, for some members, even a Country Party prime minister, but Cameron was soon content to accept Menzies' offer of five ministerial Country Party places – three full portfolios and two assistant ministerships. A meeting of the Country Party the following week endorsed this agreement.

Menzies had agreed to consult the Country Party leader in his choice of portfolios but retained the right to choose them. The Country Party's Harold Thorby, who had openly opposed Menzies' leadership days before, would be made health minister and postmaster-general but Menzies was able to delay any acceptance of Page for a ministerial position. On 8 March, the *Sydney Morning Herald* reported that the negotiations had been 'harmonious', adding that after the two and a half hour meeting the two leaders 'were both in an extremely good mood'.[21]

On the day Menzies and Cameron met, the government released a statement, reported in large headlines, that the Second AIF would be significantly expanded with a Seventh Division recruited for overseas service and an additional 16 000 troops to make up an army corps. With aircraft from overseas, the Second AIF would have an army cooperation squadron of the RAAF attached to it. Other increases to the war effort included up to two 'new age quotas' to be called up for compulsory military training. The announcement was couched in positive terms as one of action and determination, with Menzies revealing that these preparations had been weeks in the making and that the government 'was not prepared to withdraw any of them simply because the fortunes of a by-election had gone against it'.[22]

As bushfires raged in Victoria, with temperatures breaking all records, the week was one of peril and caution in the mood of east-coast Australians. There was far more afoot for national concern than the wrangling in high office over leadership and ministerial allocations. By week's end, the towns of Torquay and Mortlake had been all but wiped out, and 200 Victorian homes had been destroyed, along with massive loss of stock and farmlands. All this followed the destruction of the historic 1939 bushfires, with debt (both financial and social) from heat and fires eating at public finances and morale generally.[23] Drought years had also set in. In faraway Washington, on 6 March, the former member for Corio, Dick Casey, presented his credentials to President Franklin D Roosevelt. As Casey left the brief meeting, he was asked by reporters if Australia intended to purchase more US aircraft, to which Casey replied, 'We have to watch our dollars'.[24]

In 1970, giving the inaugural RG Menzies Lecture, Sir Percy Spender reflected on the UAP Menzies had inherited and concluded that while the parliamentary UAP in its early years had 'contained men of outstanding ability', by 1939 the parliamentary party 'was composed of men, some of whom, in mental outlook, were streets apart'. There were, he added, 'more than just one or two who secretly harboured the disapproval of Menzies which Page publicly manifested'. Spender also pointed to a lack of breadth in UAP political philosophy by 1939, with just 'opposition to Socialism and Communism and a faith in the principle of free enterprise' offering policy direction.[25] With the outbreak of war, and finally over his initial hesitancy at deploying Australian troops overseas, Menzies was being given a second chance.

Labor pains

A solidified non-Labor coalition at once realigned the political landscape. For a moment following the Corio by-election on 2 March, Labor came into its own as a serious contender for government at the 1940 federal election, but it too was still experiencing factional divisions that threatened its chances.

Among the state branches of the Australian Labor Party, the NSW branch dominated by sheer size. Jack Lang's Labor in New South Wales had split federal Labor since 1931, but by 1939 it was itself under threat from a far-left faction, headed by NSW Labor Council president Jack Hughes and NSW Labor Party general secretary Walter Evans – both of whom had strong links with the Communist Party of Australia (CPA). Lloyd Ross wrote that, of the three Labor parties in New South Wales in 1940, 'it seemed to Labor activists that the one led by Curtin was the smallest ... The Hughes–Evans state Labor Party seemed to hold all the cards'.[26]

A brief period of Labor unity had been achieved after the

federal conference in May 1939, but the outbreak of war and the Nazi–Soviet Pact that preceded it by days impacted on the attitudes of the far-left faction. Its Soviet heroes had joined forces with their dire right-wing enemies – how to respond was a conundrum. During the NSW annual state conference, at Easter 1940, the left faction forced through a motion later called the 'Hands off Russia' resolution. The reasoning behind the motion was that, in spite of the Nazi–Soviet Pact, Russia was not at war with the Allies. Curtin was forced to rationalise the resolution in a statement he made in Melbourne on 4 April, even as the federal executive repudiated it. The stage was set for further division.

With news of the invasion of Norway on 10 April, Russia's helping hand to Germany could no longer be ignored. Curtin's antipathy to the war melted quickly. In May, Germany captured the Netherlands and Belgium; by the end of June, France had surrendered and the British had evacuated Dunkirk in dramatic scenes. A special federal Labor conference that month reassessed all of Labor's defence policy, finally resolving to support a national war council in cooperation with the Menzies Government. In New South Wales, however, the Hughes–Evans faction was growing. And Jack Lang, replaced as state Labor leader by William McKell in August 1939, would not go quietly. By April 1940, in reaction to the Hughes–Evans contingent, Lang had mobilised a group to oppose the left, calling itself the Australian Labor Party (Non-Communist). The new breakaway party had gathered support from five House of Representatives MPs and two senators. Labor leader John Curtin, clearly furious, told the press the move was 'carefully planned, incapable of excuse and treacherously determined upon' and a stab in the back for Labor. He added that the divisive Lang had seen Labor lose election after election for a decade and had become 'the principal political asset upon which the UAP has relied for attacks on Labor in the federal parliament'.[27]

War games

Both Menzies and Curtin had their frustrations to bear from the subversive attacks on the war administration during 1940 from the CPA. For all their differences, Curtin and Menzies were on the same side as regarded the Allied effort to defeat Hitler and ensure the security of Australia. Left-faction Labor MPs, led by Maurice Blackburn, opposed the extremes of the regulations under the National Security Act, which was enacted within days of the declaration of war in September 1939, but for all their claims of erosion of civil liberties its opponents complained about the wording of the act itself rather than the legislation's enforcement during the first months of the war.[28] CPA publications and a variety of propagandising activities to oppose the war were a different matter.

From the outset, communist pamphlets and messages spoke out at the 'Imperialist' war, accusing Britain and France of aggression and subversion against the Soviets. At the outset, after the Nazi–Soviet Pact, CPA propaganda ran the line that Britain and France were 'ruling circles' trying to force Germany and Russia into conflict. According to such spin, the Soviet Union had avoided conflict by signing the pact. The line came direct from Moscow. David Lovell and Kevin Windle have comprehensively documented in *Our Unswerving Loyalty* how Moscow and the Comintern dominated the CPA from 1929. Lovell and Windle conclude that, after August 1939, the CPA spoke a '"defeatism" that justified the Australian government's decision to declare the party unlawful in 1940'.[29]

Rationalisation of Soviet self-interest ruled the CPA's message that Soviet Russia needed to survive the effects of dominant imperialists – Germany, Britain, France – in their efforts to 'repartition the world'. After Australian troops left for the Middle East, the CPA spread the word that the AIF was being used to protect the oil interests of British capitalists. As events in Europe changed the balance of power, the message continued to evolve. By the time France fell to the Nazis, the CPA was openly opposing the war effort and the Australian system of government, and calling for a 'people's government' and a 'real people's war against fascism'.[30] By the time of the federal election in 1940, both Curtin and Menzies had been labelled by the CPA as a 'fascist monster'.

The CPA was a problem for the War Cabinet with regard to the regulations under the National Security Act, but Menzies hesitated to move against the spread of CPA propaganda. Intelligence sources, however, advised increasingly that CPA activities were undermining the war effort. The Military Board and Naval and Air boards also wanted action taken to curtail the free association of the CPA. On 3 April, Menzies critic Earle Page accused the government of handling the communists with 'kid gloves' and went on to contrast Australia's approach with that of New Zealand and France, where, said Page, '3400 Communists had been arrested, 2778 dismissed from paid positions, 159 publications suppressed and 695 Communist groups and their auxiliaries dissolved'.[31] In early 1940, various authorities were instructed to intensify surveillance and action against individuals involved in any action that could be construed as subversive. Menzies was still wary, however, of any infringement of 'rights and privileges of innocent persons', as he told the War Cabinet.[32]

The subversive actions against the war effort by the far left and the CPA should not be underestimated. From the time of the Nazi–Soviet Pact, as far as the CPA saw things, the Allied war effort was the enemy. CPA activists in the ACTU worked to stir widespread industrial disruption, and they succeeded. For the Menzies Government, this undermined solid support for the war effort, at this point directed to faraway Europe and not so easily seen as of immediate danger to ordinary Australians. CPA activists also threatened Labor unity. Curtin had led a rearguard action against the radicals in the ALP from the time the Menzies Government passed the National Register legislation in May–June 1939 to ensure that manpower and resources were used efficiently and that fit and able men could not evade military training. As Hal GP Colebatch argues, after the introduction of the National Register 'the ACTU wanted the parliamentary Labor Party, which had opposed the Bill, to lead the unions in defying the law and refusing to comply. This was in the circumstances virtually sedition: had the parliamentary party obeyed the ACTU, Australia would have been ungovernable'.[33]

Curtin supported the government in its administration of the National Register and strongly condemned the ACTU in caucus. Communist agitation against the war continued, however. Slogans such as 'five bob a day murderers' were flung at Australia's enlisted men, and there were outbreaks of violence at communist rallies where groups of soldiers occasionally came to blows with the comrades. At one rally in Sydney's Domain on New Year's Day 1940, a crowd of 15 000 heard a dozen speakers over some hours argue against the war, sometimes drowned out by boos and cheers from the crowd, the most prominent attacked with rotten tomatoes. The *Sydney Morning Herald* reported that throughout the meeting, police restrained a group of some 200 uniformed soldiers from physically attacking those on the podium.[34]

During 1940, strikes in vital industries such as coal bedevilled the Menzies administration. In mid-March, unions on the coalfields of New South Wales began a strike that would last two months, crippling industry, seriously threatening the NSW economy and depleting supplies of fuel for motor transport. The railways, affected not least by shrinkage in coal freights, cut back on train services, while tram services were also cut. Such was the antipathy of unions to the Menzies Government, Labor MP Eddie Ward, when challenged later, could supply exact figures on industrial action that showed 855 disputes, on average eight a week, had occurred between September 1939 and Menzies' resignation at the end of August 1941. This record had abated with the establishment of the Curtin Government after October 1941, which Ward put down to the soothing effect on the unions of a Labor administration and their chaps in power.[35] It also coincided with the end of the Nazi–Soviet Pact from late June 1941, after Germany invaded the Soviet Union.

The tenor and antipathy of unions to a conservative government was industrial war, inspired by communist propaganda and militant rallies that emphasised the greed of 'warmongers' such as industry leaders and their conservative mates in control. Hal GP Colebatch has described the extent of union action through 1940. By 4 April, 35 000 workers were idle from the coal strike. A day later watersiders went out for a week over extra smoko breaks instead of loading food for the AIF in the Middle East, even as the Nazis invaded Denmark. There were strikes in mid-September in munitions factories and at Port Kembla and Newcastle, as Australian pilots died in the Battle of Britain ('6000 days for Hitler' according to one commentator, referring to the working days lost for the men on strike). In the Amalgamated Engineering Union 6000 downed tools and stopped work on naval ship construction at Cockatoo Island. There was even a strike by workers making army uniforms.[36] Thousands of workers stood idle, again and again, in industries vital to the war effort, disrupting or threatening to disrupt the smooth administration of state and federal government. Families went without, and food-relief programs swung back into action as they had in the years of depression. Industrial war had become Australia's domestic battlefield as its troops died in North Africa, Hitler worked his way across Europe and Mussolini invaded Greece – in time another graveyard for Anzacs.

Whether or not it is an indication of Menzies' faith in his skills of arbitration or belief in his ability to be persuasive, the lengthy coal strike of 1940 also saw Australia's prime minister attempt a meeting with striking miners at the small town of Kurri Kurri in the Hunter region of New South Wales. When Menzies arrived at the King's Theatre, however, he found just a small crowd; most of the town's citizens were at a meeting on the local sportsground called by union leaders to boycott the prime minister's meeting. Undaunted, Menzies headed to the sportsground where, as the *Canberra Times* reported, he 'forced his way through the packed audience on the ground to the boxing ring in the centre where threats and insults were hurled at him'. It was a courageous but futile move. He made fine debating points in defence of the arbitration system as the protector of the worker (an argument John Curtin was at the same time urging on the ACTU). He reasoned that it was not worth jeopardising Australia's security and the livelihoods of workers for a few hours' less work a week, when the union could still seek a variation of the award through arbitration. It was of no moment, as the assembled miners voted to repudiate the prime minister's stance and continue their strike.[37] Three weeks later, relief funds running out, the unions voted to return to work and accept arbitration.

Such activities of alienated workers and CPA operatives wore at the government. In April, Menzies stepped up surveillance of agitator groups and also announced that CPA members, 'who are considered by federal officials to be guilty of acts of disloyalty or other activities likely to impair the nation's war effort', would be interned (without trial).[38] On 19 April, an announcement that communist publications would be subject to rigorous censorship and forbidden to comment on the war or associated subjects sounded the end of the communist press for the duration. Minister for Information Henry Gullett elaborated on the government's move unequivocally, saying the government had been loath to encroach on Australia's freedom of speech and the press, but the move was 'special action taken against an enemy in our midst openly working for the defeat of the Allied cause and the destruction of our Australian overseas troops'.[39] Finally, in mid-June, after the fall of France, the government declared the CPA illegal, along with nine other groups, most of which were branches of the Italian Fascist Party.[40] All groups would be dissolved immediately, and police raids followed around Australia.

That other war

If Australians were uncertain about the strength of their war commitment in 1940, it was understandable. After a decade of financial stress and deprivation, the idea that further hardship had to be faced in a return to armed conflict did not stir the patriotism of the First World War. While Japan was an aggressor much closer to home, it was still at a distance and in others' backyards. The shock of the fall of France in June and the evacuation of Dunkirk certainly took national awareness up a notch, as did the replacement of Neville Chamberlain by Winston Churchill as UK prime minister on 10 May after the Allies had failed to prevent Norway, a neutral country, falling to the Germans.

Norway's port of Narvik was strategically important for the shipment of Swedish iron ore in the winter months and had been in Churchill's sights as well. Ironically, it had been Winston Churchill, as first lord of the Admiralty, who had masterminded the Allied attempt to secure Narvik, but it was the more conciliatory Chamberlain who took the blame, leading to a devastating loss for him in the House of Commons in the debate that followed. Afterwards, Chamberlain offered his resignation to the King. Discussions between party leaders had resolved that Labour would not join a national government led by Chamberlain. From that point, it was up to the King to choose a successor. As was its custom, the Conservative Party did not elect a leader to be prime minister as such. Chamberlain had the right to offer a name to the King, as the man who could command a majority in the House, but it was the King's job to agree, or not, to the name suggested.[41] Foreign Office chief Lord Halifax refused Chamberlain's offer to be his successor, writing later:

> Churchill would be running Defence … and I should have no access to the House of Commons. The inevitable result would be that, outside both these points of vital contact, I should speedily become a more or less honorary prime minister living in a kind of twilight just outside the things that really mattered.[42]

It was agreed between Chamberlain and the King that the only other man who might command the required majority in the House was Winston Churchill. Historian Lynne Olson has written of the moment, 'Although Hitler had no way of knowing it, he had just suffered his first major defeat'.[43] And while events over the next year would suggest quite the reverse, with Winston Churchill any thought of appeasement was gone.

Within weeks, Europe began to shake with the advance of the Germans across Belgium and France. Churchill's baptism of fire made defence of Britain his priority. The colonies were of marginal interest to him – as he saw it, Australia, India, Canada, New Zealand or South Africa enjoyed safety nets of distance Britain could only dream about. Indeed, in Churchill's view, it was time for the Empire to help defend Britain as never before. As early as 8 May 1940, with Australian convoys heading for the Mediterranean, the Australian War Cabinet had considered the possibility that 'diversion of convoys to the United Kingdom [might] become necessary'.[44] In a lengthy cable to the secretary of state for Dominion Affairs the same day, Menzies made clear his government's concern at the safety of Australia's men and ships so far from home, largely left to orders from the British military high command.[45] The cable gave stern warning to Anthony Eden that Australia would not tolerate any lack of information or insouciance towards it, Menzies conveying the government's concern that it 'found the review of the Chiefs of Staff disappointing' and adding that often the Australian press had more up-to-date information on the progress of battles and the war generally than did the Australian Government.[46]

In the Pacific, however, by July 1940 Menzies would succeed in having his own way regarding Australian representation in Tokyo – and this after months of deferring to Whitehall, where opinion had not, until then, favoured a separate Australian mission in Japan. Hope remained that Japan could still be influenced to stay its move south. In June, a cable from the Australian Government to the Dominions Office raised concerns over the fate of French possessions in the Pacific, as 'this might furnish a precedent to Japan for action in the Netherlands East Indies'.[47] Tensions had increased over the fate of French Pacific territories, with Casey, in Washington, eventually cabling words from the president offering sympathy and continued materiel support, but adding 'these statements carry with them no implication of military commitments'.[48] Advice coming from Casey also suggested that, as the war in Europe intensified, the United States would begin a transfer of its Pacific fleet to the Atlantic.

Australia's chief justice, Sir John Latham, was selected to open Australia's new Tokyo mission, but he managed to retain his seat on the High Court as he did so. PG Edwards has suggested this was a blow to Menzies, as there 'were rumours circulating that Menzies had his eyes on the Chief Justiceship as a refuge from the growing number of his political enemies'.[49] But Latham had needed some persuasion to take up the job, and might well have had reservations as to how long good relations with Japan would last. As it happened, the mission did not actually open until late

December 1940, by which time Japan had signed a pact with the Axis powers, leaving the Australian mission holding very limited influence. By the start of the Pacific War, less than a year later, Latham had returned to Australia.

The evacuation of Dunkirk and the fall of France had sent the new Churchill administration in London into overdrive. With Winston Churchill as prime minister, the Labour and Liberal parties had accepted the formation of a Conservative-led national or coalition government with Labour leader Clement Attlee as deputy prime minister. In South-East Asia, meanwhile, the repercussions of the European war left colonial powers, France and the Netherlands in particular, greatly weakened. In late June, the Japanese took advantage of the situation, moving into northern Indochina from the territory it already controlled in southern China. At the same time, Japan demanded that the British and French withdraw from the Shanghai garrison and the Hong Kong frontier, and that Britain cease providing supplies to China along the Burma Road.[50]

With no assurances of anything more than materiel assistance from the United States, and strong recommendations from the UK's ambassador in Tokyo, Sir Robert Craigie, to consider offers from Japan favourably in return for peace, Whitehall ceded to Japan's request – and then turned to Australia for help in the defence of its possessions in Malaya, asking that Australia send one division and two squadrons of aircraft. This coincided with a request from Brigadier General Blamey in the Middle East for reinforcements there. Increasingly, Australia's divided responsibilities, as a loyal dominion, were becoming problematic.

An election date needed to be set and a budget loomed after that. Treasurer Percy Spender had warned the premiers at a Loan Council meeting on 27 May that loan funds for civil use would need to be cut. As a result of that meeting, a coordinated plan was agreed to by the premiers whereby the Commonwealth and states would 'secure maximum defence effort' and 'maintain and improve employment in all states'.[51] Looking back on his time as treasurer until October 1940, Percy Spender admitted to the difficult task it was: 'In time of war, particularly in the transition period between peace and war, a Treasurer should not expect to escape criticism. I certainly did not expect to, and I was not disappointed'.[52]

By 9 August, press reports were coming through of the Luftwaffe's ambitious attacks on the Royal Air Force in the British Isles – otherwise known as the Battle of Britain – with savage attacks from the air on airfields and industrial complexes. A *Sydney Morning Herald* headline on Saturday 10 August read 'Signs of Approaching Zero-hour. World Wide Repercussions'. In one day, as the attack began, sixty German planes were gunned down for the loss of fifteen RAF planes on the ground. The enormity, however, of any German plan to continue such attacks could be realised in the fact that – as the *Sydney Morning Herald*'s military correspondent reported – 'Germany lost no more aeroplanes than her factories probably replace, on the same day'.[53]

While Menzies pondered a date for the 1940 federal election, the full seriousness and implications of the European conflict had still to have an impact on ordinary Australians. That Hitler might invade England and take control of Westminster was for many inconceivable, and news of the worsening situation came only with delays in much of the news reports alongside a belief that the British Empire was impregnable. As division over Australia's approach to the war effort continued, Menzies could be forgiven for feeling his days at the helm were numbered.

5

War on all fronts

You may say that all this tedious narration scarcely suggests that there is a war on, that we are in great danger and that nothing but a unanimous and maximum effort will save us. It is all too true. To be compelled at a time like this to devote about half your waking hours to avoiding political disaster is enough to drive you to despair.

– Robert Menzies to Dick Casey, 8 December 1940[1]

Reviewing his first full year as Australia's prime minister, Robert Menzies might well have resorted to the Latin he knew so well and described it as his *annus horribilis*. His lengthy letter in December 1940 to Dick Casey ('My dear Dick'), Australia's head of mission in Washington, was very much a download as to his burdens by the end of that year. Even so, Menzies was still capable, in his weariness, of an occasional wry humour at the ironies:

When you add to these circumstances the fact that our organisation in NSW – made up of the Telford Simpsons and the Horsfields – were just as willing to support Evatt as they were to support me, you will understand how … we went within a touch of sweeping victory in five states and lost it all in New South Wales.[2]

Throughout 1940, the tenor of public debate and discussion in the press centred on a general feeling of 'something must be done'. There was criticism of the government's orders for munitions supplies. In May, the government appointed steel magnate Essington Lewis as Director-General of Munitions, and coordination improved. Even so, the 30 000 rifles Australia was able to send to Britain after the Battle of Britain, when many British soldiers were drilling with dummy rifles, was only possible because production had been steady and efficient before Lewis came on board.[3] The Western allies were undoubtedly well behind their German and Italian dictator aggressors in the production of arms, but in the lean and financially depressed 1930s, Western democracies had sought peace and trade for the betterment of their citizens, who viewed with abhorrence any idea that taxes should be raised to build machines of war.

But war had come nonetheless, and as the various authorities – from government ministers to heads of departments and the services, along with business advisers – set in place plans for a new Australian military industrial complex, opinions clashed and Whitehall pulled rank. There was genuine dispute over what sort of aircraft the Australian Government should invest in, and from where. Under Lyons, the well-run BHP and partner's Commonwealth Aircraft Corporation (CAC), in spite of its monopoly, had long suffered difficulties arising from the Uniformity of Armaments with Britain regulations, being hampered by requirements to deal through British suppliers and agreements. When, in November 1938, British aircraft could not be supplied, Lyons had thumbed his nose at Britain and ordered fifty Lockheed Hudson bombers from the United States. These were the first-line military aircraft Australia needed, and quickly. But even as this occurred, High

Commissioner Bruce in London was busy working to get up a British-inspired proposal for Australia to build Beaufort bombers for the British. Lyons subsequently agreed to the plan, overriding his earlier work in developing a steady relationship with the United States over aircraft manufacture.

A drawn-out tussle among those in charge of the Australian aircraft industry then ensued. With the new Menzies Government, the CAC found itself left out of the British Beaufort bomber proposal as it went ahead in Australia. Disputes arose in back rooms over what sort of engines should be used and from where they should come. The Australian aircraft industry, Andrew Ross writes, became 'the prisoner of British technology. The idea of borrowing from the most advanced technology (i.e. American) and modifying it for uniquely Australian requirements was now effectively undermined'.[4]

Beyond the issue of munitions and war preparedness, public opinion was also difficult to gauge. The feeling of being 'at war' was not so strong in a majority of the population for many months after the declaration of war. Even so, Menzies' prevarication over when, and if, Australian troops should serve abroad had come under fire from the press – urged by their more 'win the war' proprietors – as lacking the strength of leadership. With Labor opposed to overseas deployment, the prime minister found himself caught in the middle.

At a function to open the annual conference of the Australian Women's National League in Melbourne on 25 September 1939, Menzies was so intent on answering his critics that he forgot to open the conference, and had to return to the stage to do so. He spoke out strongly at 'ill-informed attacks' on the government at a time when 'there were secrets that the people cannot know – secrets that even members of the Cabinet cannot know'. People had to trust the government, and he wanted no hysteria at 'the tragedy of it all', adding forcefully, 'In the last war there was never any question of attack on Australia. But we are not in that happy position today. In the last war Russia, Italy and Japan were our allies. They are not our allies today'.[5] For all that, by mid-1940, while there was foreboding over what might happen if Japan advanced on Singapore or, worse, moved onto the islands of the Netherlands East Indies, to a large extent this remained a threat for the future. Trade talks with Tokyo were continuing, and hope remained that Japan could be mollified. The national mood changed, however, with the German advance though western Europe in May and June. At this point, the 'something must be done' collective picked up their pace.

Newsprint wars

Armchair critics abounded, encouraged by the struggles and disputes within and between the major political parties, which suggested, unfairly in the case of the Menzies Government and the ALP leadership, that neither side was capable of a united and focused war effort. On 7 June 1940, Sydney's *Daily Telegraph* featured a front-page 'editorial' headed 'Please read this, Mr Menzies'. Rudely critical, its first two sentences pulled no punches: 'Read this with your breakfast in Sydney this morning, Mr Menzies. Of course, had you an efficient Air Minister we would not have to write it'. The leader continued, shock-jock style, with a hysterical tone and a volley of opinion: 'Spend £100 000 000 if necessary, but get planes, and guns, and tanks – and get them as quick as you can. We have the money and we want safety'. According to the writer, Australia was 'as unprepared, muddled and confused as Britain was 18 months ago'. The same paper had been similarly unimpressed with Menzies on 15 May, heading its leader that day 'We need leadership as well as courage'.

On 21 August, with an election about to be announced, the *Sydney Morning Herald* took a huge swipe at Menzies and his government. Its editorial accused Menzies of not placing 'national needs before party exigencies' and went on to turn back on him his words in May, when appointing Essington Lewis, that Australia needed 'big men' as never before. Taking up the phrase, it argued that the time had come for Menzies to strategise the entry into politics, and Cabinet, of men of strength and character who would energise the government:

> it will not be sufficient to recruit new blood for Cabinet office; there must also be a vastly better recruiting of members for the parliament which will be required to support a broader-based and reinforced Ministry and they should come from as wide as possible a range of national activity and enterprise.

For anyone with an ounce of knowledge as to how party politics worked, it was a presumptuous and ignorant gibe. But it stung its target. Menzies went straight to his desk and handwrote the draft of a lengthy letter to the *Sydney Morning Herald*'s editor, Hugh McClure-Smith.

In *Company of Heralds*, Gavin Souter makes clear why the friendship between Robert Menzies and the *Sydney Morning Herald*'s proprietor, Warwick Fairfax, had run aground in print. From the Lyons era on, the *Herald* had championed Robert Menzies, giving him favourable copy, and standing by him as he resigned from the Lyons ministry in March 1939 as well as during the stressful weeks as he became UAP leader and was attacked by Page. Warwick Fairfax himself – using his byline 'A Political Observer' – had thrown Menzies bouquets, pointing out that his forthrightness might even be the dawn of a new era in politics.[6] But from February 1940 this warmth towards Menzies from the Fairfax offices in Hunter Street, Sydney, had begun to chill. *Sydney Morning Herald* editor McClure-Smith stood Menzies up for a lunch date that included Warwick Fairfax and Fairfax General Manager RAG (Rags) Henderson, and had earned himself a roasting from the *Herald* owner. The meeting had been arranged because there were serious matters Fairfax wanted to discuss with the prime minister. One was newsprint rationing, the other Ezra Norton's desire to publish a rival daily late-afternoon newspaper to be called the *Daily Mirror*. As Henderson saw it, and put to Menzies on 4 April: 'if the government takes the view that it is permissible to license newsprint imports for new publications at the present time, it is outrageously unfair to restrict the consumption of existing newspapers in order to permit a competitor to start'.[7]

The relationship between Ezra Norton, publisher of the infamous Sunday newspaper *Truth*, and the society media magnates in Sydney was, to say the least, testy. Warwick Fairfax and Frank Packer dominated the mainstream Sydney media. But by 1940 Fairfax was thick with profits while Consolidated Press, run by Packer, was in financial difficulty, with its investment in a new women's magazine – the *Australian Women's Weekly* – not yet profitable. In a rare show of solidarity between rivals, in February 1940 Fairfax agreed to increase the price of a copy of the *Sydney Morning Herald* by more than a third to allow Consolidated Press price rises that would improve their profit margins. There was no such solidarity between rivals Norton and Packer. On Derby Day 1939, Norton had lashed out at Packer, literally, and had been forced to apologise to the Australian Jockey Club. Packer had published unflattering pictures of Norton in his paper the *Daily Telegraph* and his new *Sunday Telegraph* was eating into profits at *Truth*. Norton would hit back as the war gained momentum, running a photograph of 'Captain Frank Packer' whiling away his days at the races with the comment 'Captain Packer will be leaving for the front shortly'.[8]

It was Ezra Norton's friendship with the UAP's Eric Harrison and his lobbying of Labor leader John Curtin that had helped get his *Daily Mirror* a favourable response from Minister for Trade and Customs, Senator George McLeay. In late March, Cabinet agreed to the proposal. Opposition to the idea from the other three Sydney newspaper owners was pronounced – hence the letter to Menzies from Fairfax's general manager on 4 April. Loss of advertising was the key worry – especially as further newsprint rationing had curtailed page space. And more was to come. The war with the government would be bitter, although on the eve of the election the *Sydney Morning Herald*'s editorial advised readers to vote for the Menzies Government in both houses. As it turned out, Norton would have to wait until January 1941 for his *Daily Mirror* licence and, as the other proprietors had feared, the *Daily Mirror* would prove a runaway success.

It was the threat of a new Norton newspaper in Sydney that kept the relationship between government and the Sydney press a brittle one, right through to Menzies' resignation as prime minister. In May 1940, the major east-coast newspaper proprietors held discussions at the *Sydney Morning Herald*'s offices and resolved to offer the government their agreement to curtail their newsprint consumption by 35 per cent. The offer was accepted, but if it was intended to encourage the government to refuse Norton his licence, they would be disappointed. On 14 May, the *Sydney Morning Herald*'s editorial summed up the negotiations over newsprint with the following remonstration of the Menzies Government:

> While negotiations were going on with the Government …
> it was learnt that the Government proposed to issue a licence
> for the supply of newsprint for the production of a new daily
> newspaper. This appears to 'The Sydney Morning Herald,'
> and to other proprietors mentioned above [John Fairfax,
> Associated Newspapers, Consolidated Press, David Syme and

Co.], to be both anomalous and unfair … any newspaper proprietary contemplating the production of
a new paper during wartime, must be perfectly well aware
of wartime needs and difficulties and that the unlimited right
to start new journals is entirely inconsistent with the need of
restricting newsprint consumption …

A year later, on 17 July 1941, Warwick Fairfax would take up
the cudgels personally in a letter to Menzies, writing that he was
astonished the prime minister had not realised that to grant a
licence to Norton 'from the very beginning' was an act as 'rotten
as a worm eaten log'. There was no largesse about the public
interest from this newspaper baron, who wrote:

If you contend that the work of Mr Harrison [Eric Harrison
MP] in the government is more important to the community
than the welfare of the 'Herald', and if it is a fair example of
the way in which you conduct the government, I am afraid
our paths are likely to diverge further.[9]

A fortnight earlier, the *Sydney Morning Herald* had published its
opposition to the new minister for trade and customs, Eric Harrison, who had been responsible for Norton gaining a licence
and who had imposed deeper cuts to newsprint consumption.
The Sydney press also openly campaigned against Harrison in
the 1940 election, only to see him defeat his UAP rival Norman
Cowper, whom both the *Sydney Morning Herald* and the *Daily
Telegraph* had backed. In a further letter, on 29 July 1941, Warwick Fairfax wrote that he regarded the *Herald* as a 'public service' and that he had never been particularly interested in 'making
money'.[10]

Menzies' letter to McClure-Smith on 21 August 1940 began,
'My dear Hugh, If we were not friends I should not bother to

write this letter to you'. But it cut to the chase quite smartly, with Menzies accusing the *Herald* of pursuing a policy to advantage the Labor Party. Taking up the press suggestion that the prime minister needed to bring into his Cabinet and parliamentary team a number of 'big men', Menzies went on to give McClure-Smith a short lecture on the nature of party politics: not only had no one been able to give him names of any such 'big men' he might consider, but it was quite counterproductive for a prime minister to try to influence preselections – 'Everybody with the slightest practical acquaintance with elections will agree that there could be no more certain method of securing the defeat of my nominees'.[11]

At the editorial level, undoubtedly much of the public criticism of the Menzies Government came from a frustration among professional circles that the war and the administration of Australia were in something of a stalemate. JB Were and Son stockbroker Staniforth Ricketson had observed the bias against the government, which often arose from ignorance and sometimes from personality preference, in the minutes of his meeting – attended on Menzies' behalf – with *Argus* editor JB Aitken in Melbourne on 27 May at Rags Henderson's office. Ricketson had pointed out to Henderson and Aitken that the managing director of *The Argus*, EG Knox, was on record as saying he would 'get Menzies'. At the meeting, Henderson showed personal preference for the views and military record of Country Party leader Archie Cameron, causing Ricketson to opine in his notes, 'it was palpable that Mr Henderson knew nothing really of the "tonnage" of Mr Cameron ... even in my day at the "Argus" when we had him to lunch with us we formed a very definite notion of Mr Cameron'. As to the constant press advocacy of a national government, and Menzies' failure to form one, Ricketson could only remind Henderson and Aitken of Menzies' invitations to the Labor Party to accept positions in a national government and their refusal. In his notes of the meeting, Ricketson concluded, 'I think they were eventually brought ... to the view that, by Mr Curtin and two or three of his colleagues joining Mr Menzies, it would only result in these men being regarded as converts, with a net result of splitting the union movement throughout Australia'.[12]

For Menzies, the erudite master of communication and authority, life as prime minister in 1940 was a rude shock in the rough and tumble of public opinion. Kevin Perkins, in his biography of Menzies – a book, as we have seen, that owes much to the recollections of Menzies' foe Bill McCall – relates an anecdote from the late 1930s where McCall, then a friend of the big man, made a joke of 'Menzies PC' (privy councillor), suggesting the initials stood for 'probationary constable'. Menzies was not amused and Perkins writes, 'Menzies had a good sense of humour provided the joke was on someone else. ... he could dish it out but not take it'.[13]

Although it was a time of war, as far as the Australian press was concerned, no Australian prime minister could be exempt from frank and open public opprobrium. Menzies' predecessor, Joseph Lyons, had assumed his role of Australian prime minister as a local hero in January 1932 and become popular enough to be the first Australian prime minister to win and survive three consecutive federal elections. But he had taken the rude thrusts of cartoonists and editorials in his stride. His was a different political blooding – first as Labor premier of the struggling state of Tasmania, then as a Labor minister and acting treasurer in a turbulent period for Labor, and finally as a survivor of exile from Labor and regeneration among his one-time conservative opponents. Menzies, on the other hand, had received his federal leadership amid rancour and discord among his colleagues. True, Menzies himself had made enemies within his party during Lyons' last year, first through his public criticism of Australia's political leadership and then by his resignation from the ministry as Lyons struggled to retain unity in a party riddled with opposing personalities. More than a year on, Menzies was getting his own taste of being the public whipping boy and it rankled.

In his letter to McClure-Smith on 21 August 1940, Menzies, unusually, let his guard down on paper. Whether reliable or not, rumours often did the rounds that the prime minister was ready to throw in the towel. He certainly showed no desperation to be at the helm in his offers to Labor to form a national government – and was ready to serve under Curtin if need be. The war effort was Menzies' principal concern. And he was still somewhat divided over his full career possibilities – an appointment to chief justice, state or federal, ranked well on his scale of future options. By mid-1940, sustaining his enthusiasm for the job of prime minister had become a strain, and this showed towards the end of his letter to McClure-Smith:

It is indeed ironical to think that the government's danger of defeat … does not come from its opponents but from the destructive activities of a relatively small group of men who have failed to realise that if the people are persuaded that this government is a bad one they will certainly install another government which will not be made up of angels of light but of Curtin, Ward, Brennan and company … I tell you quite honestly that my own defeat would, as such, leave me cheerful. As Prime Minister I have sweated day and night, under recurrent difficulties and disappointments, and sometimes disloyalties. I have gone on in spite of it all, doing my indifferent best, sniped at and loftily admonished, until I sometimes curse the day I entered politics.[14]

A party at war

Such was the low morale of the public by the middle of 1940, that in parliament on 28 May, ALP leader John Curtin stood up for the efforts of the Menzies Government in its war leadership, saying that events in Europe were being misconstrued as somehow the responsibility of the Australian Government. He criticised the voices pushing this sort of argument, saying they were undermining confidence in government and lessening respect for national leadership. As to Australia's participation in the Empire Training Scheme for pilots, Curtin admitted, 'I see no way by which Australia can now effectively organise an air force … except in complete collaboration with the Empire air scheme'. He was also prepared to give credit to the government for its efforts, especially on the 'factory' side since the outbreak of war.[15] As Paul Hasluck has recorded of 1940, 'June and July were months of frequent public meetings, patriotic rallies and resolutions calling for action'.[16] In general, there was much clamour but little focus on a genuine path for that clamour. In Hasluck's view, there was 'something rather indecent about the glee which Australian writers and speakers seemed to display whenever they found that something was going wrong, and the lesser concern either with what had been done or remained to do'.[17]

The personality-ridden UAP was not immune from the public mood either. Old divisions around Lyons, Hughes, Menzies and Page remained. Some in Sydney persisted in blaming Menzies for Lyons' physical collapse, others just resented a Melbourne strongman taking over as leader. The break with the Country Party still rankled, although now bandaged over with a new coalition and portfolios for Country Party leaders. Then there were the malcontents, such as Bill McCall and Sir Charles Marr. And the public mood added energy to those who argued that Menzies was not the man for the job – that he was aloof, not a man of the people, lazy or could not unite the differing factions.

A UAP conference, held in Melbourne on Saturday 25 May 1940, brought together a lot of the unhappiness within the ranks of the party. Such discontent, however, reflected much of the unease within the wider community over a perceived stalemate at the head of government. Notes kept of 'lobbying preceding the conference' are revealing.[18] NSW party operatives Telford Simpson and HW Horsfield held discussions with Western Australian UAP operatives Stanley Perry and JJ Simons, and the minutes of these discussions reveal much about the chatter and personal bias put about against Menzies.

The conference had been called at a request from the prime minister. The two 'Westerners' were asked by Horsfield and Simpson what they meant by the 'gathering storm of protest against the PM's inactivity and failure to measure up to the needs of the war crisis'. Their response was that he had failed to form a national government, which 'everybody' was demanding. They also referred to Menzies' failure to grasp 'the Fifth Column menace'. They intended to question him on this and insist upon answers. Menzies was all too clever, they added, and evaded issues with responses such as matters 'will be attended to' while he had no intention of doing anything. When asked who might replace Menzies, their answer was the 77-year-old Billy Hughes – who they said 'apart from his deafness … was as good as ever'. They also queried Menzies' legitimacy as leader by arguing that he had won the vote for leadership off the back of votes from senators – as if senators were not genuine UAP members. While much of what the WA representatives said was more grist to the mill for the two NSW operatives, even they had to query the suggestion that Menzies was responsible for the failure to create a national government – as the note taker observed, the westerners 'spoke as if the creation of a national government could be carried out if the PM willed it'. The conclusion of these lobbying discussions was that the conference was to be used to goad the prime minister, especially as word had gone round that he was close to throwing it all in or, as the note taker put it, 'was to be put on trial by the conference'. That was the plan – which Menzies foiled yet again, as the notes of the meeting reveal in a final paragraph:

> The same night the PM delivered an arresting and appealing speech at the Melbourne Town Hall which spiked the guns of those who were apparently after his head. His well reasoned and convincing explanation to the conference of the Cabinet's difficulties and achievements disarmed or cowed those who were hoping to bring about a change of leadership through the conference.

In *Politics and a Man*, Percy Spender recalls how as treasurer in 1940, he had been forced to present what would decades later be termed a 'mini-budget' on 2 May, which increased taxes substantially, taking effect from July. In Spender's view, the tax increases were a bare minimum, the war effort making huge spending increases necessary. He also believed, however, that the average Australian had enjoyed 'comforts and security for so long' that it was nigh impossible to distract the national consciousness to the feeling of real endangerment: 'Even after Dunkirk, there was in Australia no unity of opinion, no sense of need for national sacrifice such as existed in Britain'.[19] Spender also believed that with unemployment and interest rates falling, and with prices kept down and business 'buoyant', taxes could be raised further to better finance the war effort. On 12 June 1941, Spender wrote at length to Menzies outlining his estimation of shortfalls; both he and the prime minister had become worried about 'the increasing menace of overseas developments in relation to a) our power to defend Australia and ... b) our power to supply and reinforce our military forces abroad'.[20]

This lack of an energised national consciousness in support of the war hampered government at all levels. While CPA and left-leaning operatives eroded industry and government at an industrial level, the Treasury faced 'too many [who] felt no need to make any personal sacrifice. More taxation was to be opposed; it would, so it was asserted, create more unemployment'.[21] Even so, significant voices were clamouring for greater commitment to the war. As countries in western Europe fell to Germany, rallies and meetings called for more to be done. Within the UAP, such sentiment rumbled quietly against its leader. As August approached, debate ensued in the press over whether the election due in 1940 might be postponed because of war and the debates over how Australia should respond.

On 25 July, *The Argus* reported that a proposal to seek powers to delay an election in an emergency had become a dispute in Cabinet. Country Party leader Cameron had made a public statement that he would oppose any decision to delay an election. There was no resolution to use emergency powers, even though Labor leader Curtin had no objection to such powers being used if needed. Cameron was forced to qualify his public statement. It was a case of jitters all round, with a new Labor 'split' reported in New South Wales as the federal executive of the Labor Party moved against the left in the NSW state executive and suspended all officials. *The Argus* reported this on 3 August as a 'bombshell' that would 'precipitate one of the biggest crises and the most confusing situations in State Labor history'.[22] By 8 August, the press was forecasting an early federal poll, not later than 28 September, with a headline in *The Argus*: 'Election probable next month. Effort to stabilise government'.[23]

The cold wind

With the exception of 1975, no election campaign in Australia's history has begun amid such drama as that of 1940. Abroad, the news continued of the Battle of Britain as Hitler made plans to invade, albeit plans he would later shelve as British pilots fended off the Luftwaffe at great cost. The Soviet Union, meanwhile, in the first weeks of August, annexed the Baltic states and reaffirmed the Nazi–Soviet Pact. In Australia, by the end of July the process of accepting applicants for the RAAF had been streamlined after complaints about huge backlogs for interviews in Sydney. Sir Donald Cameron, chairman of the NSW recruiting drive, could now confirm that, 'the authorities in Sydney have at last caught up with the long list of men who have applied to join the RAAF'.[24] But with the continued push for more talent in Cabinet, the forthcoming election opened the way for more contests in UAP seats.

Former NSW premier Bertram Stevens, who had entertained federal hopes since Lyons' last year, was one such contender. Stevens was pushed by UAP operatives in Sydney. For the Sydney UAP, Stevens, should he make it to Canberra, had long rivalled Menzies as a potential federal leader. On 9 August, the *Sydney Morning Herald*'s editorial devoted much of its two columns to urging efforts to bring new talent into the government 'to improve its calibre', saying this was 'one of the best reasons why an early election should be held'.[25] A report in *The Courier-Mail* on 15 August revealed that the UAP in New South Wales was about to change its policy to allow multi-candidate contests in all UAP-contested seats. This would mean that, weeks out from the election, preselections would be overturned, allowing more than one UAP candidate to contest any one seat. It was also reported that Bertram Stevens would stand if this happened. NSW premier Alexander Mair, alarmed at such disruption within the party so close to an election, called for the government to see out its full term, which he said could be as late as the following January.[26]

As the air battles over Britain began, Australia's newspapers were already speculating on a federal election being called by week's end. But it was the loss of an Australian plane, near Canberra, that would become the focus of the Menzies Government's real concern and sorrow that week, a concern that would shake the War Cabinet and the UAP/Country Party administration. It followed a weekend in Melbourne for the prime minister. On Sunday, before he left Melbourne, it was suggested to Menzies that he return to Canberra with three of his senior ministers – Geoffrey Street, Henry Gullett and Jim Fairbairn – on an RAAF plane leaving Essendon airport on Tuesday morning, rather than go back sitting up in a train. Gavin Souter has recorded the important decision Australia's PM made:

> After sitting up all night in the train on Friday 9 August, and attending War Cabinet right through that weekend, he planned to leave for Canberra again on Sunday night. His private secretary, learning that three other ministers would be flying from Melbourne to Canberra by R.A.A.F. Lockheed Hudson on the morning of Tuesday 13 August, suggested this as a possible alternative to another uncomfortable night in the train. But the Prime Minister insisted on the Sunday night departure.[27]

The most vivid account of the tragedy that befell the Australian Government on 13 August 1940 is given in Andrew Tink's *Air Disaster Canberra*. His forensic analysis of the crash of the Lockheed Hudson – which was carrying three senior Cabinet ministers, Chief of the General Staff Lieutenant General Sir Brudenell White, an army staff liaison officer, the air minister's private secretary and four members of the RAAF – offers persuasive evidence that Air Minister Jim Fairbairn, who had piloted warplanes in the First World War and was an experienced aviator, may well have been at the controls. The plane was delayed ten minutes on the tarmac at Essendon aerodrome – a delay that can be traced back to the possibility that the air minister pulled rank and changed seats with the copilot, Richard Weisner, to take over as copilot himself. And so it was that, flying into Canberra air space at around 10.40 am that Tuesday, the Lockheed Hudson, carrying what the waiting officials on the ground had been advised were VIPs about to arrive, appeared briefly over Canberra aerodrome at 9000 feet (2740 metres) only to circle gradually to the north, lose height and then disappear.[28]

Even for the newspapers, with daily reports of world war as the main news, the crash registered as a national disaster. For the prime minister, it hit like a knockout blow. Writing many years later of his emotions at the time, Sir Robert Menzies prefaced his words by describing his 'special feeling' for the three colleagues he lost that day. Then,

> A knock came on my door, and somebody walked in. There had been a dreadful air crash, almost within sight of my windows. Gullett was dead; Street was dead; Fairbairn was dead; … Sir Brudenell White, whom I had recalled from retirement to be Chief of the General Staff, was dead. And dead with them were other younger men whom I knew and for whom I had affection.
>
> This was a dreadful calamity … I shall never forget that terrible hour. I felt that, for me, the end of the world had come.[29]

Looking back, it was Menzies' view that this tragedy had harmed his first term as prime minister more than anything else. He had enemies in the UAP ranks, but these three friends had been his cushion against those foes.

A week after the air disaster, Menzies announced to parliament that Australians would go to the polls for an election for the House of Representatives and half the Senate on Saturday 21 September. Immediately there was a jostling for the seats held by the newly dead UAP ministers, with a report that there would be a number of government candidates for the seat of Henty previously held by Gullett. Pattie Menzies was present in the visitors' gallery at the sitting to close parliament on 22 August, a sign perhaps that this was a more than momentous occasion: there was no guarantee the government would be returned. In their speeches to end the session, the respective leaders of the two major parties – Menzies and Curtin – praised each other in turn, showing an old-fashioned courtesy somewhat foreign to parliaments seven decades later.

Neither major party was in particularly good shape for a federal election. In New South Wales, three Labor parties were contesting seats. The UAP, with criticism of a weak front bench, was allowing candidates to nominate for seats within a few weeks of the election. The governing parties were also rent with division both within the coalition and within each party. Maintaining unity on all sides was difficult. The UAP and Country parties opted for a single campaign-opening speech to be given by Menzies in the Camberwell Town Hall, even as division opened up over contestants for the seat of Flinders, now vacant with Jim Fairbairn's death. Menzies made clear he was not in favour of the Victorian Country Party premier, Albert Dunstan, contesting Flinders, given he had been supported by Labor in his term as premier. At the same time, Earle Page was maintaining his personal campaign for a national government to be elected on the floor of parliament.

The press continued to speculate on the fresh talent that might be enlisted for seats – giving the impression that the sitting UAP members were inadequate. Menzies' travel to election meetings was restricted by his need to attend War Cabinet meetings in Melbourne, so it was decided he would not be able to campaign in Queensland or Western Australia. As HV (Bert) Evatt resigned from the High Court to contest the seat of Barton he, with a flourish of self-importance, in a telegram to former UAP minister and chief justice John Latham, gave off something of the bombastic and intimidating tone his future parliamentary colleagues would come to expect:

> I would also suggest in interests High Court as institution
> that you should frown on any attempt fill vacancy before
> incoming Govt has chance of review stop If govt took this
> step I should have to publicly denounce as scandalous abuse
> of power then matter would become direct election issue
> stop Owing to rush here it would be great convenience for
> me if two rooms which I occupy could be left at my disposal
> until successor appointed though of course I should not be
> occupying them in any way … EVATT Justice High Court
> Sydney.[30]

Evatt would be another factor constraining Menzies in the year to come.

The 1940 federal election saw a record number of candidates stand, both as a result of the splinter Labor Party groups in New South Wales and the additional UAP candidates in multi-candidate seats. Of these candidates just five were women, none of whom would win. Robert Menzies had five opponents in Kooyong – one from the ALP and four independents. In three NSW seats there were eight candidates, another two had seven, and a further five had six. New South Wales had become Menzies' Achilles heel, partly because of UAP resentment in that state at having a Melburnian for party leader and partly because, even while Labor had split, the preference flow from the differing

Labor candidates would strengthen whichever Labor candidate pulled ahead. And while the UAP and Country Party cast Menzies in the mantle of Churchill, Labor stigmatised him as in essence embodying the indecisive Chamberlain. With a little over a week to go, a bitter controversy arose over the UAP's use of a poster showing Churchill with Menzies, which Curtin described as 'a political outrage', since both major parties were loyal to the British Government and striving to bring all Australians to the United Kingdom's defence.

As the campaign wore on, Curtin sounded more and more as if he had never opposed sending Australian troops to Europe; his message in support of the war was no longer ambiguous. In a cable to the British Labour leader, Clement Attlee, which Curtin read out to a crowd of 2000 in the Sydney Town Hall on 13 September, he ramped up his support for Britain:

> We admire the steadfastness of our kith and kin in this great crisis. Australian Labor stands solidly and unitedly for a more vigorous national effort in conducting unflinchingly and irrevocably this life and death struggle which is yours and ours. We will stand and fall together.[31]

Historian David Day has written that, in view of the Labor splits in New South Wales, 'the election on 21 September proved to be a triumph for Labor'.[32] This overstates the result somewhat. Considering the UAP and its coalition partner had been in government since January 1932, had suffered the loss of their popular leader Joe Lyons and also been diminished by infighting, especially in New South Wales, the election result was better than the UAP might have expected. As Menzies wrote to Dick Casey on 8 December, 'The election was a curious affair'. In Western Australia, Labor leader Curtin had barely held his seat of Fremantle. During the campaign, Labor had promised what

Menzies described as 'a series of social benefits of exactly the same character and extent as would have been offered in a time of peace'. Against this, the parties around Menzies had offered 'not one solitary promise of any description'.[33]

The result saw Labor win seven seats from the UAP/Country Party, and Gullett's old seat of Henty go to an independent, the former mayor of Melbourne Arthur Coles, who had taken the seat by default when the UAP had failed to find a suitable candidate. Counteracting that, the UAP picked up three Labor seats – two in Tasmania and one in South Australia. The nation was split down the middle, with Labor (including Lang Labor's four seats) and the UAP/Country Party holding thirty-six seats each. Bert Evatt had won Barton, Menzies describing his campaign to Casey as 'vicious and personal' and heralded by an admiring press 'led by the *SMH*'.[34] As for Menzies' old rival Bertram Stevens, he had – in spite of the solid support of the *Sydney Morning Herald* – 'got the poorest vote that any UAP man has had in that district for fifteen years', while in Kooyong Menzies had attained a record majority and his independent rivals had 'all lost their deposits'.

High drama and the closeness of the election result meant that it was not until some three weeks after election day that a meeting took place to resolve the deadlocked result. Within the Country Party, Jack McEwen had put his name forward to challenge the mercurial Cameron. As Cameron looked likely to lose the leadership, Page came back into the frame, abandoning Cameron and playing his own game. In a ballot to choose between Page and McEwen, the vote was tied (Cameron had stormed off, refusing to vote) and Fadden had emerged as acting leader for the interim. A meeting of all parties on Wednesday 16 October, referred to by *The Argus* as a 'historic gathering', began in Canberra. A week later, Labor finally rejected yet again any idea of a national government, so Menzies reluctantly agreed instead to an Advisory War Council with Labor appointees. Then Menzies formed a minority government with the support of the two independents, both from Victoria – Arthur Coles and Alexander Wilson (the member for Wimmera). Parliament resumed on 20 November.

It was a precarious result all round. As Menzies related to Casey in his letter, the budget session that immediately followed was fraught with brinkmanship. The UAP member for Swan had died suddenly after the election, and the by-election for the seat was yet to be held. To pass the budget, Menzies needed not only the independents' votes but also the vote of the speaker. Demands for an increased payment for wheat from independent Alexander Wilson and for an increase in old-age pensions, and a refusal by Labor to accept the government's cut-off point for exemption from income tax, provided the stumbling blocks. On the Labor side, Evatt had scores to settle for not being chosen for the Advisory War Council by the Labor executive. He gathered support in the Labor caucus for a tilt at the government over the budget, seeing a chance to bring down the Menzies team and have Labor installed in its place without a federal election. Curtin, preferring not to have to govern under such tumultuous Labor conditions, managed to reason with Menzies to increase the old-age pension payment and the income level for tax exemption. The budget was passed.

Menzies' summary to Casey of his last few months of 1940 shows a shrewd political head watching an unfortunate national scenario unfold. Labor was changing and becoming more intense, his own side just hanging on. As Menzies saw it,

> there is no doubt that there is a first class split developing
> in the Labor Party. Evatt is in a tremendous hurry for office
> and his consecutive defeats in his own party have made him
> bitter. Incidentally, he has gone to great pains to make himself

a good fellow with some of the weaker brethren on our own side.[35]

That observation on Menzies' part was not lacking in perception, but in the coming year it would be his own side that failed the unity test, forcing Menzies' demise while Evatt pushed his reluctant leader into government.

6

War at a distance

The invitation extended to the Australian Prime Minister (Mr. Menzies) to remain in England during the present crisis is a timely recognition by the United Kingdom Government that the time has come for closer consultations and contacts with other members of the British Commonwealth ... The course of affairs in the Balkans has not been in accord with expectations.

– *Canberra Times*, 21 April 1941, p. 2

Reflecting on Australia's choices in the early 1940s, as both Robert Menzies and John Curtin led a country at war in difficult circumstances, historian Geoffrey Blainey commented that Menzies had been torn by his divided loyalties. Britain and Australia were allies but, in 1940–41, Britain was overextended, its back to the wall, while the prospect of Japan cutting off Australia from its major trading routes became increasingly real. 'As a war goes on', mused Blainey, 'you take different positions as your war aims alter according to battle positions'.[1] And, as war went on, this was true of Robert Menzies as much as of others.

Various historians have emphasised Menzies' expressed sorrow at committing Australia in September 1939 to support Britain in another European war. Judged against a backdrop of the carnage, so recent, of the First World War, to see such a declaration as 'tragic' should not be considered a weakness. Yet Menzies has been called to account on occasion for his mixed feelings. Some of this has to do with arguments about appeasement, which as we have seen was a popular approach across all levels throughout the Western world, especially after the Munich agreement with Hitler on 30 September 1938. As negotiated settlements with Hitler proved worthless, a great divide opened among British politicians over the value of conceding yet more to an obvious predator. A group of UK Conservative MPs around Winston Churchill, Duff Cooper and a young Harold Macmillan continued to ginger up the political debate with arguments against selling out and Britain's lack of resolve in the face of the Nazi regime. Prime Minister Neville Chamberlain, however, would hold onto the party leadership even as his belief in appeasement was reduced to tatters. And, as war was declared, many still clung to a view that Britain should go neutral and negotiate with Hitler more on his terms. George Bernard Shaw was one such, preferring this to 'making more mischief and ruining our people in the process'.[2]

During the 1930s, Australia's UK high commissioner, Stanley Bruce, had continued to emphasise to Australian leaders that negotiated peace was what the modern world needed – and that the League of Nations was the best instrument to achieve this aim. Menzies, like most others, abhorred the thought of another world war. For conservatives such as Menzies, the real enemy from a democratic perspective was Bolshevism, with its erosion of Western institutions through such means as militant trade unions. Throughout most of the 1930s, Germany was seen in the United Kingdom as a bulwark against socialism. Even as the troops were called up, voices continued to argue for a negotiated peace. Chief among them was former UK prime minister David Lloyd George, who rose in the House of Commons on 3 October

1939 to argue for peace negotiations with Hitler. Challenged by Duff Cooper, who accused him of preaching surrender, Lloyd George gave the defeatist's reply, 'Tell me how can we win', then went on to belittle Britain's military preparedness, saying the country was heading for defeat.[3]

As Australian prime minister, Menzies believed he needed to visit his troops – whether to boost their morale or his standing at home, or even to win favour with the British, can only be guessed at. Then there was the ongoing matter of supplies of aircraft and Australia's tussle with the United Kingdom over orders, along with the problem of ships needed for Australia's exports. The latter was also a considerable matter, the importance of which Australia was finding hard to impress on its British partners amid the crisis in the Mediterranean and the Atlantic.

The Menzies' trip to Britain and North America in 1941 had reasonable cause – even if High Commissioner Bruce had offered a wily, even prophetic, few words of advice in a communication on 5 January, warning that Churchill was a dominant personality in the War Cabinet. The cost of making the journey, both for Menzies personally and Australia, might not be worth it.[4] But the situation around Singapore was dire, Britain having put it at the bottom of the list of its priorities, with home defence and Europe the immediate focus. There was also Churchill's wilful denial that Britain's South-East Asian post at Singapore needed any reinforcements. In addition, Australia was beginning to play a significant role in Libya and the desert war, where a successful push against the Italians had seen ports taken from Bardia to Benghazi, the surrender of tens of thousands of prisoners, and the Allies advance 500 miles (800 kilometres). Of the Bardia victory, Glenn Wahlert has written: 'Approximately 40,000 prisoners were taken and most accepted their lot. Many ended up as trustee prisoners on Australian farms'.[5]

After the federal election in September, with the budget

finally passed and concern growing over the Japanese advance in South-East Asia, Menzies made arrangements for a lengthy trip to Britain and the United States, leaving Sydney on 24 January 1941 on a Qantas Empire Flying Boat. With the kangaroo-style hops of aircraft at this time, Menzies and his party made significant stops, among others, at Darwin, Batavia (Jakarta), Singapore, Rangoon (Yangon), Calcutta (Kolkata), Karachi, Bahrain, Basra, Tiberius, Jerusalem, Gaza, Cairo and Alexandria. In Egypt, Menzies made trips to Australian troops out of Bardia, Tobruk, and El Adem. After this, his flights to England took him by way of South Africa through Khartoum, Lagos, Freetown, Bathurst and then, breaking records in a flight of twenty-six hours, to Lisbon from Bathurst (southern Africa). From Lisbon, Menzies entered the United Kingdom, landing at Poole on 20 February after crossing snow-covered Devon.[6]

By any standards of the time for trips abroad by Australian prime ministers, this one was extraordinary. Menzies had, in a few weeks, made contact with significant areas of South-East Asia, the subcontinent and the Middle East. He had touched base in parts of Africa and held discussions in Lisbon that seasoned him for perspectives on Vichy France and the delicate position of the United Kingdom regarding Franco's Spain. By the time he arrived in London, Menzies could hold his own with the best at Whitehall.

Menzies was not normally a diarist and in fact not keen on personal diaries, but on his overseas trips he kept a diary – in 1935, 1936, 1938 and 1941. These diaries reveal both the private and public Menzies but do not go as far as anything approaching intimacy. From them, a reader gains an appreciation of Menzies' eye for weakness in others alongside his ability to acknowledge qualities in people he may not have agreed with. His criticisms of 'tropical service Englishmen' in British posts in Asia balance his admiration for abilities he found in Englishmen employed in non-British territories in the Middle East: 'These mysteries under which Englishmen hold posts of authority in non-British countries are quite beyond me, but the breed is superb'.[7]

The Menzies diary for 1941 reveals him to be a well-educated Australian of British stock who is very much a member of the British Empire. As Judith Brett has noted, Menzies' love for England should be viewed through the prism of Empire loyalty, not the experience of Britain itself.[8] For many Australians, this was the case. Australians at the time were familiar with the Union Jack being flown on occasions alongside Australia's ensign, either red or blue, and a sense of Britishness pervaded mainstream political groupings. In September 1938, for example, Labor leader John Curtin had questioned the Lyons Government's recruitment of Danish workers, saying, 'The government needs to look at this matter more from the viewpoint of the future of Australia as an English-speaking community, and as an outpost of the British race, than merely from the narrow economic outlook'.[9]

While in London, over some ten weeks, Menzies joined the British War Cabinet as a dominion premier. Moving among his well-heeled contacts, experiencing the bombing in London and port towns such as Plymouth, and joining in public and private discussions, Menzies became as concerned with playing his part in the defeat of Hitler and the defence of England as with the defence of Australia. In his mind, they had become one, and this was a reasonable view, given that the United States had not shown any indication it wanted full-scale involvement in the European campaigns and was still convinced it could negotiate or appease Japan, which was continuing its threatening expansion into southern Asia.

In those days of fragile international communication, and while Britain was so caught up in its fight to the death at home, being heard from the other side of the world was extremely problematic. Churchill was focused increasingly on getting the

United States to enter the war effort – at least with materiel support while the Lend-Lease Bill sat with Congress. (The Lend-
Lease Bill, by which the United States supplied aid to the Allies,
was eventually signed by the president in March 1941). The big
Churchillian picture was for the United States to fully support
the Allied effort in combat as it had in the First World War.
Churchill is said to have rejoiced at the bombing of Pearl Harbor
in December 1941, and 'slept the sleep of the saved and thankful'
that night.[10] Preoccupied with attempts to negotiate the United
States into the conflict, Churchill believed Singapore could only
be taken 'after a siege by an army of over 50,000 men, who would
have to be landed in the marshes and the jungles of the isth-
mus'.[11] On 1 December 1940, the Australian Government had
cabled Dominions Secretary Viscount Cranborne, making clear
its grave concerns over the lack of reinforcements at Singapore.[12]
Just a day before, Cranborne had visited the Australian Associated Press offices in London's Fleet Street and expressed his
admiration for the expanded news services enabling Australia
and New Zealand to be so up to date in their coverage of overseas
war news.[13] For all that, impressing on London an Australian
perspective was not so easy.

After the loss by the Free French, supported by the British,
of Dakar (in French West Africa) to the (pro-German) Vichy
French in late September 1940, Menzies had cabled Churchill
(via Bruce) to say how 'disturbed' he was over the 'Dakar incident
which has had a very unfortunate effect in Australia'.[14] Menzies
referred to the attack as 'half-hearted' and incurring a 'damaging loss of prestige'. He then complained at his government's
knowing 'practically nothing of details of engagement and nothing at all of the decision to abandon it until after newspaper publication'. It had been 'humiliating'. He ended by adding, 'must
say frankly that Australian Government profoundly hopes that
difficulties have not been underestimated in Middle East where

clear cut victory is essential'. This soon brought a stiff rebuke, on 2 October, from Churchill, who accused Menzies of implying the United Kingdom had a 'half-hearted Government'. Churchill pretended surprise at Menzies' attitude: 'I thought indeed that from the way my name was used in the Election [21 September 1940] that quite a good opinion was entertained in Australia of these efforts'. Churchill apologised for nothing, concluding, 'I feel it due to your great position and the extremely severe tone of your message to reply with equal frankness'.[15] This was not an Empire leader to cross. Churchill would remember Menzies' criticisms as he refused three months later to agree to Viscount Cranborne's proposal that he consult the dominions in military decisions: 'It would certainly not be possible to consult the Dominions ... about any direct military operation, even when their own troops were liable to be engaged'.[16]

In December 1940, Australia had its work cut out convincing the United Kingdom it needed more consideration from its 'Mother Country'. The political landscape in Canberra had also changed, with a more aggressive Labor opposition whose newly elected MP Bert Evatt did not agree with his leader John Curtin's reasonable approach to the government of the day. Curtin was not ready to assume the role of prime minister with such a slim margin, nor while he led a divided Labor group. The breakaway Labor MPs (Non-Communist Labor or Lang Labor) would only return to the Labor caucus in March 1941. Bert Evatt, on the other hand, had taken to Canberra parliamentary politics with the energy of a convert to a new religion, racing off to Western Australia to campaign for Labor in the 21 December by-election for Swan. Evatt announced at a meeting in the Perth Trades Hall that if Labor won Swan, John Curtin would be Australia's prime minister within ten days.[17] The Country Party retained the seat, but Evatt was now aligned with a group of Menzies' opponents in the UAP calling for a national government. After the two

Labor parties healed their differences in March 1941, Evatt was made a member of the Advisory War Council.

A chancy undertaking

Menzies was accompanied on his lengthy overseas trip in 1941 by Frederick Shedden, then head of Defence Co-ordination, John Storey from the Aircraft Production Commission and two secretaries, Norman Tritton and Samuel Landau. Pattie Menzies came to Rose Bay to farewell her husband. As they left Sydney, Menzies wrote in his diary, the 'whole business is distressing to Pat who has vast courage but knows that for once in my life I am off upon a chancy undertaking'.[18] Heading out across the Timor Sea from Darwin, at dawn on Monday 27 January, Menzies wrote, 'Australia is behind and the great adventure has begun.'[19]

It was a journey fraught with operational dangers, flying across half the globe in short hops, making on-ground assessments of not only the vulnerability of Singapore ('the interesting material at Singapore was human – and disturbing')[20] but numerous important outposts along the way – all the while armed with a new movie camera. Menzies was a strange mixture of high hopes and pleasure at the 'adventure'. Ahead lay consultations and arguments in London, and the risk of not attaining the outcomes for Australia he hoped for. His diaries reflect part observer and part player, a man who has never known failure, a man who believes he has the goods to bring back what he wants.

As Menzies observed the lame defences of Singapore, overseen by English officers headed by Sir Robert Brooke-Popham, he affirmed his rejection of any softening on Japan: 'We must as soon as possible tell Japan "where she gets off".[21] Appeasement is no good. The peg must be driven in somewhere. I must make a great effort in London to clarify this position'. The complacency among the British officers at Singapore startled Menzies:

'Why the devil these generals and people should be ignorant of and not interested in the broad principles of international strategy I cannot understand. All the talk on those aspects was by myself, with Shedden feeding me with material'. Churchill also had concerns about the Chamberlain supporters he retained in his ministry, those who might be convinced that surrender and peace terms were a better option against Hitler than fighting to the death. With the publication, from the 1960s onwards, of personal diaries and other historical records of the period, it has been revealed that the battle for Britain was also a battle for Churchill to maintain his unswerving fight against Germany.

Assuming the prime ministership in May 1940, Churchill not only faced a war crisis with the evacuation of Dunkirk, the fall of France and the Battle of Britain, but also needed to play a deft game of mollifying his high-Tory opponents who had continued to support Chamberlain.[22] In Andrew Roberts' *Eminent Churchillians*, the cosy network of that power play is vividly described. Not only did the King and Queen prefer Chamberlain, Churchill had also strongly backed Edward VIII in the abdication. High Tories supporting Chamberlain doubted Churchill's judgment and temperament, and had scores to settle over his long-held criticisms of the Tories in general. In late February 1941, Robert Menzies landed among this rich mix of rivalries and personal resentments crisscrossing London politics. He was noted as a fine speaker, a dominion leader with style and a moderate voice to challenge the war doggedness of the prime minister. In his third volume on the Second World War (published in 1950) Churchill himself revealed how Menzies 'had not been satisfied either with the organisation of the Cabinet or with my exercise of such wide powers in the conduct of the war'. Churchill added that Menzies had raised this with him on 'several occasions' but Churchill had disagreed and given his reasons why.[23]

The clash between Menzies and Churchill would result from

Churchill's obsession with the Mediterranean and the Atlantic to the exclusion of the Pacific, as well as from the disasters surrounding Churchill's Greek campaign, where the British high command, in a high-handed way, pushed Australian troops to serve with little regard for the views of Australian political or military leaders. But as he headed for Britain, Menzies had no intention of having a fight with Churchill. His confidence in his own ability to persuade and advocate his cause, as an accomplished barrister of long standing, spurred him on. Menzies remained a loyal supporter of Churchill as the senior partner he had to mollify.

As he left Australia in 1941, Menzies carried a view of Churchill as he had seen him in 1935 – a political force but out of favour at Westminster; 'I therefore looked forward ... to seeing him in command, at the height of his powers', Menzies wrote.[24] He was thus caught, abruptly and within days of his arrival, by Churchill's apparent indifference to Australia's Pacific plight. As he sat in his first meeting of the War Cabinet, Menzies would not have been reassured by the prime minister reporting to his Cabinet colleagues that he had just met with the Japanese ambassador in London, who confirmed that Japan 'had no aggressive intentions against Australia, Singapore or the Netherlands East Indies'. This, he said, was supported by the UK ambassador in Tokyo, who had spoken to the Japanese foreign minister.[25]

Such a difference of view would lead to weeks of tension between the two leaders, whatever their personal dealings. But there is no evidence whatsoever that Menzies had headed to the United Kingdom with a support base readying him to 'break the political deadlock in Britain, crush Churchill's power and end the war'.[26] Menzies' arrival was heralded by a few press paragraphs, which described him as one of the Empire's young and talented 'premiers'[27] – something to be expected in an age when the prime ministers of British dominions had real constitutional influence in British law.

Not surprisingly, Menzies would discover in London that there were divisions of opinion among leading figures in the British administration over the conduct of the war and even whether the only aim should be continuing war until the enemy was defeated. Chief among those providing succour to the would-be peacemakers was Lloyd George who, while he would tell Menzies over lunch at his home in Churt in Surrey on 26 April that he believed Britain would not lose the war, was convinced at the same time that it could not be won.[28] For all that, Lloyd George merely sat back chewing on his opposition to Churchill, and fuelling chatter in clubs and restaurants among opponents of the prime minister in Conservative ranks. Robert Bruce Lockhart, Director General of the Political Warfare Executive, described Lloyd George, after visiting him at Churt on 19 March 1941, as 'a vain old man who cannot bear to see others wielding the power he once had and ... is waiting for the opportunity to be a Petain'.[29] As the months of war played out, Lloyd George never laid a glove on Britain's war-obsessed leader. During a debate over the failure of the Greek campaign on 7 May 1941, Lloyd George made a serious challenge to Churchill in a House of Commons speech that was interrupted by a number of contradictory interjections from Churchill – who went on to win the debate by 447 votes to three.[30]

Churchill outsmarted his opponents by rallying ordinary Britons with his courage. Smoother minds such as Menzies might privately have bemoaned Churchill's boyish obsession with 'maps and charts, working out fresh combinations'[31] and despaired at the yes-men around him, whom Churchill also held in contempt. But he could not match the bulldog prime minister's ability to outrun his circling opponents, and was even a little envious, making an entry in his diary that '[Churchill] reveals his real opinion of the Chiefs of Staff in terms I could not have equalled! He knows they are Yes-men, and does not love them for it'.[32]

No evidence suggests that Menzies' feelings regarding Churchill went further than private frustration and sporadic public stances. Churchill had the call, and would tolerate no obstacle – even that of a popular and questioning Australian prime minister at a time when Australia was one of Britain's few allies lending the military support Britain so desperately needed.

Political leaders travelling abroad move through a daily program of lunches, dinners and meetings. Menzies, for example, dined with Churchill at Chequers on six weekends during his weeks in the United Kingdom – as Churchill's private secretary John Colville records, 'week-end after week-end ... he [Menzies] fell into a category to which Churchill attached importance when he was off-duty, that of men "with whom it is agreeable to dine"'.[33] For a historian, it is important not to read too much into the casual, if informed, responses from meetings with public personalities. Arch-Conservative MP Henry (Chips) Channon's diaries contain brief mentions of Menzies in 1941 – both for his value as a 'raconteur ... full of sense and charm'[34] at dinner in Lisbon on 3 March and, earlier, much the same in Cairo. He also noted Menzies' naivety in relation to Churchill, as they travelled together out from Egypt: 'He says he does not intend to be blitzed by Winston, but he will be'.[35]

Labor MP Hugh Dalton who in 1941 was minister for economic warfare in Churchill's national government, dined with Menzies occasionally and diarised that he thought him good company. Each found the other surprisingly genial as representatives of their opposite side of politics. They had first dined together in Melbourne in 1938 at the Athenaeum Club, after which Dalton recalled, 'He said, "I am delighted to meet a member of the British Labour Party who has a sense of humour." I replied, "I am equally delighted and astonished to meet an Australian conservative who has some intelligence." '[36] To Dalton, Menzies was a Churchill man, but one who could also work with reasonable political opponents. Dalton had no qualms about offering advice to Shedden, over a private lunch on Anzac Day while Menzies was speaking elsewhere, that in his view the best thing the embattled Menzies could do was return to Australia and let Labor leader John Curtin form a national government in which Menzies could serve.[37] Not surprisingly, Shedden saw no sense in the suggestion. Menzies had made national government offers to Curtin already only to be rebuffed. Whether Curtin led an Australian national government or not, he could not be sure his own side would stand united if he agreed to join one.

Churchill

In all the writings on the time, one factor is never disputed: that Winston Churchill was at the controls in London, in a total war scenario. Without convincing Churchill of Australia's need for reinforcements at Singapore, nothing would eventuate. It was Menzies' confidence that he could break through the Churchillian mindset in Australia's interests that pushed him on. Chips Channon and Stanley Bruce might predict that Menzies would be outsmarted by the UK prime minister but Menzies would have to test these opinions with his own judgment.

Winston Churchill had taken over as leader of Britain's national government on 10 May 1940. The days leading up to his accession have been well recorded – the defeat of Neville Chamberlain was bitter and the debate over the rout in Norway saw him lose the confidence of the House, where the Conservatives held a clear majority. Churchill began by offering Chamberlain the position of chancellor of the Exchequer until harder heads talked him out of it. But in making up his ministry, Churchill gave the pro-Chamberlain faction a generous number of positions. Lynne Olson records this in detail in her study *Troublesome Young Men*. Chamberlain also retained leadership of the

Conservative Party until his death in November, a few months later. And, once at the helm, Churchill showed little preference for that handful of Conservative colleagues willing to walk in the wilderness to oppose appeasement. The best jobs went to others. Olson records that

> of the thirty-six ministerial posts disclosed by May 15, twenty-one were given to men who had served under Chamberlain. Not only did Halifax [Chamberlain's preferred successor as prime minister] remain as foreign secretary, but Rab Butler, one of the most aggressive proponents of appeasement in the government, stayed on in the Foreign Office as undersecretary …
>
> Churchill also wanted Lloyd George in the cabinet as minister for agriculture and tried to persuade Chamberlain not to oppose the appointment.[38]

As published diaries and biographies of key players at the time reveal, the United Kingdom may have been under armed attack and facing its greatest ever peril through 1940–41, but for the movers and shakers around Whitehall – its civil service and the parliament – life was very much business as usual. In the black-outs, most chiefs of staff and senior bureaucrats could walk on familiar central London streets to their homes, clubs or apartments not far from their offices. Weekends were still spent, more often than not, in country hideaways, catching up with wives and enjoying long walks in the countryside. Within departments, the speed of having to match the enemy's obvious military superiority meant pressures weighed. But competition for the best civil service posts continued unabated.

Appointments to the top came as much from personal favour as from any sense of who was the best man for the job. Robert Bruce Lockhart had enjoyed his rise in the civil service but was not 'cut out by nature of experience to be a manager or administrator'.[39] And Kenneth Young describes the department Bruce Lockhart controlled as 'chaotic', where 'its members plotted and quarrelled and were consumed by "inter-departmental" strife and jealousies, as was reported to the Foreign Secretary'.[40] On 26 July 1940, Bruce Lockhart recorded in his diary that Max Beaverbrook, then minister for aircraft production, had 'advised me strongly to get out of the F.O. [Foreign Office]: "Rotten show, didn't count anymore, would do nothing for me." If I came to him I could be his liaison with government departments, other ministers, etc.'[41]

Atop all this intra-government jockeying sat Winston Churchill, an old hand at the vagaries of Whitehall and used to having his own way. Even his supporter Lady Violet Bonham Carter described him as 'by temperament an intellectual autocrat. He never liked having other people's way. He infinitely preferred his own'.[42] For all that, as for many who lead nations, Churchill made choices about people as much to protect his position as to best govern. In the case of Lloyd George, having not succeeded in bringing the old malcontent into the circle, and having learnt from Beaverbrook of Lloyd George's defeatist views on the war, Churchill tried to move him to Washington after the death of the British ambassador, Lord Lothian, in December 1940. Lloyd George declined to go.[43] Halifax went instead, thus getting another of the old pro-Chamberlain Tories out of Churchill's way. But even as he did it – knowing his key lieutenant Beaverbrook wanted the Washington post himself – Churchill dispatched a letter to Beaverbrook revelling in the fact that the Ministry of Air was at war with Beaverbrook's own Ministry of Aircraft Manufacture, saying, 'it is more in the public interest that there should be sharp criticism and counter-criticism between the two departments'. This upset Beaverbrook – 'as he saw it, Churchill was putting him on the same level as his deadly opponents'.[44] In this way, Churchill disappointed loyalty and crushed opponents. Beyond the elites of Whitehall, however, Churchill was a hero even as Britain faced month on month of crisis – a Gallup poll in late July 1940 reported that 88 per cent of Britons approved of him and his leadership.[45] With a confidence only inexperience could encourage, Robert Menzies was about to meet his match.

The War Cabinet and the Greek campaign

Menzies, as a dominion prime minister, was entitled to join the War Cabinet while in London. His first attendance was at 5 pm on Monday 24 February. His diary records that the serious matter for discussion of Australian troops being used in what he referred to as 'the Greek adventure' took just forty-five minutes – it was agreed the AIF should spearhead the expedition, subject to Australian Cabinet approval. This decision would dog Menzies for weeks as the campaign became a military disaster – but in his diary he noted that, before the Cabinet meeting on 24 February, he and Shedden 'both favour scheme – Bruce is more doubtful'. The meeting also confirmed for Menzies that Churchill dominated War Cabinet discussions, with few other voices making any sort of mark. 'I was the only one to put questions', diarised Menzies, 'and feel like a new boy who, in the first week of school, commits the solecism of speaking to the captain of the school'.

Confidential annexes to the minutes of both this Cabinet meeting and the following one on 27 February, however, indicate that Menzies was equivocal in his feelings about the commitment of Australian troops to the Greek campaign. The Italians had invaded Greece in October 1940 but had not yet taken control; the fear that the Germans would come from the north-east and capture the port of Salonika, thereby threatening Britain's hold on the eastern Mediterranean, was a realistic one. These Cabinet notes reveal the pressure was on, especially from

115

Churchill, who spoke about 'going to the rescue of Greece' with hope that the action would 'bring in Turkey and Yugoslavia'. He added that 'General Wavell had recommended' troops be sent to Greece. The news from Libya was good and, since the general was 'inclined to understatement', the prime minister felt Wavell's opinion 'must have considerable weight'. The secondary hope for Churchill was that 'the reaction of the United States would also be favourable'.[46]

Menzies did query the advice about the likely success of the military venture – could the Allies' shipping 'maintain the strain'; could the Australian forces used be properly equipped in time or put in a defensive position in time? The responses from Churchill were entirely positive, and the vice chief of the Imperial General Staff, Lieutenant General Sir Henry Pownall, assured Menzies that Australia's General Blamey 'would have been called into consultation on this question'. But Churchill only tolerated the new boy's interruptions briefly and soon brought him to heel, telling him that 'in the last resort' the matter of committing Australian troops 'was a question which the Australian Cabinet must assess for themselves on Mr Menzies' advice'.[47] When the response from the Australian Government was cabled back to London, it was clear that Australian troops were to be committed with reservations hanging over the decision. It was a resolution being made in haste and under pressure from a senior partner.[48] Even the Canadians and the United States were not to be told of the plan until the timetable for the advance had been drawn up.

The Allies' military campaign for Greece struck problems from the outset, with the Greek commander General Alexandros Papagos failing to respond with troops along the defensive line planned. Foreign Secretary Anthony Eden, who had been responsible for pushing 'the Greek adventure', urged Churchill on, using harsh warnings about repercussions for Britain if it backed away. This most risky and ultimately disastrous campaign was thus continued until its tragic finale – troops, large numbers of them Australians and New Zealanders, facing defeat, retreat and inadequate evacuation backup over some weeks. Menzies would not only be appalled at the whole adventure – it would shake his faith in Churchill's judgment.[49]

By 22 April, *The Times* was reporting trouble for Menzies in Australia over the failure of the Greek campaign. Bert Evatt had made an 'outspoken statement' on the lack of consultation with the Advisory War Council and was demanding that parliament be recalled with suggestions the council should be 'endowed with emergency executive powers'. Evatt also opined that the question should be asked if it was time for Labor to take over the government.[50] In an insouciant move, however, Menzies ignored the warnings, making an entry in his diary for 22 April: 'Make a press statement for Australia, to steady the malcontents'. He had already ignored his wife's cable on 12 March warning him to come home.[51]

Menzies continued to have confidence in his ability to persuade – after all, his trip was dependent on a change of heart at the centre of the Empire regarding the need to support Singapore more fully in Australia's interests. Over the commitment of troops to Greece, however, Menzies was unaware that bigger interests than his own were at work in military decisions about Empire forces. His protests during War Cabinet meetings on 6 March over the contradictory information regarding the advisability of a Greek venture had forced Churchill to cable Eden in Cairo for greater consideration of Australia and New Zealand's point of view, and for a more detailed assurance the AIF had every chance of success in Greece.[52] The cable mollified Menzies when he read it at War Cabinet the following day. Assured he would receive more reliable information (he never did), Menzies cabled Fadden to advise the Australian Cabinet to agree to the expedition. Menzies was, however, unaware that the British commanders had already given orders for Australian troops to embark for Greece three days before his cable to Fadden.[53]

Ireland

At lunch on his first Friday in London, with Bruce and a group of ministers, including Hugh Dalton and Ernest Bevin, and various trade and government officials including Maurice Hankey, Menzies had noted in his diary how 'all present are plainly anti-R.C.' in reference to their very 'free talk' about southern Ireland.[54] Chamberlain had handed back to Ireland its three deep-water, west- and south-coast ports at Berehaven, Lough Swilly and Cobh, under the Anglo-Irish Agreement in 1938. With Ireland taking a neutral position on the war, Britain was at a serious disadvantage in not having access to those ports so close and vital to the Atlantic war.

At Chequers a day after Menzies' first London lunch, Churchill gave his own 'free talk' of Eire's taoiseach, Éamon de Valera, describing him as a 'murderer and perjurer', which led Menzies to write in his diary 'why should the British people, (and the Australian) be prejudiced and perhaps defeated by this fantastic Southern Irish neutrality?' As no scholar of Irish history, and with his experience of Australians of Irish heritage such as Joe Lyons, Menzies had little understanding of the deep divisions he would stumble over as he entered British politics.

The Irish position by 1941 was that of a newly emergent nation still entrenched in the aftermath of its war with its former British occupier. Eire in the south by then had its own constitution, but partition continued to ensure that the IRA had strong backing, a force against which southern Ireland's leader Éamon de Valera needed to work deftly to maintain unity in Eire. Clair Wills in *That Neutral Island* offers both political and cultural analysis of the Irish mindset:

The IRA numbered nearly five thousand at the end of the
1930s [and] ... wider European issues were eclipsed by
Ireland's immediate grievances ... any attempt by de Valera
to take Ireland into the war on the side of Britain would
have met with fierce resistance from the IRA. And many
of de Valera's own supporters were convinced that entry on
Britain's side would have meant the occupation of the ports
and airfields by British troops − a renewed invasion.[55]

Menzies listened to his urbane British contacts, and their harshness about the Irish, all of which disturbed his sensitivities − as
it might for someone who had entered a room only to witness
its occupants halfway into a fierce argument. With his Anglo-
Australian and 'new world' Empire perspectives on Britain, such
ancient European scars and sores did not register as they might
have.

Menzies had prolonged his stay in the United Kingdom.
While he could not compete with US Republican Wendell
Willkie − who had arrived in London towards the end of January 1941 to a press meeting with 200 journalists and shortly after
some 500 letters inviting him to visit or speak[56] − Menzies had
made his presence felt in speeches and visits to factories and
regional localities. His address on the Pacific to the Foreign Press
Association on 3 March to a packed audience had gone down
well, he thought, although the Australian press had accused him
of appeasement when he argued for firmness and cordiality in
relations with Japan. By 4 March, Menzies was being approached
by publisher George Harrap to write a book on his impressions of
England, and before he left for home he would have a collection
of his UK speeches published. Trade talks continued to be positive, although no definite contracts had yet materialised, in spite
of his very positive address to the War Cabinet on Australia's war
effort on 10 March, in which he demonstrated the benefits for the

United Kingdom in investing in Australia for the construction of 'heavy bombers or whatever type the British Empire required east of Suez'. He had also argued that there was 'no reason why the United States car should be allowed to capture the Australian manufacturing possibilities'.[57]

But there was no movement in the Foreign Office, nor with Churchill, to make the Pacific a priority. A meeting with Parliamentary Under-Secretary for Foreign Affairs Rab Butler and Permanent Under-Secretary of State for the Foreign Office Alexander Cadogan on 26 February left private impressions that explained the gulf between Australia and the United Kingdom over Japan. Cadogan's diary entry summarising the meeting with Menzies, Bruce and Shedden and presumably talking about the need to secure Singapore is, simply, 'What irresponsible rubbish these Antipodeans talk!'[58] Across London, at the same time, Menzies made his own diary entry, 'Frankly, drift seems policy of FO but I hope that Anthony Eden may satisfy me more'. Eden wouldn't. Only First Sea Lord of the Admiralty AV Alexander showed slightly more empathy in their meetings, the first of which took place on 8 March, when Menzies at least managed to get Alexander to explain the 'preliminary steps which were under discussion for sending battle cruisers and aircraft carriers into the Indian Ocean for the protection of trade routes'.[59]

For all that, Menzies continued to register that the Foreign Office's outlook regarding Japan – as Churchill's – was unchanged. At the War Cabinet meeting on 31 March, Churchill reported that the Japanese ambassador to the United Kingdom was 'friendly to us' and that he had agreed to allow the ambassador to meet the Japanese foreign minister in German-occupied France. Oddly, Churchill then added that he would be giving the Japanese ambassador a 'sealed letter' asking frank questions for the Japanese Government to answer 'before embarking on war against us'.[60]

During Menzies' weekend at Chequers on 8–9 March, he met US emissary Colonel William J Donovan, who had been to Eire and spoken to de Valera. Donovan impressed Menzies as he reported his views of the problem with de Valera; as Menzies noted in his diary, Donovan believed there was a need for a 'personal contact between Dev and Churchill'.[61] Donovan seemed to believe dáil member James Dillon, who opposed neutrality, could lead local Catholics of like persuasion to pressure de Valera to be more conciliatory to the British. Ireland was increasingly isolated and its farmers were suffering. Wendell Willkie had also met with de Valera while visiting the United Kingdom, flying into Dublin one morning late in January and getting back to London for afternoon tea with the King and Queen the same day. Churchill had told him his meeting with de Valera would be useless, and it was; the transitory nature of Willkie's visit would not have been lost on hardened Irish republican de Valera.

Donovan's, no less than Willkie's, was an amateur's hope, but it seems to have influenced Menzies, who told the War Cabinet on 24 March that he was trying to arrange an interview with de Valera to put before him 'a statement of views which had been accepted by his colleagues in Australia'.[62] Menzies argued that he realised the visits of Wendell Willkie and Colonel Donovan had been 'valuable', but they had not been made public. He intended to make public a statement on Eire and its war position after his meeting in Dublin. The War Cabinet concurred that this should happen – there is no record of Churchill's feelings on hearing of Menzies' intentions. Undoubtedly, Menzies sought to achieve some breakthrough that would assist him with Churchill in his case for greater consideration of Australia's defence.

On Friday 4 April, Menzies travelled by train from Belfast to Dublin, arriving at 11 am for a meeting with de Valera followed by lunch. With no blackouts, Menzies found southern Ireland 'queer', but as Clair Wills records,

Visitors rhapsodised over the startling sea of lights in Dublin Bay ... and not only was there light but there were things in the shops ... Steak, cream cakes, knickerbocker glories, bacon and eggs, butter, cosmetics, jewellery, leather goods, all were in plentiful supply, and at bargain prices for the British visitor.[63]

Dublin had become the city well-off Britons would visit for a weekend, a place to enjoy a day or two away from dark and embattled England.

De Valera and Menzies spent what Menzies recorded as a 'long conference, followed by lunch' after which the minister for finance and education, Seán O'Kelly, hosted Menzies for a tour of the Wicklow Mountains. Menzies' entire visit, including accommodation at the Shelbourne Hotel and security, was provided by the Eire Government.[64] On Saturday 5 April, Menzies drove around Dublin with an escort named Beeton from Irish External Affairs, whom Menzies labelled 'a bigot', after which he lunched at Leinster House, where Eire's government offices are housed.

The visit mirrored many that Dublin had witnessed, as the *Wicklow People* reported on 10 April: 'quite a relay of distinguished foreign diplomats and politicians visiting Dublin in recent months ... a recognition that we are on the map'. Menzies referred in his diary to the group at lunch on 5 April as the 'Cabinet', but correspondence in the file on his visit suggests that invitations to such lunches were a bone of contention. The *Wicklow People* had fun reporting Menzies' lunch, suggesting that opposition leaders might have been invited but refused to attend. It then mused on why or why not the members of the opposition might have boycotted the luncheon. A couple of letters in the file show that one member of the dáil, William Davin, was very upset that his name had appeared in a newspaper report as having attended when he had not. Excuses came from both

Top Inaugural meeting of the Advisory War Council after the 1940 election: *(L to R seated)* Jack Beasley, Billy Hughes, Robert Menzies, Governor-General Lord Gowrie, John Curtin, Frank Forde; *(L to R standing)* Norman Makin, Percy Spender, Artie Fadden. State Library of Victoria

Above The Advisory War Council meets in Canberra, 1940: *(L to R)* Jack Beasley, Norman Makin, Frank Forde, John Curtin, Robert Menzies, Billy Hughes, Percy Spender, Artie Fadden, Harold Holt. State Library of Victoria

Left A political team always: proud father James Menzies with his son Robert Menzies, who was sworn in as prime minister of Australia on 26 April 1939. Menzies family collection

Top The War Cabinet meets in Victoria's old Legislative Council Chamber in 1940: *(L to R)* John McEwen, Frederick Stewart, Geoffrey Street, Archie Cameron, Robert Menzies, Frederick Shedden, Billy Hughes, Percy Spender, Senator Harry Foll. State Library of Victoria

Above left From peace to sudden war: Prime Minister Robert Menzies watches anti-tank gun training at Ingleburn, New South Wales, on 3 April 1940 after troops from Australia's Sixth Division began leaving for the Middle East. Fairfax

Above right A believer in his powers of advocacy, Robert Menzies visited striking workers during Wollongong's 'pig iron' dispute in 1939. He would try his hand at this sort of on-site dispute resolution during the miners' strike in April 1940. Fairfax

Top left Robert Menzies addresses Australian troops in the Western Desert, North Africa, February 1941, flanked by General Thomas Blamey (*left*) and other officers. Australian War Memorial

Top right Robert Menzies on his way to Britain at the Piazza Benito Mussolini in Tobruk, 1941, with Fred Shedden (*left*) and General Thomas Blamey. National Archives of Australia

Above This photo, taken by Damian Parer in February 1941, shows Australian Prime Minister Robert Menzies visiting an Australian general hospital in the Middle East, where he was surrounded by an excited crowd of Australian nurses. Australian War Memorial

Top left Trade and support for the Empire inspired Robert Menzies' message to audiences during his visit to Britain in early 1941 – here he is addressing factory workers at Coventry. Menzies family collection

Top right Robert Menzies' visit to England in 1941 made him a popular figure with the press – especially for his morale-boosting speeches to a nation under siege. Australian War Memorial

Above In April 1941 Robert Menzies witnessed Britain under siege from the Luftwaffe bombings – here he is filming the destroyed Lancashire Cricket Club buildings. State Library of Victoria

Defying the onslaught, 12 April 1941: the day after Bristol suffered heavy attack from German fighter bombers, as chancellor of the University of Bristol, Winston Churchill conferred honorary degrees on Robert Menzies and US ambassador John Winant. Australian War Memorial

Robert Menzies, 1941, meeting pilots and staff from the Royal Australian Air Force at a coastal command station in the south of England. National Archives of Australia

Top Arriving in New York, May 1941, Robert Menzies speaks to the press accompanied by New York City Council chairman Newbold Morris (*on his right*), Australian minister in Washington Richard Casey and Fred Shedden (*on his left*). National Archives of Australia

Above left Back in Australia to 'play politics': Robert Menzies with his wife Pattie Menzies after landing at Rose Bay Flying Base on Saturday 24 May 1941. Fairfax

Above right Menzies speaks in the House of Representatives on 27 August 1941 – on the eve of his announcement that he was resigning as prime minster of Australia. Fairfax

WEATHER: Fine, Unsettled Later

SALES 251,906 DAILY

99'6
PERMITTED IN TRAINS
LONDON BABY CARRIAGE
MANUFACTURERS PTY LTD
CENTURY BLDG
SWANSTON ST. CNR
LT. COLLINS ST.

The Sun
DAILY AT DAWN
NEWS ~ PICTORIAL

Registered at the G.P.O., Melbourne, for transmission by post as a Newspaper.

No. 5906   Melbourne: Friday, August 29, 1941   (20 Pages)   2d.

Order your
OVERSEAS
HAMPER
NOW — for Christmas Delivery to
Civilians and Members of the Services
Overseas. Full particulars from
THE *Mutual* STORE
HEADQUARTERS FOR HAMPERS

MR. MENZIES RESIGNS TODAY

MR. FADDEN SUCCEEDS

NEW MINISTRY TO MEET FEDERAL HOUSE

CANBERRA, Thursday. — After a day of momentous negotiation and meetings, the Prime Minister (Mr. Menzies), tonight, announced to his Cabinet colleagues, and later to a joint meeting of the two Government parties, his decision to resign the leadership of the Federal Government.

The two Government parties met tonight and at 11 p.m. unanimously elected the leader of the Country Party (Mr. Fadden) to succeed Mr. Menzies as Prime Minister.

Mr. Menzies will interview the Governor-General (Lord Gowrie) tomorrow morning and formally tender the resignation of his Government. He will advise the Governor-General to commission Mr. Fadden to form a Government. Mr. Fadden will accept the commission.

Mr. Fadden will spend the week-end in reconstruction of his Cabinet and the new Fadden Government is expected to be sworn in at the beginning of next week.

It will proceed immediately to prepare the Federal budget and will meet Federal Parliament, which adjourned earlier today, for the pre-budget recess on September 17.

Mr. Fadden, who has been in Federal Parliament for only five years, will become Australia's second Country Party Prime Minister, but the first Country Party member to lead a Government in an administrative programme.

Sir Earle Page, another Country Party member, was Prime Minister for two weeks after the death of Mr. Lyons in 1939.

Mr. Coles Walks Out

THERE was a dramatic scene at the meeting of the U.A.P. tonight when Mr. Coles, M.H.R., on hearing of Mr. Menzies' decision, announced that he would withdraw from the party.

Mr. Coles entered Parliament at the election last September as independent U.A.P. member for Henty. For the past six months he has sat in the U.A.P. as a member of the Parliamentary party. It was understood, however, that he felt free to leave the party at any time.

When Mr. Coles withdrew, another member was sent hurrying after him to try to induce him to return, but in the meantime Mr. Coles had left the House and had returned to his hotel.

In resigning the Prime Ministership, Mr. Menzies was not so far resigned leadership of the United Australian Party. This issue may arise later.

(Continued on Page 3)

THE FEDERAL TREASURER (Mr. Fadden) all smiles as he left the House of Representatives on Wednesday.

BIG DECISIONS FOR JAPAN

Another Cabinet Crisis Looms

SHANGHAI, Thursday, AAP. —Diplomatic quarters say that the Japanese Cabinet is facing a crisis, says the correspondent of United Press.

Cabinet, they say, probably will have to decide within a fortnight whether to seek a rapprochement with Britain and America or give way completely to a militarist Government.

Diplomats said that the root of the trouble was the failure to solve problems arising from British and American freezing and embargo actions or to halt United States shipments to Vladivostok.

If Prince Konoye is unable to get British and American aid to revive trade and manufacturing and build up depleted war stocks he will probably have to resign in favor of a militarist Cabinet which might seek access to raw materials by force.

Chinese Offensive

MEANWHILE, Japan admits for the first time in months that the Chinese are on the offensive, tending to confirm reports that Chiang Kai-shek ordered a general offensive in North, Central and South China which began on August 19, Chinese Independence Day.

The Domei Newsagency said Japanese troops repulsed an attempt by the Chinese 40th Division to attack Kaoshun, 25 miles east of Wuhu, which is west of Shanghai, two days ago and also that the Japanese had crushed Chinese preparations to attack Japanese garrisons 50 miles west of Thing Shah in Anhwei Province.

GERMAN OFFENSIVE LOSING IMPETUS? LENINGRAD HOLDS

Exclusive Sun Service

LONDON, Thursday. — The third great German offensive of the Russian campaign, which has now been under way for three weeks, is still raging along the whole length of the Eastern Front, but now appears to have lost its impetus.

Reports from the battlefront are still contradictory and confused, but no new place names have been used officially by either side for 24 hours.

The latest Russian communique repeats that there is stubborn fighting at Kingisepp, Smolensk, Gomel, Dnepropetrovsk and Odessa.

Nor do the Russians confirm Swedish reports that Soviet forces have reoccupied Gomel. The Stockholm correspondent of the Daily Telegraph said General Koniev's forces had re-entered Gomel.

Moscow still neither confirms nor denies German claims to have captured Velikie Luki, a rail junction on the central north front, the industrial city of Dnepropetrovsk on the Lower Dnieper, and to have cut the Moscow-Leningrad railway.

Moscow says that in the drive against Leningrad the German advance has been slowed almost to a standstill. Russian troops are savagely contesting every metre of ground.

In the Ukraine it is clear that the Germans have failed to cross the Lower Dnieper. The defences of Odessa are still holding the enemy.

Military observers say that if it is true the sting has gone from the German push, it is extremely unlikely that they will be able to mount another before winter. Time is now a great ally of Russia.

The Russians claim to have inflicted extremely heavy casualties on the Germans in the Gomel area. They estimate enemy casualties at 80,000 dead and wounded and claim to have destroyed 200 tanks, 100 planes, and thousands of motor transports.

In an unnamed sector the Russians also claim to have routed the 132nd German Division, which left 6000 dead on the field.

CONTRADICTORY REPORTS

Exclusive Sun Service

LONDON, Thursday. — Latest information from Moscow is that the Germans nowhere have crossed the Dnieper below Kiev or, indeed, below the Gomel district, says the Stockholm correspondent of The Times.

HOWEVER, Berlin claims that the German army has crossed the Lower Dnieper River and captured the industrial city of Zaporozhe, near the great Dnieprogres Dam.

Moscow makes no mention of the German claim in the latest communique.

Budapest Radio says that Hungarian and German troops have broken Russian resistance at bridgeheads on the Lower Dnieper and at some places have crossed the river and are established on the east bank.

The German claim that General Kleist's Army captured 83,000 men after the battle for Uman is exaggerated like other recent German figures, but if it represents all the Russian prisoners taken in this area it is a smaller sacrifice than was feared would be necessary.

It is noteworthy that the German report mentions Kleist's army and not von Rundstedt's as hitherto, lending color to the report that von Rundstedt has been killed.

Pending further news, Tallinn, capital of Estonia, should not be considered lost, although it is impossible to ascertain even approximately the number of Russians are there. Presumably it is large and the Russians will hold the city if possible.

Red Fleet units are reported to have joined in the fighting near Tallinn.

The operations at Hanko, in south-west Finland, appear to have stabilised as they have been since July.

Finnish claims represent Wiipurt as practically captured, but the most competent view is that the city can and will be held for a long time.

BULLET NEAR LAVAL'S HEART

Exclusive Sun Service

LONDON, Thursday. — Latest reports from Vichy say that the condition of pro-Nazi Pierre Laval is more dangerous than was at first thought.

ONE of Laval's wounds is an inch above his heart, and the doctors decided not to attempt to remove the bullet at present.

Marcel Deat's condition is even worse. He has perforated intestines.

Laval and Marcel Deat and another pro-German were shot by Paul Colette, 20, at a swearing-in ceremony of French volunteers to fight with Germany against Russia.

The German Government has rushed two specialists to attend Laval.

According to Berlin radio Colette admitted joining the Anti-Bolshevik Brigade so that he could get within range of the "French quislings."

Three onlookers are reported to have been wounded by bullets from Colette's revolver.

(Wave of Unrest—Page 3)

The Sun (Melbourne) headlines Menzies' resignation as prime minister, 29 August 1941. Fairfax

Top left Robert Menzies with his legal mentor and close friend Sir Owen Dixon in 1947. Newspix

Top right Robert Menzies, opposition leader in 1948, visited Britain and was critical of the Attlee Labour Government – here he is handing out Australian food parcels, accompanied by his daughter, Heather, on his right. Heather Henderson

Above Robert Menzies enjoys an early victory for the Liberal Party in the Victorian state election, 8 November 1947, with the member for Hawthorn, Frederick Edmunds, and a Liberal campaign organiser. State Library of Victoria

sides in the wash-up. Best of all was a note, handwritten by JP Walshe, secretary of the Department of External Affairs, that appeared below a minute to the secretary explaining that Liam Burke of the Fine Gael Party had given reasons why its members would not attend the lunch. Walshe annotated: 'Mr Davin gave no notice of his intention to stay away. When rung up from the Dail … he said he wouldn't go to a lunch for a "bloody orange-man"'.[65] Old sores healed slowly, if at all. Another opposition figure, having replied he was coming, developed a sudden tooth-ache and sent apologies.

For all his efforts, southern Ireland's 'troubles' had smothered Menzies' attempts at persuasion. He had achieved little more than a few days of sightseeing and pleasant exchanges. In his public statement to the Irish press, as he finished his brief trip, he refused to say whether he and de Valera had discussed 'the ports'. On 7 April, under a heading 'Mr Menzies on Atlantic battle: "of course Britain will win"', the *Irish Times* reported that the Australian prime minister had used an anecdote about a judge who, after listening to a barrister summing up, declared he was little wiser. The barrister replied that while no wiser, the judge was 'better informed'. Menzies told the press he felt like the judge in relation to Eire. As to the rationing of tea and bread of which the Irish were complaining, all he could say was that 'everybody seemed to be living a very full life. Brown bread, he always heard, was better than white'. On the question of shipping, which bedevilled the Irish, Menzies emphasised that he understood but it was going to be a problem as long as the 'enemy carried on his depredations in the Atlantic approaches'. And he finished – when asked how the Irish in Australia regarded the war – by saying that the Irish in Australia are '100 per cent behind the war effort'. Those four parting shots delivered, with his barrister's sense of moment, Menzies returned to Liverpool on what he described in his diary as a 'rough journey in a "Rapide"'.

As public statements go, Menzies' response to the Irish press was not one with success to its name. Menzies' few days in Ireland would form the background to a confidential report, rather than a public statement, on Ireland for the War Cabinet on 9 April.[66] In the report, he gave information about Ireland in general and its politics, some of which would not have been new to members of the Cabinet, along with his impressions of de Valera. The taoiseach, in his 'long dark frieze overcoat and a broad-brimmed black hat' had left a definite mark. Menzies liked de Valera in spite of his 'exaggerated self-consciousness' and lack of understanding of the war effort. Menzies had come away with an impression that one of Ireland's motivations for neutrality could be its fear that it was without defences and could be bombed by the Germans. For all that, de Valera told Menzies that he believed Britain's cause in the war was 'a just one' and that in spite of Eire's distrust of the English, he and around '80 per cent, at least, of the people of Eire' would like Britain to win. One can only imagine the cynicism in the War Cabinet at this. But Menzies also expressed a somewhat naive hope that better engagement with the taoiseach and his ministers might bring results – especially if Britain could look at the 'whole question of the defence of Eire'. Some members of the Irish Cabinet had begun to realise that 'neutrality has its defeats no less than war'. Menzies was also staggered to find that de Valera and the Northern Irish leader John Andrews had never met.

The effect of this report on Churchill is not recorded, except for an entry in Menzies' diary on 10 April: 'Winston describes my paper as "very readable" – a most damning comment'.[67] Certainly, Churchill would have seen it as the words of an outsider offering advice to the better informed. Britain in 1941 did not recognise Eire as a sovereign state and its neutrality was regarded as repudiating the 1922 Anglo–Irish Treaty – and by Churchill himself as an illegal act. In January 1941, Churchill had written to Dominions Secretary Viscount Cranborne saying that while bases in Eire were not as yet vital to Britain's survival, 'the lack of them is a grievous injury and impediment to us'.[68] And he added disturbing thoughts regarding a worsening situation in the Atlantic, saying, 'Should the danger to our war effort through the denial of the Irish bases threaten to become mortal ... we should have to act in accordance with our own self-preservation and that of our Cause'. Without realising it, Menzies had harmed his standing with Churchill.

7

Menzies' dark and hurrying day

In the smoking-room, Winston sits down and has his glass of
Bristol Milk and is prepared to answer questions. Members
cluster round him rather ingratiatingly. 'How well you are
looking, Prime Minister.' He does in fact look better than I
have seen him look for years. All that puffy effect has gone
and his face is almost lean, with the underlip pouting defiance
all the time. He says: 'Yes, I am well. I am in fine trim. More
than I was this time last year. We are doing well. We have a
real Army now. We have tanks – good tanks. We have guns.
In the air our position is not merely absolutely, but relatively,
stronger.'

– Harold Nicolson, diary, 1 April 1941[1]

For Labor sympathisers and many among the Australian left,
Robert Menzies was never quite Australian, and represented
an Anglo dependence on things British. From this developed a
jaundiced account of Menzies' time in London in 1941 as that
of an ambitious dominion leader looking to score a plum British
appointment, even the prime ministership itself. To go down this
path, however, is to leave aside a wider world of British politics
with its spider-web network of relationships and myriad government, business and political associations underpinned by lunches,

126

breakfasts, drinks at clubs, weekend retreats and countless professional and private exchanges, and to see through a very narrow lens. From the British perspective, Australia's Prime Minister Robert Menzies encountering Britain and its leaders over a few months in early 1941 is a very small part of history for the time.

In the ABC-commissioned Screen Australia/360 Degree Films' television documentary on Menzies and Churchill, moments recorded by Menzies in his diary take on unrealistic momentum for the sake of a good story. Reconstructions of exchanges between Menzies and UK officials, including Churchill, create a dramatic effect, but they are often inaccurate and exaggerated. A 'heated exchange' between Menzies and Churchill over the evacuation of troops from Greece takes place 'in the living room at Downing Street'. The Churchills did not live at Number 10 Downing Street from the beginning of the blitz in 1940 – it had, as Churchill's daughter Mary Soames has recorded, become 'unsafe for habitation'.[2] In January 1941, US visitor Harry Hopkins described Number 10 in a letter to Roosevelt as having 'most of the windows out – workmen over the place repairing the damage'.[3] The Churchill family and staff were accommodated instead in what became known as 'the Number 10 Annexe', a series of offices directly over the underground War Cabinet rooms, which could be accessed by an internal staircase. Occasionally, Churchill would have the press photograph him leaving Number 10, as if he still lived there, but only to give the impression to an anxious population that things were going on normally.

In 1941, Churchill and Menzies were part of a professional milieu where any exchange at a business level was conducted in the formal way, whether at a social gathering or an office meeting. Real-life negotiations, crisis or not, would also involve other senior figures, and in government-to-government meetings staff would take minutes. The mechanics of government have a particular style. Even on weekends at Chequers, meetings with the British prime minister were semi-formal occasions, as opposed to the conviviality of good friends or associates spending time together for purely social reasons. Menzies might stroll about with a Churchill relative or guest while staying for the weekend but the actual times he would see Churchill were at arranged moments of the day, usually over dinner, drinks or lunch. Any London meetings were carefully managed into a very crowded diary. Frustrations on Menzies' part did come out at War Cabinet meetings, and he spoke up with the manners such a meeting requires, even if his annoyance was barely veiled. On Monday 14 April, as Churchill told the War Cabinet Tobruk 'must' be held, Menzies dared to question with what.

At a lunch on 21 April in the War Cabinet rooms with Churchill, Eden and Attlee, which Menzies referred to as 'very amusing', he drew Churchill's ire by suggesting the British prime minister needed 'Chiefs of Staff who will tell him he is talking nonsense'.[4] But, amid the 'amusing' joviality around the lunch table, this then became a spirited conversation, where Churchill tipped a bucket on Menzies' chiefs of staff for being 'yes-men', agreeing with him even while ignoring his advice. There wasn't a blazing row. Churchill was capable of keeping anyone who crossed his path very much in their place, even the larger-than-life Beaverbrook. It may have made Menzies angry at times but, as a prime minister himself with a difficult team of opponents in Canberra, it also fascinated him. After a War Cabinet meeting on 3 March at which Churchill was not present, Menzies diarised: 'I must discover the secret of having my cabinet unwilling to decide any important question in my absence'. On 4 March, Menzies noted how well the War Cabinet and the ministries worked: 'Get through 3 times the work we do. Chiefs of staff *do* confer'. And, again, on 26 March, as Menzies reflects on how Winston could reduce his Cabinet colleagues to 'look and sound like 6th form boys', he comments, 'I wish I knew the secret'.[5] It was what Menzies biographer Allan Martin described as a love–hate relationship.

An Australian abroad

Historian Robert O'Neill has written that

> There is very little direct evidence as to what Churchill thought of Australia, New Zealand, and Antipodeans generally. He mentioned them rarely in his speeches and writings and then only briefly … there was simply not enough knowledge in his head of what the Pacific dominions thought and offered for them to achieve even a small fraction of the attention that he paid to the state of affairs in Europe and to Anglo-American relations.[6]

O'Neill goes on to argue, 'The fact that he [Churchill] made only the briefest of factual references to Menzies in his memoirs and official papers suggests that Churchill rarely gave the Australian Prime Minister a second thought'.[7] Indeed, it was this lack of engagement that pushed Menzies to extend his stay in Britain, in his quest to get the British to back Singapore with strengthened defences, along with a sandbag campaign to salvage the evacuation of Australian troops from Greece to Crete. How could he return home empty-handed?

In the early part of 1941, as Mary Soames relates, the Churchills entertained a continual trail of important visitors to London. Americans got super attention from Churchill; as Soames writes, 'Winston deployed all his personal warmth and charm to win their friendship' as well as to convince them of 'the firmness and effectiveness of Britain's stand'.[8] They came as representatives of President Franklin D Roosevelt: Harry Hopkins, Averell

Harriman, Wendell Willkie and the new US ambassador, Gil Winant. All but Willkie spent many weekends at Chequers. Harry Hopkins spent twelve evenings with Churchill in his first two weeks in the United Kingdom and later recorded that Chequers was the coldest house he had ever visited.[9] There were also the other dominion leaders: Field Marshal Jan Smuts from South Africa, Mackenzie King from Canada. The atmosphere around the political elites, even at the height of the war, is well recorded in Harold Nicolson's published letters and diaries. As a parliamentary secretary and censor at the Ministry of Information, Nicolson had both the opportunity and time to observe. Influential visitors, ambassadors, representatives of foreign royal families in exile, business leaders – all came to pay their respects, plead for help, negotiate deals, seek advice, play the diplomatic game.

Nicolson's jottings for 27 March 1941 give the flavour:

In the morning two things happened. (1) I read a telegram
from Belgrade saying that Subotic [Yugoslav Minister
in London] was sending information to his government
regarding our attitude. (2) An hour later I learned that the
Yugoslav Government had been arrested by [anti-German
General] Simovic. (3) An hour later I had to lunch with
Subotic. You admit this was an awkward concatenation.
When I arrived I found my old friend Tilea [leader of the
Free Romanian Movement] as the first arrival. He whispered
to me, 'Be careful, they are not pleased.' I said nothing.
Then in pranced the Turkish Ambassador and seized a glass
of sherry. '*Je bois,*' he said, '*à la santé de Sa Majesté le Roi
Pierre II et à l'alliance Balkanique.*' [I drink to the health of
His Majesty King Peter II and to the Balkan alliance.] The
Subotics put on a blue face.[10]

By the end of the day, however, Nicolson was musing on even happier news – the fall of the Italians' main stronghold in Eritrea: 'What a triumph! Truly it is all over'. Not that this would last for long. On 4 April he notes, 'The Libyan news is worse than I had supposed'. On 3 April, adding personal grief, he had written to his wife, Vita Sackville-West, telling of his concern for her at the news of Virginia Woolf's suicide. Life in London was a strange and heady broth. And the men at the top belonged to a deep seam of upper-class blood, saturated with cosmopolitan and Eurocentric links and relationships. They oozed the confidence of being born to rule. Menzies may have been a good match for his British colleagues, but he was a visitor rather than an insider.

Churchill presided over and dominated this rich pot. His private secretary in these war years was a young diplomat, John Colville, who kept and later published diaries of his time serving three British prime ministers. His descriptions of Churchill at Chequers alone give pictures of intellectual arrogance alongside a desperate doggedness. As Churchill entertained his influential visitors, he regaled them in fireside performances of his views on the war, as on the evening of 26 January 1941:

> We sat in a circle, [Marshal of the Royal Air Force Viscount] Portal, [Harry] Hopkins, Jack Churchill, myself and Prof. [Professor Frederick Lindemann, science adviser], while the P.M. stood with his back against the mantelpiece, a cigar between his teeth, his hands in the armpits of his waistcoat. Every few seconds he would start forward, trip over the marble grate, walk four or five paces, turn abruptly and resume his position against the mantelpiece. All the while a torrent of eloquence flowed from his lips, and he would fix one or another of us with his eye as he drove home some point.[11]

Among ordinary Britishers, even in late 1940, Churchill was a hero. Menzies writes of this in his diary: 'The people have set him up as something little less than God, and his power is therefore terrific'.[12] And no amount of flattery was too much for him to hear. Colville records how on a cold day in Dover, Harry Hopkins told Churchill he had overheard a workman tell his mate as he caught a glimpse of the prime minister, 'There goes the bloody British Empire'. Colville writes, 'Winston's face wreathed itself in smiles and, turning to me, he lisped "*Very* nice." I don't think anything has given him such pleasure for a long time'.[13]

Into this political mix came Robert Menzies, ready to prove others wrong in their estimation of his sway with this autocratic British prime minister. Both David Day and the 360 Degree Films docudrama based on his book give a swagger to Menzies that did not resonate so loudly around Churchill's table. Chips Channon, married to a Guinness daughter, dined with Menzies in Cairo at the British Embassy, where he noted in his diary that the Australian prime minister was 'jolly, rubicund, witty, only 46 with a rapier-like intelligence and gifts as a raconteur'.[14] Showing a lack of intimate familiarity with London social circles, Menzies had noted of the same occasion that he had dined with 'Other house guests, Lord & Lady Glenconner, Capt Hon T. Cope – 12th generation descendant of Sir Edward Cope … and one Channon MP from London – agreeable but indeterminate'.[15] The personable Chips Channon continued to cross Menzies' path; they travelled by plane together on the long south-western detour across Africa and through Lisbon to England, Chips recalling that 'the excitement of the Menzies' Australian entourage was touching to see as they approached England for the first time'. As he chartered a car back to London, Channon realised that 'the Kangaroo party' had disappeared.[16] On 3 March, Menzies accepted Channon's invitation to dinner – 'one of the gayest and most riotous festivals I have ever arranged', Channon recorded – where Menzies again impressed as 'immense, a raconteur … full of sense and charm'. And he caught up with Channon for drinks at the Dorchester on 1 April. All round, Chips Channon and Bob Menzies hit it off, with their love of fine wine and conversation – even if Menzies' 'robbing Paul to pay Peter' quip over the fate of Prince Paul of Yugoslavia in the face of Italy's advance irritated Channon. He was upset the quip had 'gone around London'.[17]

This was Menzies at large and on the town. Hugh Dalton, another of Menzies' social contacts in high places, observed that this charming dinner-guest prime minister could go weak at the knees before the largest political figure in London. Arriving at Chequers for a weekend stay on 2 March, Dalton was under-whelmed by the line-up of other house guests:

> I found only Menzies, several women – Mrs Churchill and, I think two daughters – various underlings, the Prof [Frederick Lindemann], [Churchill's principal private secretary, Eric] Seal and [Churchill's aide-de-camp, Commander Tommy] Thompson. PM in great form. Complained that his beer was not cold enough. Spoke in favour of onions, of which we had a good supply.[18]

As usual, Churchill was doing most of the talking. Apart from a long discourse on rights and property, nationalisation and some time mocking Halifax and his 'draft on Peace Aims', the prime minister was worried about Britain's tremendous loss of ships. And he complained that troops were 'eating too much' and 'could do with less rations'. In all of this, Menzies did not seem to have been playing his part as the talented raconteur. Dalton noted that Menzies had been 'rather silent at lunch, a little overawed'. And when Churchill had shot at him the suggestion that 'Hitler says that 16 million Jews ought to go and live in Australia. What do you say to that?', Menzies 'had no quick answer'.

Dalton expected more from Menzies, but Churchill was making a jab at the Australian leader for his pro-appeasement attitudes and Menzies could sense it. He knew when not to take the bait. For all that, Menzies was outshone and outdone by Churchill in front of other guests.[19] They were by no means equals. A week later, Menzies was at Chequers again and on the day the Lend-Lease Bill passed, with General Charles de Gaulle a house guest. John Colville recorded that conversation moved from a discussion of the German character and how to deal with retribution, to analogies from ancient Greece, outback Australia, and Rome and Carthage. Churchill compared England and Carthage, saying Carthage had lost because 'they lost command of the sea'. Menzies countered, arguing that the Carthaginians had 'not had a Winston Churchill'. Colville, obviously conscious of Menzies' attempt to flatter Churchill or simply make known his personal admiration, observed in an aside that Menzies had forgotten Hannibal.[20]

Collision not conspiracy

Menzies came to London not to save the Empire but to save Singapore and thus Australia. He was not ambivalent about the war.[21] Having doubt about going to war is not the same as being uncertain which battles should be fought. Even after the United States entered the war in Europe and the Mediterranean in 1942, there were differences of judgment, Churchill believing the North African theatre should be their priority before pushing the Germans back in Europe, the Americans favouring a European advance. Churchill stood his ground and prevailed. Australian troops would play a hero's role in that part of the successful North African campaign. Curtin had retained Australian forces in the Mediterranean, even while he believed the Pacific was Australia's priority. It had been a decision of the

Menzies Government that Australian troops would serve in the Middle East, and Curtin had reminded a meeting of the Advisory War Council on 18 March 1941 that if the policy of the Labor Party had been followed Australians would not have been sent.[22] Menzies was appalled at the lack of focus on the Pacific coming from Whitehall. That Menzies and Churchill were on a collision course is not surprising – but it was not a case of peacemaker (or Lloyd George–style appeaser) against warmonger, just a clash over priorities.

Churchill ruled by collisions, even as his enthusiasm and theatrical advocacies caught Menzies' admiration for him as a war prime minister. Menzies' diary notes, on his first weekend in March at Chequers, 'he [Churchill] is pacing the floor with the light of battle in his eyes. In every conversation he ultimately reaches a point where he positively enjoys the war ... Churchill's course is set. There is no defeat in his heart'. And, on 31 March, as ships still sank but some victories in the Mediterranean gave heart to the Allies, Menzies expressed his admiration again, 'Winston's attitude to war is much more realistic than mine ... War is terrible and it cannot be won except by lost lives. That being so, don't think of them'.[23]

Whether Menzies was on his mission out of his personal ambitions in government at home and to shore up his support within coalition ranks, or was ready to risk his career by leaving Australia in order to secure Singapore is not the question. The fact is that seriously improved defence capabilities for Singapore were at the top of Menzies' priorities for his meetings in London. This was reinforced as he travelled. At home, meetings of the Advisory War Council in the first two weeks of February saw members trying to ease political differences collectively; working to change public perceptions about the seriousness of the war; and absorbing new information coming to them from the Dominions Office and John Latham in Tokyo, who had advised that Japan was set on a course to move progressively southwards even if it meant war.[24] Curtin himself was chief among those pushing for a more urgent response at all levels to likely and imminent localised hostilities.

Menzies was welcomed to the United Kingdom by a number of reporters in the British press as something of a pop figure in their drab and besieged country. And he was welcomed – like any Australian prime minister – by Australian troops in the Middle East. It certainly flattered him – and certainly he loved it, after his tribulations with the press in Australia. This is not sufficient evidence to argue, however, that such praise and publicity might be connected to leading figures in the UK Government (most of whom had been supporters of Chamberlain and the idea of peace negotiations) seeing in Menzies a replacement for Churchill. Or even that the accolades went to Menzies' head and gave him thoughts along such lines. It was a parallel universe, not a connection. There is also no evidence to argue that 'the British public apparently read with rapt attention of this larger-than-life figure rushing to London to lend his support'.[25] This is overdone commentary and speculative. Menzies was hardly rushing to lend a hand. Australia was already involved, with its troops in real support in the Middle East. And, before Menzies' visit was half over, Australian troops were part of the Greek campaign, even if it was a move Menzies had deep reservations about.

Menzies' mission had a second priority, which he also found difficult to achieve. He had come to the United Kingdom to attract British investment in Australian-made aircraft. This aim stood significantly alongside his attempts to persuade Whitehall, and Churchill in particular, that the Empire in the Pacific was desperately undefended and that additional reinforcements were needed fast. Newspaper reports of his visit illustrate the relativities of his task. Local politics, everyday life and the alarming headlines alerting the public to devastating Atlantic and

Mediterranean battles, smothered isolated press reports on Australia's prime minister. A perusal of national dailies for the weeks Menzies was in the United Kingdom is instructive here.

Towards the end of his visit, as Menzies became more desperate in his mission and spent time dining with leading press figures, his popularity was somewhat overwritten by one or two journalists who were seeking to stir the political waters. Menzies was a striking figure from an important dominion who talked up courage and a will to win for Britons in his speeches. The slim volume of his UK speeches was published at the end of his visit, its publishers believing his words held inspiration for UK readers. That Menzies spoke of the war as one where Britons and Australians were standing together was to be expected. In 1937, then Australian prime minister Joe Lyons and his popular wife, Enid, on a visit to London, were also pursued by the UK press as something exotic and fresh with a message of dominion loyalty to spread. Not surprisingly, Menzies was noticed, praised and seen as a figure to give heart to Britons at a time they had so few allies. And, in all of this, he did allow himself to be used by a small group in London to ginger up disquiet about Churchill's handling of the war effort. As Churchill's obstinacy about war aims and tactics persisted, those seeking to prevail over him, and some who conferred with Menzies, left the Australian prime minister thinking that a full-time dominion presence in the War Cabinet might be a way to stir Churchill regarding the importance of defence in the Pacific.

Menzies' diary in 1941 offers no evidence that he was at any stage contemplating a tilt at Churchill's leadership. But throwaway lines from a few men about town, impressed that the Australian prime minister had views and the ability to communicate them independently, did add to rumours. On some rare occasions, there were suggestions he could be better used in the war effort to raise morale in London than by returning to a faraway place most

Britishers thought was safe and secure, and unlikely to be endangered in the war. While he was in London, the idea of an imperial conference was mooted among Churchill critics who dealt with Menzies – alongside the idea of greater involvement in decisions about the war by dominion prime ministers, such as Mackenzie King and Jan Smuts. Menzies discussed such ideas in his meetings with the Canadian prime minister in Ottawa on 7 May.[26]

At lunch on 11 March, press baron Lord Kemsley (Gomer Berry) told Menzies expansively, 'We must not let you leave this country!' In his diary, Menzies was scornful of the comment, knowing full well that media types were mostly concerned with selling newspapers. He noted cynically, 'Lord knows what journalistic stunt he will be working'.[27] This diary entry shows that Menzies took the comment as it was meant – a press baron trying to seduce an attractive public figure to make news, to agitate against the dominant Churchill. There had been talk around Menzies that very day of the chances for Labour after Churchill, but no suggestions as to who might follow on the Conservative side. Even Menzies knew the lack of names meant simply that Churchill was there for the long haul. In early May, after Menzies had left London, a bitter Lloyd George would come a cropper in the House of Commons trying to create a division in Conservative ranks over the failed Greek campaign.

David Day has speculated on what might have been discussed at a meeting between Menzies and Kemsley three days later over tea at the Ritz, writing,

> we can only presume that Kemsley went further into his plans
> for Menzies' prolonged detention in London ... powerful
> press support, together with the possibility of a political
> vacuum if Churchill fell from power, may well have provided
> the basis in Menzies' mind for the idea that it was not beyond
> him to make a bid for Downing Street.

But, as Day himself writes, this is only presumption. No one has any record of what was discussed. Menzies was giving good copy, and he was the Australian prime minster with connections both in the Antipodes and around London. He was also a good friend of Clive Baillieu, Keith Murdoch and Warwick Fairfax, all of whom would have had associations with the press baron. Menzies also knew most of the top businessmen in Australia. And he was good company. Whatever they discussed, we simply do not know. The same is true of a meeting Menzies had with Beaverbrook to inspect aircraft. Certainly, Beaverbrook used his friendship with Menzies to encourage him to speak up at the War Cabinet and challenge Churchill, but this does not indicate any sort of move to take Churchill out. In spite of being Churchill's friend, Beaverbrook resented the way he dominated. And here was an Australian prime minister, erudite and strong in argument, who, unlike other members of the War Cabinet, could challenge the bulldog without any fear of losing his job.

It has been suggested that Menzies considered a career in England in response to his precarious position in Australia, 'torn between these two widely separated futures'.[28] Yet in response to the idea that a few British MPs would look forward to his defeat in Canberra so he could try out for London, Menzies wrote in his diary (in Latin), 'Every unknown a magnifico'.[29] All the evidence suggests that Menzies never took such comments seriously, however much he may have envied the comfortable gentlemen of Whitehall with their country homes and roles in the action. Connections between Australian prime ministers and the smart crowd in London had been in place for years. Lady (Nancy) Astor, with her eclectic Cliveden social set, had begged Enid Lyons to visit her home in London during the Lyons couple's time there in 1935.

Over his various London visits, Menzies continued the connections he, Bruce and Lyons had first established in the Silver

Jubilee year, adding more with each visit. The Astors, prominent appeasers, switched their support to Churchill during 1939, Nancy Astor voting with the rebels against Chamberlain. Menzies was about to stay with the Astors when, on 20 March 1941 in Plymouth, Nancy Astor led the official party welcoming the King and Queen to a gala day.[30] As dusk settled, Plymouth suffered the first day of a sustained German air attack, which Menzies recorded when another night raid came the following day. He and Nancy Astor kept her household 'entertained' in the cellars while the bombs fell for a second night.[31]

For Menzies, and many Australians of his generation and beyond, Britain was a place where he felt at home, in a professional and intellectual sense – even if his amateur films, when shown to Mackenzie King in Ottawa, left King with the impression Menzies had not grasped the full implications of the global conflict at hand, noting in his diary: 'These beautiful estates, etc., in England, titled ladies with their shelters, privileged positions, etc., these are things that the people are out to destroy'.[32] Yet Menzies never forgot where he belonged. On 16 April, after deciding the day before he should remain in London a bit longer and with *The Times* reporting this decision favourably, Menzies wrote in his diary that he had mixed feelings: 'desperately homesick – go out and buy Heather [his daughter] a pearl necklace'.[33]

Straws in the wind

Taking his leave of the United Kingdom by plane from Bristol to Lisbon en route to Ottawa on 3 May, Menzies was not a happy Australian prime minister. His final days in London are recorded in his diary, where he noted on 30 April, just before leaving, 'Great argument in War Cabinet. I protest against W.C. deciding what advice to offer USA regarding moving Pacific fleet … to the Atlantic, *without* reference to Australia, though I was in

London!'[34] Something of his last moments is also described in the diaries of Maurice Hankey, Cabinet secretary from 1916 to 1938. Hankey had lunched with Fred Shedden on 30 April and two days later had encountered Menzies on Park Lane after a lunch at Grosvenor House for the Iron and Steel Federation, at which Menzies had been the guest speaker. Hankey and Shedden had talked of Menzies' frustrations in the War Cabinet, at his not being able to get Churchill to contemplate any plan for troop evacuation in Libya, if needed, where a majority of the forces were Australians and New Zealanders. On 1 May, Menzies had come to the lunch direct from another War Cabinet meeting and, according to Hankey, made 'acid remarks' at the beginning of his speech about time use in those meetings.

In the street, after leaving the lunch, Menzies caught up with Hankey and his wife and downloaded his frustrations at Churchill's dominance of the War Cabinet, suggesting the only answer for the dominions was to 'summon an Imperial War Cabinet and keep one of them behind, like Smuts in the last war, not as a guest but as a full member'.[35] Hankey, as Allan Martin among others has recorded, had wielded great influence between the wars, even becoming a full member of Cabinet under Chamberlain in 1939. But with Churchill his influence was much diminished. Hankey, whose mother was Australian, had befriended Menzies on a trip to Australia in 1934, later becoming an influential contact during Menzies' visits to London.[36] In the busy days before his departure, Menzies was clearly reaching out in desperation, hoping even someone of Hankey's lessened influence might offer him a way to break Churchill's obstinacy.

This was no play for power on Menzies' part. His diary entries show that he was flattered by talk around him, from Beaverbrook and others, that he could make a valuable contribution in London. But his major worry, as he faced his departure, was his responsibilities as the Australian prime minister. As an Empire man, Menzies was concerned at Churchill's direction of the war and its consequences for Britain, but his chief worry was that his long weeks in the United Kingdom had delivered very little assurance of Australia's defence in the Pacific or that the interests of Australian troops in the Middle East and Mediterranean were being properly guarded. The debacle in Greece only emphasised the shabby way Whitehall had pushed the Australian leadership into sending its troops there – the blame for which later was described by Anthony Eden as falling 'unjustly' on Menzies, who had endorsed the move with 'courage' as being 'what he believed to be right'.[37] By way of small compensation, Menzies had later prevailed in having Thomas Blamey appointed deputy commander-in-chief of the British forces in the Middle East. But as the military situation in North Africa deteriorated for the Allies, Churchill refused to make plans for any evacuation. There had been a successful evacuation of 13 000 from Greece on 25 April – to Crete. But Menzies' diary on 28 April shows he had lost his admiration for Churchill's ability to take a hardened approach to war dead: 'Winston says, "We will lose only 5000 in Greece". We will in fact lose at least 15000. W. is a great man, but he is more addicted to wishful thinking every day'.[38]

It is also wishful thinking for Menzies' critics to try continually to interpret events around him during his London visit in the context of his being the spearhead of a move to topple Churchill. There is, as Allan Martin has verified through exhaustive research for his two-volume biography of Menzies, simply no evidence for the thesis. False hope notwithstanding, Menzies and his advisers were working to get concessions for Australia in trade and defence while facing a distracted and embattled Churchill. David Day's conjecture that, in his last couple of weeks in London, 'Menzies would make frantic efforts to extinguish Churchill as Britain's driving force' is contradicted by Day's own admission that Menzies himself had a torrent of mixed feelings towards

Churchill: indeed a love–hate relationship. Within lines of arguing that Menzies was making 'frantic efforts' to depose Churchill, Day admits that Menzies had reversed his negative views of Churchill after news came through of Allied victories in North Africa and the Mediterranean. In fact, the trajectory of Menzies' feelings about Churchill is very much linked to how well or how poorly the war was going for the Australian forces around the Mediterranean.[39] Good news for Australian troops meant good news at home for the Australian prime minister.

Anyone with an informed understanding of how British politics worked, especially the selection of a Conservative prime minister, would conclude that there was no chance Winston Churchill would be overthrown. Certainly, Lloyd George had his own delusions of a return to the top job. Those who hung about Lloyd George, however, had no influence. The chairman of London's Daily Mirror Newspapers, Cecil King, met with Lloyd George in April. There was a discussion between them of an imagined scenario where Churchill would be forced to 'accept the guidance of a Cabinet of five or so members without portfolio',[40] none of whom, however, would be Menzies. It was all to become a sad little sideshow around a bitter and ageing sell-out man. Menzies' visit to Lloyd George was the idea of Australian businessman WS Robinson, who had met Menzies in London. By the time he visited Lloyd George, Menzies was desperate for any help in getting through to Churchill. Lloyd George steeled him up – and Menzies no doubt flattered Lloyd George. It made no difference to the situation at large.

Fred Shedden had been with Menzies over some months when he lunched with Hugh Dalton on 25 April. Shedden had come to admire Menzies and his abilities. Indeed, he was by then quite a fan. He had also absorbed fully the prime minister's frustrations over Australia's point of view not being heard in the War Cabinet. The two men formed a bond, as travellers often do. But it was the excess of a loyal minder, and nothing to do with actual plans afoot, that led Fred Shedden to opine of Menzies in his notes on the visit of 1941 that 'in the British Empire there is no one on the horizon who approaches him as the successor to Churchill. (Radical as it may sound, why should not a Dominion statesman lead the Empire in a war?)'[41] Rhetorical question or not, Shedden was letting his thoughts get ahead of reality. In a later draft he deleted his suggestion that a dominion prime minister might lead the Empire in a time of war. These musings of Shedden are evidence only of a loyal lieutenant's overexpansive imagination. Shedden would continue in his departmental role just as loyally under John Curtin as prime minister. His musings regarding Menzies and his taking on any UK leadership role were never supported by reality, planned or otherwise, in any diaries, memoirs or correspondence of the main players.

Menzies' encounter with Maurice Hankey did, however, spark a small move for greater effort to challenge Churchill's domination. Soon after, Hankey met with Lord Chancellor Viscount Simon (formerly Sir John Simon) at the House of Lords, a meeting that encouraged Hankey to request that Menzies make a final appeal to Churchill to accept more advice, even an Imperial War Cabinet. Menzies did have words with Churchill, but it changed nothing, as Shedden reported over tea with Hankey on 2 May. At this point, Hankey gave Menzies a letter to deliver to Halifax in Washington. He also wrote, at length, to Sir Samuel Hoare (a strong Chamberlain supporter and by then UK ambassador to Spain) on 18 May and downloaded his apprehensions: 'Menzies, the very able Australian PM soon discovered that the Government is a "one-man show", and did not half like it'. Hankey would write to Hoare again on 11 September in similar mood:

I am very critical of the present regime. At the same time I believe the PM keeps a fairly strong hold on public opinion –

not as strong as a year ago, but strong enough; and in parliament … he always gets away with it on the day. But Menzies went back to Australia disquieted at the way things are run, and Australian opinion is still very sour at the lack of air support to their troops in Greece and Crete and at the deterioration of our relations with Japan.[42]

Halifax's reply to Hankey's secret letter, hand-delivered by Menzies in May, supports the evidence that those seeking to restrain Churchill, and who saw Menzies as an influential figure who might bring more force to bear on the bulldog prime minister, were a small minority. They certainly did not see Menzies as a replacement. As Halifax told Hankey, writing on 25 May 1941:

> I got your secret letter by Menzies. And have been a fair deal disturbed. Not hardly surprised by it … Menzies opened up freely to me when I saw him here and I devoutly hope that he might get back. The whole trend of events – and what we may expect to be coming – seems to me to make it of very great importance to have someone a) of that calibre & b) of the Dominion, in at Cabinet decisions.[43]

Halifax went on to suggest that Hankey have a good talk to Anthony Eden, who was capable of standing up to Churchill. Other than that, he could only suggest speaking to Lord President of the Council Sir John Anderson, whom he doubted would be much use in an argument but was capable of asking questions. Halifax seemed more concerned about the exhaustion of the chiefs of staff: 'The things that Menzies told me which disturbed me more than anything was that Chiefs of Staff are at a point of fatigue or surrender of their judgment which prevented them standing up if they were doubtful'.

In Ottawa, where he made a fine impression and won praise

from Mackenzie King, Menzies put forward his idea of what King referred to as 'a conference of Prime Ministers – some kind of Imperial Cabinet'.[44] Menzies then briefed the Canadian prime minister on his experience of the War Cabinet, its failings in his view, and Churchill's dominance and lack of consideration for dominion interests. He referred to his meeting with Lloyd George – how he had taken heart at the encouragement the aging ex–prime minister had given him to pursue his Imperial War Conference idea. Mackenzie King, however, advised Menzies to be wary of being away from his own jurisdiction for long. Their discussions eventually appear to have persuaded Menzies of the impossibility of a 'continuous' dominion presence in London. King diarised on 8 May that Menzies had agreed as he left that 'the most he would think of now was a meeting for some special occasion when some practical thing was to be done'.[45] It was highly unlikely, in King's view, that dominion prime ministers would want to be away from their cabinets, and in London, for any length of time. Within weeks, Menzies' idea of a dominion conference would be scuttled by both King and Churchill. Although Churchill had become aware of Menzies' criticism of his role in the War Cabinet, there is no suggestion in any of the documents that Churchill ever imagined Menzies was deluded enough to try to take his job. Churchill simply viewed Menzies' criticism as dominion impertinence, and he had removed far bigger opponents over far larger issues. A dominion prime minister could be kept in his place quite easily.

Clearly, Menzies' weeks in London had left him with deep misgivings about the progress of the war. This is not to be mistaken for ambitions on his part to save the Empire or topple Churchill – an assertion both demeaning of Menzies' intelligence and simplistic as a theory. In the 360 Degree Films docudrama commissioned by the ABC and Screen Australia, the hearsay of Campbell Stuart, a Canadian newspaper magnate who worked in propaganda programs during the wars under the British Ministry of Information, is taken as further evidence of Menzies' ambition. Stuart visited Mackenzie King in Ottawa in mid-May 1941 and spoke to him of Menzies' desire to take Churchill's job. As Gerard Henderson has shown in published correspondence with the producer and lead writer of the show, 360 Degree Films' John Moore, the so-called evidence from Campbell Stuart is 'hearsay upon hearsay ... a report of what Mackenzie King claims he was told by Campbell Stuart about what Stuart maintained to be Menzies' attitude'.[46] Mackenzie King recorded that Campbell Stuart had told him, on 15 May, that

> he thought Menzies' ambition was to be Prime Minister
> of England, and that there were perhaps in England some
> who would be prepared to accept him. He did not think
> England would accept Beaverbrook ... He thought Churchill
> liked Menzies and might be prepared to take him into the
> Cabinet.[47]

This is meaty stuff but not in the least reliable. On 15 May 1941, Stuart opined to Mackenzie King that Churchill liked Menzies enough to have him in the Cabinet. Yet David Day has argued that, at the very same time, Churchill was ensuring that Menzies would not return to London to help advise on the war effort. Both cannot be right. Stuart Campbell was not always regarded as an entirely reliable witness in Whitehall circles – he was one of a number around Whitehall whose imagination and sense of his own importance sometimes got the better of him. On 26 July, Robert Bruce Lockhart noted in his diary that Duff Cooper, whom Stuart denigrated from time to time and who had, in turn, no time for Stuart, had a story (confirmed by Beaverbrook) that while in Canada Campbell Stuart was said 1) to have told Mackenzie King that he had been sent to Canada to prepare for evacuation of British government and 2) to have said to Lord Portal (with whom he travelled out to Canada) that H.M.G. [His Majesty's Government] were not satisfied with Lothian [Halifax] and had sent him (Campbell Stuart) out to report on him. These stories were told to Winston who is very anti-Campbell but was honest enough to say that such *bruits de malveillance* were not evidence.[48]

Those who have been caught by the imaginative idea that Robert Menzies had any ambition to topple Churchill ought perhaps, when deciphering historical evidence, to take a leaf out of Churchill's book in this instance. London was rife with rumour and gossip, inflated and bruised egos, would-be chiefs and armchair critics – and the war was not going well.

8

The enemy within

September 1941, Monday 1, – Had Menzies to lunch at
Scots. He said that last Monday Fadden had rung him to say
that as Labor might reject his offer that they shd be ready. He
knew they must have plotted. When they met first [Harry]
Foll then [Harold] Holt sd there must be a change. At length
all but 7.

– Owen Dixon diary[1]

If Menzies had any inflated thoughts of how he might play a
more effective role in London's war decisions, his arrival back in
Sydney on 24 May 1941 after such a long time away from Australia soon brought any heightened sensitivities of his own imperial contributions to a halt. His weary comment as he arrived
home, that he regretted he would have to 'play politics ... at a
time like this' would be prophetic, even if it gave off an unfortunate sense that he wished he was back in London.[2] In spite of the
full comment having the added words 'however cleanly and however friendly' and being made in the context of an impassioned
plea for all parties to work together, it gave off an irritated air.

Menzies had landed back in Australia on the day of the
Boothby by-election in South Australia following the death
of its local member Jack Price, one of the last survivors of the

breakaway Laborites who had joined the UAP with Joe Lyons in 1931. The result would be a UAP victory but, as Menzies arrived before the count, the tenor of the election campaign, as divided as any, hung over politics. It was also Empire Day at a time of major threat to Britain. Reports of the celebrations in the press described crowds of thousands drawn to gatherings where vice-regal and political speeches 'emphasised the unconquerable spirit of the Empire and the certainty of victory'.[3] NSW Labor premier William McKell, however, captured the true mixture of emotions, saying:

> To-day we are celebrating the Empire spirit, the spirit that is keeping the British people undismayed and resolute in the face of terrible trials, the spirit of Dunkirk, the spirit of the A.I.F. that carried them through Libya, and the spirit which is now being shown at Tobruk and Crete.[4]

At Rose Bay after alighting from his seaplane, embracing his wife Pattie and greeting his father-in-law Senator Leckie and other dignitaries – including Premier McKell, Artie Fadden and Bert Evatt – Menzies conducted a press interview and then made a nationwide broadcast. All press reports recognised exhaustion in the prime minister (he had brought back 230 pounds [104 kilograms] of official papers, *The Argus* reported), but his radio broadcast lacked none of his usual vigour in its urgent call for unity among the political groupings in Australia. 'The effectiveness of Australia's voice is impaired by our political position', he told listeners.[5] The prime ministerial plea for unity would fall on deaf ears; Labor was committed to maintaining a separate opposition. Moreover, the somewhat strident prime minister's message for unity was undermined by widespread knowledge of UAP/County Party divisions, papered over on Menzies' arrival as he thanked Fadden for all he had done as acting prime minister.[6] But even as he did this, Menzies was aware, via a communication from Percy Spender, that various members of his government were discussing his removal.[7] Strongest among his critics were sections of the Country Party and, while Page was thereafter always considered to be foremost among these, it is most likely that Fadden harboured his own ambitions, even as he remained openly loyal to Menzies. His feelings towards Menzies at the time come through in the claim in his autobiography that Menzies had not thanked him on his return to Australia. This is not true – press reports, both of the day Menzies arrived and of speeches made afterwards, and parliamentary records, show that Menzies made public his gratitude and praise for Fadden's work in his absence.

For all that, it was soon evident to Australians at large that Menzies was back at his job, rousing audiences with his speeches of appeal for national unity. For him, there was a renewed hope that he might push the Labor Party to reconsider a national government. He would not give up trying. As Menzies put it to Bruce in a cable on 13 August, 'government stocks rose very high' at his being back.[8] The populace was ready for strong leadership and Menzies gave every impression he was their man. His message was uniform – what he had seen and learnt while away convinced him that Australians needed to be roused to empathise with Britons and support more enthusiastically the war effort in a coordinated and overt way. He had much work to do to bring what he had learnt to the work of government in Australia. And he wanted the people of Australia to take from his experience a keenness of understanding at the peril that faced the Empire – or, as he put it in his arrival broadcast, 'If I can in the next few weeks translate what I have seen into words to move the Australian people to the dangers – the great terrific dangers – of this war, then I shall feel that I have brought back something that has justified you in sending me abroad'.[9] As Vin D'Cruz has argued, until Pearl

Harbor, 'Menzies viewed the threat to his purpose directly as a European threat or indirectly as one that was a European derivative ... German victories ... would trigger the Japanese assault. Till the last moments before Pearl Harbour [sic], it seemed that his assessment was the correct one'.[10]

For Australians generally, capturing the sentiments of UK citizens, with their feelings of endangerment and privation, was not easy. By July 1941, the number of Australians in employment had reached a wartime peak. Paul Hasluck documented that, with unemployment plummeting, the nation had gone on a spending spree, especially after the long years of financial austerity in the 1930s. In June 1941, the principal retail outlets in Brisbane, Melbourne and Sydney increased their average sales by 47 per cent over June 1939; in August 1941 the increase was 38 per cent over August 1939.[11] Price control also worked to the consumer's advantage. And, it was a good time for banks, with spare cash filling their coffers. On 27 February 1940, chief manager of the National Bank of Australasia, Leslie J McConnan, could write, 'Cash has simply been pouring in during the past couple of weeks and for the first time I have been in this Chair I am relieved of the anxiety of not having sufficient funds'.[12] In many respects, ordinary Australians were operating on different levels. In public, they absorbed the rhetoric about the peril facing the Empire alongside assurances that even as Japan advanced through South-East Asia there would be some restraint at Singapore. In private, most were enjoying boom times not known for a generation. Paul Hasluck argued that 'Perhaps the one quality that was lacking was demand – a demand that was itself the voice of mutual confidence, a confidence of a leader in his people and an expectation of their confidence in him'.[13]

The prime minister was welcomed home to Melbourne by a crowd of thousands filling footpaths along Collins Street from Spencer Street Station to the packed Town Hall, where 2500 heard him speak. *The Argus* of 2 June reported that 'almost every city building was hung with flags'.[14] As was Spencer Street Station, 'where several thousand people, including 100 Air Force men, awaited his arrival'. He was cheered with shouts of 'Good old Menzies!' and 'Good On You' hanging in the air. This was the sound of the national and party unity Menzies had envied in Mackenzie King's Canada, where he had noted in his diary how King 'has a loyal following. They stick to their leaders here. He has been P.M. 14 years and Liberal leader 23'.[15]

Parliament resumed for just three days, and was then recessed until 18 June, just enough time for Menzies to report to the House the significant developments around his long trip abroad and allow debate over the campaign in Greece. During the recess, the government would reorganise the departments of the public service in preparation for an announcement by Menzies of his 'prospectus for an unlimited war effort' to coincide with the next parliamentary sittings.[16] In his lengthy speech to the House of Representatives on 28 May, Menzies tried to draw his listeners into empathising with their fellow Britons, so many of whom were experiencing daily privations alongside horrors Australians could barely imagine. Menzies' months in the northern hemisphere had strengthened his message on the war – he wanted to bring that experience to the war effort in Australia. As he did so, the prime minister's own battles with journalists and press barons were not far from his mind; he included a shot at Australian newspaper magnates upset with the government's rationing of newsprint, saying that British newspapers, even if limited to 'four or six pages', continued to come out daily. He concluded: '1941 will be a year in which the British people all over the world will struggle and struggle to avoid defeat'.[17]

Politics at play

The problem for Menzies was that, even while Labor leader John Curtin had modified his opposition to Australian troops being part of the European campaign, Labor still saw Australia's defence as a Pacific matter. The European war also raised complications within Labor ranks after the signing of the Nazi–Soviet Pact in August 1939, with the left of the Labor Party compromised by its support of Soviet Russia. As the extremes of Labor saw it, the war in Europe was not Australia's affair. The war effort in the Mediterranean had now turned especially bad for the AIF. The defence of Greece by heavily outnumbered Allied troops, mostly from Australia and New Zealand, had been doomed without support from Turkey. When 28 000 Allied troops evacuated to Crete in late April, they faced bitter fighting before further evacuation, in which some 3000 Australians were left to become prisoners of war. In addition, the prime minister's rather triumphant homecoming was made all the more problematic with the Allies' early advances in the Middle East now being overturned by a more aggressive German advance under Rommel. The decision to send Australian troops abroad, and Britain's resistance to sending reinforcements for Singapore, added weight to arguments that Australia was in grave peril. The casualty lists from both Greece and Crete soon became public and distracted Australians from a huge revamping planned by the Menzies Government around five new departments. The administrative shake-up also upset a handful of disgruntled UAP/Country Party colleagues who missed out on appointments in the reorganisation. The game of politics could not be avoided as Menzies' minority government came under increasing attack from a strengthened and unified Labor.

Indeed, Labor MPs such as former Langite Jack Beasley and Bert Evatt, two of Labor's members of the Advisory War

Council, did not share Curtin's more personable approach to the government's management of the country at a time of crisis. By August 1941, Beasley and Evatt were openly ready to bring down the UAP/Country Party government in the hope of an early election to bring Labor to power.[18]

Over just three days in the House of Representatives, Menzies' attempt to bring Australians with him on the international situation did little to buoy opposition emotions for Australia's beleaguered Empire compatriots. Parliamentary discussion quickly resumed at a more localised level. For starters, how could the prime minister talk of national governments (as in Britain) and pulling together in a crisis when his own party had played politics as much as any other in the Boothby by-election on 24 May? In his reply to Menzies, Curtin assured the House that, during the prime minister's trip abroad, he and his Labor team had supported the government's war efforts, adding that neither he nor any of his colleagues 'engage in idle, cheap or miserable political disputation'. Two days later, Labor's Frank Baker (the member for Maranoa) gave the lie to all that by attacking Menzies and his government for failing to overcome poverty, allowing war-profiteering scandals and leaving eight of the returned soldiers from Bardia and Benghazi to travel from Sydney to Brisbane in a second-class compartment.

The gloves were off, and just days after the prime minister's return to Australia with a call for national unity. In the same debate, the member for Batman, Frank Brennan, took the discussion to a new low by quoting Archie Cameron's description of the divisions in conservative ranks as 'a stew of simmering discontent, spiced by insatiable personal ambitions and incurable animosities', going on to call Menzies' speech to the House an 'interesting travel talk' of a journey at a time when the prime minister's 'tour of duty lay here in Australia', adding that Canada's prime minister, Mackenzie King, and South Africa's prime minister, Jan Smuts, had not left their homelands in this time of war, and concluding by accusing Menzies of never having 'advanced an Australian ideal' or 'contributed anything to a wider or more deeply based Australian status'.[19] The prime minister, Brennan asserted, was a 'butler' to the British Government. Brennan's speech was full of bile, accusing Menzies of being an Anglophile lackey who had deserted Australia. Such an extreme Labor view was never voiced by Curtin, but it stayed on the record and hit a chord on both sides of the House as the uncertainties of minority government and the war situation continued.

Labor opposition to Menzies may not have cut through so sharply had something of the 'stew of simmering discontent' Brennan pointed to not held more than a grain of truth. In *The Government and the People, 1939–41*, Paul Hasluck describes the UAP in 1940 as 'a coalition of pieces rather than parties' resting on 'a mass of shifting discontents'.[20] Furthermore, by late July 1941 'There were signs, too, that the leader himself had become sick at heart at the constant struggle against unreason'.[21]

Menzies and Country Party leader Earle Page had never had an easy relationship. As far back as 1931, Menzies had advised media baron Keith Murdoch that he could not countenance Page as deputy leader in any new conservative party formed.[22] Page and Menzies had managed to work together after the UAP was forced into coalition with the Country Party following the 1934 election, but after the bitter speech Page made against Menzies while prime minister in April 1939, Pattie Menzies would never speak to him again. Not until June 1940 did Menzies return Page to the ministry, albeit with a lessened role. The Menzies–Page relationship continued as one of personal distrust, and Page would have been happy to see Menzies fall. For all that, on 30 May 1941, Page asked leave of the House to make a personal statement, in which he tried to make amends for his outburst about Menzies in 1939, saying the prime minister had his full support. And he lavished praise on Menzies for his efforts abroad: 'No one could have done more than he has done at the heart of the Empire to uphold the interests of all sections of the Australian people'.[23]

Page's speech was no doubt an attempt to push coalition unity at a time of national and international crisis. It was also, quite possibly, inspired by his antipathy towards Country Party leader Artie Fadden who, having stood in as acting prime minister during Menzies' long months abroad, was looking more and more likely as Menzies' replacement in any coalition leadership spill. Fadden had found appeal as a popular alternative prime minister, his amiability a contrast to the more imposing and cool Menzies. On the other hand, as suggested in *The Argus* on 31 May, Page might have been 'planning a bid to regain CP leadership'.

Across all parties there was fracture and dissent in 1941. With Menzies' resignation, the UAP lost the vital vote of Arthur Coles who, having joined the UAP in 1941, resigned from the party over Menzies' replacement. In an unpublished assessment of Coles, Paul Hasluck demonstrated that there was evidence Coles had wild notions he should lead a national government on the basis that 'a business man who had made a great success as a retail shop keeper [with GJ Coles & Co.] would necessarily also be a success in running a nation'. Hasluck also concluded that, in *Menzies: Last of the Queen's Men*, journalist Kevin Perkins inflated UAP MP Bill McCall's role in Menzies' resignation based on gossip rather than evidence, much of which was not only inaccurate but 'reveals the nastiness of McCall's nature'.[24]

Then there were Labor's trials. Its ranks, split from 1931 between traditional Labor and Lang Labor, had reunited, but scars remained. In the Advisory War Council, a body formed after the 1940 election as an alternative to a national government, former Lang Labor member Jack Beasley retained his seat after Labor and Lang Labor reunited – but only by increasing the size of the council in order to allow the newly elected and forceful Bert Evatt a seat. On no account would Beasley give up his seat for Evatt.

Personality at play

For the months during which Menzies remained prime minister, his government would be overshadowed by a political game he could not escape. Menzies' own weariness with it all, and the circus the press had made of it, was to be recorded later in a lengthy piece he wrote privately the day after his resignation at the end of August:

> [William] Hutchinson, [Bill] McCall and [Charles] Marr have been bitterly hostile, and with a Budget in the offing there has been every possibility of a fatal attack by Labor. The newspapers, notably the 'Sydney Morning Herald' and the Murdoch group, have been extremely hostile to me, the former blatantly and crudely, the latter with a little more subtlety, praising me and killing me in the same breath, the techniques being that of the skilled slaughterman who calls attention to the beauties of the beast just as he strikes it down.[25]

Pattie Menzies, with the astuteness of a seasoned political spouse from an extended political family, had foreseen the outcome many months before, as Menzies would record decades later in his political memoir *Afternoon Light*. When, in late November 1940, Menzies advised his wife of his intended trip to the Middle East and London, she had cautioned him, saying: 'If you feel you must go, you will go. But you will be out of office within six weeks of your return'. As it happened, Pattie Menzies was just under two months out in her reckoning. Unlike Kevin

Rudd in June 2010, who resigned knowing he did not have the numbers in caucus to beat Julia Gillard's challenge, with Menzies in August 1941 it was not a case of losing a majority of votes within his own party. Like all seasoned political figures, Menzies' supporters could count and quite a few believed he could have survived a UAP vote at the time. Percy Spender, in *Politics and a Man*, argued that Menzies could have hung on:

> He was weary of the whole thing and about to throw in his hand.
>
> Yet he could, in my view, still have saved the day if he had said to his Cabinet, 'We shall remain in Government. We will cast the burden upon the Labor Party to attempt to throw us from office. I shall in the meantime, continue as Prime Minister; let any Minister not willing to serve under me, stand up and say so, and he may surrender his portfolio.'[26]

Spender added that all Menzies would have needed to do from there was ask UAP members either to endorse his leadership or throw it to a vote after offering another UAP member in his place. He would have won, Spender believed, and then should have demanded loyalty and undivided support from every MP. In faraway Britain, Winston Churchill was well aware of the whisperings from rival colleagues at his dictatorial manner as he stood defiant at the helm of a besieged nation. Churchill chose to stare down his doubting colleagues; he used his speeches in the House of Commons to rouse British confidence in his autocratic leadership, to hoist himself up as the bulldog leader to see them through their trials. How very different, on the other side of the globe, was Robert Menzies. Aggrieved at the criticism being levelled against him, from colleagues, opposition and press, Menzies gave up his leadership. Battered and weary, he chose to resign, believing his coalition partner, the Country Party, would continue to erode the unity of the government, whatever fragile cohesion he might achieve within the UAP.

Diverse explanations have been offered for Menzies' 1941 nadir, for his giving up what could still have been his. Percy Joske, who attended Wesley College with Robert Menzies and was a long-time friend both in the law and politics, wrote his own memoir of Australia's most successful prime minister – *Sir Robert Menzies 1894–1978: A New, Informal Memoir*. His explanation of Menzies' actions in 1941 are candid and reflect the views of not just an observer of history but also someone with a close, personal understanding of his subject. Joske put the full onus on Menzies. He saw a leader who had got beyond his abilities at that stage of his career, a man who had not been sacked by his party but had 'sacked himself'. He laid the blame for much of the personal animosity within the ranks at Menzies' own feet, for not being more generous to Artie Fadden for his loyalty on his return from abroad, and for being 'so satisfied that no other man measured up to him and that he must get the British War Cabinet appointment as his right, that he had not considered it necessary to observe the amenities of life'.[27]

Joske saw these as the actions of a clever and successful personality who 'was still, to a degree, politically naive, and had not as yet achieved maturity'. For Joske, the Menzies Government, on Menzies' return, was in no danger. Those who had been publicly expressing discontent were not influential members and would never have voted the party out of office. On the other side, while Evatt was ready to take anything he could get, Curtin was 'not anxious to govern'.[28] Curtin led a party that was newly unified but still raw with the disputes and the splits of a decade. For him to take the reins of a minority government would have been a risky business. Better an election and a good majority.

There is much to Joske's assessment, not least because he knew Menzies' character. Perhaps, however, he was too harsh on

Menzies' sense of self-importance. Menzies' certainly was the only voice in Australia's parliament that might have measured up to Churchill – and there is reasonable evidence that his challenges to Churchill while sitting with the War Cabinet in London were not welcome to the UK prime minister, partly because they hit their mark. No doubt this also stood in the way of Menzies ever being able to transfer to a Commonwealth position. For all that, Menzies' opponents belatedly came to recognise that his proposed prime ministerial presence in London in late July or early August was a missed opportunity to influence what Paul Hasluck has called 'higher policy decisions in the Pacific', at a time when both Britain and the United States were focused exclusively on the Atlantic and Australia was at the mercy of their decisions.[29] It was a move blocked by the Labor Party at the time. At the Advisory War Council, Menzies and Curtin agreed that warships were needed, desperately, in the Indian Ocean and Pacific but, as Hasluck has shown, 'the international issue was subordinated to the domestic issue', with stirrers like Evatt and deputy Labor leader Frank Forde pushing Curtin to making trouble for Menzies at any suggestion the Australian prime minister go back to London to 'convince the United Kingdom Government, and Churchill as much as anyone, of the vital significance of holding Singapore'.[30]

Historian Geoffrey Blainey was once told by Cecil (Peter) Looker, Menzies' chief of staff in the 1940s, that Menzies was 'very difficult to handle in 1940–41'.[31] Only later did he develop greater tact and goodwill in his dealings with colleagues. Percy Spender recounts how Menzies had intimidated his colleagues in his first years as prime minister, often sending ministers away with good or bad reactions to policy documents like a gruff 'headmaster' giving a mark. Spender recalled an evening at dinner when 'Menzies was in top form', during which a senator colleague (possibly Senator Harry Foll) who had been hostile to Menzies warmed to him, telling him as they left that he should be more like that all the time and that his problem was he didn't suffer fools gladly. To which Menzies had replied, 'And pray, what do you think I am doing now?'[32] This senator, claims Spender, threw his weight into getting rid of Menzies as prime minister.

In spite of his successful return to Australia in 1941, it only took a few weeks before the Australian military losses in the Greece and Crete campaigns began to spark lively criticism of the government in the press. Menzies took umbrage at this, privately calling together a meeting with senior party officials, including Staniforth Ricketson, to discuss tactics for handling the press attacks on him. Menzies still blamed the *Sydney Morning Herald* for non-Labor losses in the 1940 election campaign in New South Wales. His difficulties with the press were also of concern in Melbourne, where notes taken by Staniforth Ricketson of a two-hour meeting he had held, on Menzies' behalf, with *Argus* representatives RAG Henderson (chairman) and JB Aitken (editor) on 27 May 1940, indicate a strong prejudice against Menzies at the editorial level. Henderson had little knowledge of or influence over this prejudice, so cockily displayed by Aitken at the meeting. Ricketson found Aitken especially to be 'entirely self-satisfied and condescending ... even patronising towards the prime minister'. He also found Henderson to be 'living in a world almost of make-believe' in terms of what might be done regarding the war effort and its political impact, believing that 'the prime minister, by waving a wand' could change a difficult situation.[33] The meeting was called at Henderson's request, but it is clear from Ricketson's notes that his conclusions that *The Argus* held a prejudice against Menzies as Australian prime minister were justified.

Calling it stumps

In mid-1941, led by the *Sydney Morning Herald*,[34] the press began a campaign for Menzies to return to join the War Cabinet in London so Australia's case could be made more strongly for British naval support for Singapore. In spite of Australia opening a Tokyo mission and appointing John Latham as Australian minister there at the end of 1940, relations with Japan were steadily deteriorating as the Japanese moved further south. At the Advisory War Council meeting on 6 August, Menzies informed members that Australia had denounced its commercial treaty with Japan and was imposing import and export controls against it – it was hoped such pressure could influence Japan towards peace.[35] Meanwhile, there was public speculation about an early election to solve the uncertainty of minority government – and this unnerved many of Menzies' ministerial colleagues, who felt he was unpopular with voters. A revamp of Cabinet had not helped, as disgruntled members of the UAP, such as William Hutchinson, Charles Marr and Bill McCall, made their disquiet public when they received no promotion. Labor MPs mocked the prime minister in the House on 1 July, suggesting his actions had put hostile colleagues like these even further offside.

Amid the pressure, on 3 July Menzies had cabled dominion leaders Smuts of South Africa and King of Canada suggesting that an overworked Churchill would benefit from a dominion leader in the British War Cabinet to support him at such a time. Neither Smuts nor King concurred, and social democrat Mackenzie King's reply, written a full month later, contained more than a few gratuitous lectures on the need for a dominion prime minister to stay with his people in times of war. It was a verbose knockback. King had resented Churchill's moves to organise an imperial conference for July to coincide with a visit to London of New Zealand prime minister Peter Fraser, and his intention to cable the other prime ministers to try to be there.[36] King made it clear to the UK high commissioner to Canada, Malcolm MacDonald, that he wanted to go alone to London and not for any imperial conference.[37] His reply to Menzies, drafted on 1 August and described in his diary as written 'almost without reference to any previous correspondence', he believed would stand 'as an important State paper in clearing up involved and difficult aspects of control of so-called Empire policies'.[38] King was wary of Menzies' attempt to obtain dominion support for his own return to London. At home, Menzies had also lost the support of Keith Murdoch who, as Allan Martin confirms, 'thought Menzies inadequate as a leader and was not impressed by the prime minister's successes in England'.[39] Murdoch had been tiring of Menzies even before Lyons died.

On 17 July UAP Victorian MP William Hutchinson, after a meeting with his parliamentary colleague Bill McCall (and reported 'others') went public with an announcement to the media that he was asking for an immediate special party meeting to discuss the leadership. He added that he believed it was time for a new leader.[40] At a UAP meeting on 29 July, Menzies was overwhelmingly re-endorsed as party leader, but there were leaks to the press that the meeting had exposed clashes, and not all members of the parliamentary party had attended. By 11 August, Cabinet was meeting to discuss the advance of the Japanese into Indochina and its threat to Thailand. Menzies' ministerial colleagues concluded he should go back to London to represent Australia's interests at the War Cabinet. While Curtin was personally agreeable to this – provided the budget had passed through parliament – Evatt and Forde took a belligerent stand at the Advisory War Council meeting that followed and made it clear Labor would not agree. Menzies sought advice from Bruce as to whether Australia's representation could be made by a minister other than a prime minister. The answer was no. So Menzies tried once more for Labor to accept a national government. After deliberations, Labor's reply was refusal. Cabinet was meeting as the message came. It was 26 August.

Menzies wrote in his personal record made within days of his resignation that for the rest of that Cabinet meeting he invited and listened to the views of his ministerial colleagues regarding the leadership. Country Party ministers Earle Page, Jack McEwen, Tom Collins and Larry Anthony were all for a new leader; the UAP's Percy Spender, Harold Holt, Eric Spooner and Billy Hughes supported that view, while Philip McBride, John Leckie, Herbert Collett and Frederick Stewart were for no change. Menzies calculated that, of those absent from the meeting, Joe Abbott would side with the Country Party while George McLeay, Eric Harrison and Allan McDonald would be loyally for no change. Artie Fadden said little but expressed loyalty to Menzies.

Menzies now felt that his leadership 'rested upon nothing better than quicksands'; his Cabinet was split down the middle, with him and against him. For Menzies, the indomitable headmaster, it was a personal Waterloo. Something cracked. As noted earlier, he went back to the Lodge for dinner with his wife and father-in-law, Senator Leckie, and spoke by telephone to his father in Melbourne, who reacted on the phone, 'breathing threatenings and slaughter'. James Menzies then convened an instant family conference, in which the siblings who were present agreed that their brother should offer his resignation. Later, as he announced his intention to quit as leader of the government, Menzies insisted his successor should be elected only by the joint ministerial parties and that, once elected, should be given unanimous support.

It was after midnight when Menzies left the joint party meeting on 28 August. Artie Fadden was the new leader of the UAP/Country Party parliamentary team. Menzies walked away with his private secretary, Cecil Looker, who recalled years later in interviews that Menzies had an arm around his shoulder and tears in his eyes. It was to Looker that he said, through those tears and quoting from an old Scottish ballad, 'Ile lay mee downe and bleed a while/And then Ile rise and fight againe'.[41] The next day, Artie Fadden became Australia's new prime minister, and the minority Country Party assumed a mantle that sounded the death rattle of the UAP, just over a decade after its foundation.

Thus in late August 1941, a phalanx of disgruntled parliamentary UAP/Country Party colleagues completed a diverse but long assault on Robert Menzies, and he capitulated. Beyond this local drama, Hitler advanced on the Soviet Union and Japan made plans to attack the US naval base at Pearl Harbor in Hawaii. A new chapter in the war and in Australian politics had opened.

9

On the wings of a phoenix

In the particular situation, brought about by many conflicting factors, in which neither single-party nor all-party government was possible, a temporary arrangement had been found by which the traditional system of parliament and party was preserved. On both sides of politics there were men who would have liked to give the nation what they called strong government by using quite different methods. The leaders Menzies and Curtin, however, were both scrupulous. The liberalism of one, founded on the rule of law, and the practical socialism of the other, rooted in the parliamentary method, made them both careful of the same tradition.

– Paul Hasluck[1]

Australians have been well served by their governments over decades. In times of strain and crisis, Australia's parliamentary system and constitutional arrangements have withstood challenges to deliver practical and reasonable outcomes. Even through the years of the first Menzies Government and the minority Curtin Government that followed, during the politically fragile years of the Second World War, the glue held.

The minority government of Menzies from 1940 to 1941 and his term as prime minister from April 1939 were not the policy failure many Labor-leaning critics have asserted. This is borne out by Paul Hasluck's extensive history of the war years. Much of the success of the Curtin years (1941–45) came not only because Australians quickly united in the face of a sudden Japanese onslaught after December 1941, but also as a result of the reorganisation of government in the Menzies years, the build-up of military resources and the growing acceptance by Curtin of Australia's responsibilities in the European crisis. Australian troops remained in the Middle East long after Curtin assumed the prime ministership when the short-lived Fadden Government fell on 7 October 1941. And this despite a tense relationship between Australia and Whitehall over the command of Australian troops.

In 1960, secure in his leadership of an enduring Liberal/Country Party government, and with yet another major split in the Labor opposition, Menzies privately penned a mock obituary posing as the *Sydney Morning Herald*'s review of his life. The newspaper had been a frequent Menzies critic over many years so the mock piece began accordingly: 'We announce today, without gloating but not without satisfaction, the death of the former Prime Minister, Robert Gordon Menzies'.[2] The piece is amusing and characteristically quick-witted, but it also lists what Menzies himself believed were his achievements in his first years as prime minister. As the mock obituary put it:

> The real test is what Mr Menzies did as Prime Minister ... we will, to be generous, abandon our usual rule that good things done by his various governments should be attributed to his subordinates and that only the bad should be attributed to him ... what do we find?
>
> In his first period of office, from 1939–1941, he saw that a war was imminent; he re-introduced compulsory military training; he led a united nation into war; he raised the second

AIF; he dispatched it abroad; after he was out of office, his successors inherited a trained and experienced AIF and used them effectively in New Guinea and the islands; he created a munitions organisation in Australia, appointed Essington Lewis as its director and helped him to assemble a great team of industrialists which his successors saw no reason to change thereafter; put into production aircraft and weapons of war on schedules which stood the test of time; went to the Middle East and visited our fighting troops as far west as Benghazi; went to Great Britain and brought messages of comfort and encouragement to the bombed people of Britain; visited America and urged the impossibility of neutrality; returned to Australia and created the Department of War Organisation of Industry, whose labours were thereafter essential.[3]

For all its personal bias, this was a reasonable summary of the work of the first Menzies Government. It might have added that, in 1941, the Menzies Government had introduced universal child endowment for second and subsequent children. The list was a remarkable tally given the disunity of the non-Labor side of politics at that time. Nearly two decades later, though, it still irked Menzies that the administration he had led in those years had not been recognised for the good work it had done. Some of this he captured in a rejoinder immediately following the short summary in his mock obituary, which opined 'with our usual perception, we perceived under this spurious façade the natural indolence of the man' – a reference to assertions from some Menzies critics that he did not work hard enough at his post and to the oft-repeated muttering throughout much of the 1940s 'You'll never win with Menzies'.

The forgotten people

With the defeat of the Fadden Government's budget on 3 October 1941 and the accession of John Curtin heading up a new Labor government four days later, Menzies called a party meeting the following day, 8 October, and resigned his leadership of the UAP. In the ensuing reorganisation of leadership positions, Billy Hughes was elected UAP leader by just one vote over the comparatively junior member for Corangamite in Victoria, Allan McDonald. And since, in a joint party meeting, Menzies could not convince the opposition to reinstall the leader of the UAP as leader of the opposition, Fadden retained that position. Within two months, Japanese bombers had sunk the Royal Navy's *Repulse* and *Prince of Wales* off the coast of Malaya, along with much of the US fleet at Pearl Harbor, and had moved rapidly through South-East Asia. UAP leader Hughes, spurred by the new sense of commitment to war throughout Australia and critical of Curtin's doubts about British support, had written to UK Conservative Leo Amery in November that the Japanese onslaught would 'put [Australia] even more on her mettle than hitherto'. Amery's reply, that 'Singapore will hold all right', reached Hughes after Singapore's surrender to the Japanese on 15 February 1942, emphasising the misguided British notions of their strength in the Asia–Pacific, which had bedevilled Menzies' advocacy in London.[4]

Throughout 1942, Hughes continued to look over his shoulder at Menzies, suspicious that he was merely biding his time for resurrection as party leader. The 79-year-old Hughes believed he had another election win in him.[5] Menzies, however, as the documents show, was at all sorts of crossroads as to his next move. He had failed to find an overseas posting on some three occasions – rival Earle Page had been chosen as the ministerial liaison in London while all other suggestions, including taking Dick

Casey's vacancy in Washington, had fallen through. Menzies was on the outer both within his party and with Empire allies – all the while assured in diplomatic terms by the powers that be of his great attributes and talents as a person of influence for the nation. Such political exile could have sent Menzies into long-term decline. Instead, he began licking his wounds as a cast-off political leader and eased immediate tensions by filming footage of the Cabinet (with his hand-held camera) just before offering his resignation to the governor-general on 30 August.[6] Returning to Melbourne, he enjoyed the solace of crowds at Spencer Street railway station. The following week, at a formal dinner in his honour at Parliament House on 4 September, he showed the movies he had taken on his overseas trip earlier that year.[7] In the longer term, however, Menzies was saved by his need for supplementary income and his appetite for professional and intellectual activity.

As allowed under rules for MPs at the time, Menzies had soon returned to the bar. On one occasion Ken Menzies, while in Melbourne on leave from his army training at Puckapunyal in May 1942, slipped into court in the hope of catching his father before he returned to base: 'I went into the court but despite the fact that I sat up the back for nearly 40 minutes you did not look around but just went on talking'.[8] Menzies' daughter, Heather Henderson, records that during the years her father was in opposition in the 1940s, he would often walk from his Studley Park home in Kew to his Melbourne city office – a distance of four miles.[9] He was, in fact, a great walker and used the time spent walking to think. Ken Menzies, tongue in cheek and writing to his father on 8 December 1941 about the deteriorating Pacific situation, referred to the Japanese advance as having 'put an end to your walking tour'. This was indeed seedtime – those years between the loss of prime ministerial office in 1941 and the concerted action to rebuild the fractured non-Labor forces in 1944.

Its fruits became obvious, if not fully clear, by halfway through 1942. Ironically, it would be radio broadcasts on commercial stations that gave Menzies the opportunity to formulate principles on which non-Labor political groups might fashion their identity in the coming decades.

Allan Martin has documented how UAP executive officer HW Horsfield had suggested to Robert Menzies shortly before he resigned as prime minister that he should follow President Roosevelt's example and overcome press opposition by use of radio broadcasts.[10] What Horsfield had in mind were Roosevelt's *Fireside Chats*. The idea appealed to Menzies but events overtook him as prime minister. Only in opposition did he take up the challenge. With the backing of Sydney radio station 2UE, which relayed the broadcasts to stations in Queensland and Victoria, Menzies began a series of weekly radio talks in January 1942 that lasted until late into 1943.

There was nothing new in 1942 in Australian radio using well-known political figures to make radio broadcasts. Dame Enid Lyons, contracted by Macquarie Broadcasting, made a series of radio broadcasts in 1939 as she resurfaced following her husband's death.[11] Joe Lyons as prime minister had made use of radio extensively during the 1930s to speak to listeners in homely evening broadcasts, on some occasions with his wife. The novelty in the Menzies' broadcasts, however, was that here was a significant political figure, who was neither prime minister nor leader of the opposition, offering his views each Friday evening on politics and matters of national importance. What's more, this all took place on commercial radio rather than with the Australian Broadcasting Corporation, where more erudite opinions might have been expected. The Horsfield suggestion had been a canny political move for a prime minister under siege to break through to swinging voters. But here now was a deposed leader of the UAP, and one with no perceived hope of returning to the leadership, making a wide-ranging series of broadcasts to the nation, in the manner of opinion pieces later to be published in book form. This allowed Menzies a freedom to indulge in breadth of thought, and eventually led him to use the broadcasts as a way to put across a new line of argument on the guiding moral values for non-Labor politics.

Unlike Labor and the trade unions, Australia's non-Labor side of politics had no strong tradition in any founding movement or manifesto. Centuries of parliamentary tradition in Britain had seen upper-class moderates and conservatives develop over time into Whigs and Tories, conservatives and liberals. But what fitted that deep seam of landed wealth and privilege had no bearing on a parliamentary democracy in a fledgling collection of colonies on the other side of the globe. In the early decades of representative government, colonial landowners and professional groups had tugged at governors' coat-tails and won seats in legislative councils. From that, as federation emerged, loose-fitting alliances had developed over financial or sectional issues of the day. The Country (now National) Party is Australia's oldest and longest surviving non-Labor party. The United Australia Party – which in 1931 had hastily developed guiding principles for unity – was built out of a financial crisis. By 1941, its financial principles still held, but the financial crisis that gave the party strength had long since passed. It was thus, in May 1942, that Menzies began to use his radio broadcasts to develop some semblance of a manifesto that could underpin the raison d'être of his side of politics'.

For more than three months, Menzies' broadcasts tackled topics of the day – the war and US involvement, the Empire and Australia's relationship with Britain, the economy at war, censorship, postwar planning and even women in the war. Then, on 22 May, came a longer talk entitled 'The Forgotten People'. A month later, Menzies began seven weeks of consecutive broadcasts entitled 'The Four Freedoms'. All of these broadcasts invoked President Roosevelt in some way although, in a remake of Roosevelt, Menzies' 'forgotten people' were of the entrepreneurial middle classes, squeezed between big government and demands for government assistance from the masses of unionised working poor – both requiring additional taxation. By contrast, Franklin D Roosevelt's April 1932 'forgotten man' was the little person hounded to death in the Depression by the failure of capitalism. To differentiate, in his first broadcast along these more philosophical lines, Menzies drew a distinction between his forgotten people thesis and what he saw as a 'false war' between rich and poor as embodied in the phrase 'What side are you on?' – a phrase that echoed the song 'Which Side Are You On', written by miner's wife Florence Reece during the Harlan coal strike in Kentucky in 1931.[12] The song's sentiments had become an inspiration for the continuing success of Roosevelt's people power.

As Judith Brett's analysis of the 'Forgotten People' broadcast illustrates, too forensic an examination can be misleading. Attempting to pick the terminology apart for consistency of definition cannot do justice to the appeal Menzies' words would have to ordinary families listening in. And Brett's attempt to assess Menzies' use of family values as the basis of individual rights in a clinical fashion fails to capture the spirit of the address. But Brett does acknowledge that Menzies' deliberate attack on the use of the word 'class' was a 'brilliant rhetorical move'.[13] It left his message distinctly as one supporting individualism and self-interest, in a positive sense, in contrast to Labor's attachment to ideas of solidarity among those of the lower strata, where working-class union action had become a weapon to wield at democratic order. Menzies had defined in a raw theoretical way a sector of the voting public who could well argue they would be forgotten by any government that leaned towards raising taxation to implement a social program. And, while it was still early days for non-Labor in 1942, as policy for postwar settlement became the rhetoric of the Curtin and Chifley governments after the 1943 election, the sentiments of the Menzies' broadcasts would eventually find their mark – especially with the referendum to extend wartime central government powers in 1944 and Ben Chifley's attempt to nationalise the banks from late 1947.

Taking off the gloves

In his *Politics and a Man*, Percy Spender describes 1943 as 'the year that was!' going on to detail a litany of disasters for the UAP/Country Party coalition in the lead-up to the 1943 election, which the Labor Party won in a landslide in August. As Spender describes it, the leadership of the UAP was a shambles: 'Hughes had been chosen as leader of the United Australia Party … He failed to give it any direction. It rarely met separately as a party, since Hughes displayed no interest in calling it together'.[14] But it was also a year when Menzies cautiously avoided the temptation to be pushed too early into a leadership challenge. Spender would come to recognise that there was 'no more astute political strategist [in Australia] than Menzies'. In his diary on 29 January, Spender recorded that 'antagonism between Billy Hughes and Bob Menzies [is] becoming very pronounced'. As the Militia Bill to enact a very limited scale of compulsory military service south of the equator came up for debate, the UAP divided bitterly.

Menzies led the UAP opposition to the bill as too limited, arguing that Australia could not expect US troops to travel thousands of miles to rescue Australia's troops and defend its shores given it was not prepared to send sufficient troops itself to all lines in the battle for South-East Asia and the islands. The bill passed but ten UAP members of the House of Representatives voted against it. In the days leading up to the vote, both Spender and Menzies had resigned from the joint executive of the UAP parliamentary party. With tension over the bill drawing to a crisis in the UAP, Menzies had written to Ken Menzies in February:

> The position of the Opposition is extremely obscure. There is no doubt that among the best men on our side there is a growing realisation that we possess neither force nor direction and that we must rebuild ourselves on the foundation of some real political beliefs (which, after all, we do possess) if we are to have any prospect of success at an election.[15]

On 19 March, Hughes received a letter signed by nineteen members of the UAP demanding a party meeting. Spender, who did not sign the letter, sensed a spill of positions was in the offing. He and Harold Holt met with Hughes and a meeting was called.[16] A spill of positions was called for, with arguments supporting a younger and more spirited leadership – a motion defeated by twenty-four votes to fifteen. Then, on 1 April, Hughes was handed a letter signed by seventeen UAP members announcing that a National Service Group, of which Menzies was a member, had been formed within the parliamentary group of the UAP. This group would remain within the party but not attend its meetings.[17]

Spender, who had declined an invitation to join the National Service Group, noted that the majority of its members were from South Australia, where Menzies had considerable support in the parliamentary team. In public, Menzies remained defiant in the face of criticism that he was making a move on his leader:

> The present issue is not Hughes versus Menzies ... [but] whether the great principles for which the party stands should be really fought for in Parliament with disregard of the electoral risks.
>
> For the past 18 months, the U.A.P. has been, for all practical purposes, dead. Some such party standing courageously for its

principles is urgently needed if the present Government is to be removed at the next election … The object of the National Service Group is to try to bring these things about. If this, for the time being, involves some disunity, that cannot be helped, for unity produced by mere inertia is useless.[18]

Menzies and his supporters might be forgiven for their desperation in the circumstances surrounding the UAP's demise. Observers of history could also be forgiven for noting that this was not the first time in politics that Robert Menzies had used a subgroup to force party renewal and his own strategies – in the late 1920s, he had led the Young Nationalists as a Victorian MP; in 1931 he had spearheaded 'The Group' that installed Joe Lyons as leader of the newly formed UAP to defeat Labor at the 1931 election; and now it was his National Service Group spurring change under Hughes. The new group energised Menzies' approach to opposition, something he did better when he was in charge of a political operation. He commented to Ken in a letter of 30 June 1943 that his regular broadcasts had 'become completely political and direct' and that the audience reaction had been 'very good'.

It is a testament to the truth in Menzies' comments to his son back in February 1943, that by the second half of the year the UAP could be such a spent force at a time when the Labor minority government of John Curtin was itself undergoing not a few strains. In August 1942, after the censorship for overseas publication of a virulent attack by Hughes on the government's military efforts, the Curtin Government was challenged by both Hughes and the press. Warwick Fairfax soon resigned from the Press Censorship Advisory Committee and John Curtin all but threatened his resignation as prime minister, telling his critics that 'Parliament could accept his Administration or get another one'.[19] He then launched personal attacks on Hughes, Menzies and Spender, all of which suggested minority government was taking its toll on Curtin. Certainly the gibe by Curtin's opponents within the Labor Party during 1941, that 'honest John' was so reasonable towards Menzies that he not only 'rented a flat in Bob Menzies' pocket but he lived in it', was no longer credible.[20] In late April 1943, a censure debate over Eddie Ward's false accusation that the Menzies Government had plans to abandon Australia above a 'Brisbane line' ended in Ward being relieved of his ministry pending the results of a royal commission into the matter. The opposition may have taken Ward's scalp and momentarily wounded the prime minister but, as Paul Hasluck has commented, this was all just the opposition's 'first gallop on a dead horse'.[21]

The 1943 election campaign, when it came late in July, pushed by uproar over the Brisbane line issue, was a debacle for the UAP/Country Party opposition. From the outset there was division in the opposition. On 22 July, Fadden opened the coalition's campaign in Brisbane, announcing policies that included postwar credits – certificates of having paid higher taxes during the war years that a taxpayer could redeem in peacetime. In a speech the following night, Menzies contradicted Fadden over postwar credits, arguing that Labor had 'substantially increased taxation' and that postwar credits could no longer be supported by a UAP/Country Party government. Thus the opening shots in this election campaign became the opposition firing on itself. In the press the following day, Fadden called Menzies' speech 'a stab in the back'. This led Menzies to point out the absence of any refunding of taxation in the coalition's 'thirty-one points'.[22] That Menzies and Fadden could be so openly at war on the eve of an election is breathtaking – surpassing even the Rudd–Gillard stand-off at the 2010 federal election.

The state of the UAP/Country Party as it approached a federal election could not have been worse. Menzies acknowledged in a letter to his son Ken on 30 June that the calibre of the

UAP/Country Party candidates was not good and that his anxiety was not about winning the election but 'the dangerous scarcity of Cabinet timbre'. Menzies, at that point, was almost convinced a narrow win for the opposition was possible – and he seemed none too keen on such an outcome, as he told Ken in the same letter:

> If we were to win three or four seats and come back much as we now are, I would not envy anybody the task of forming a government, and I would have some fear that the government when formed would not be sufficiently resolute in action. The handling of strikes, for example, requires more than fine speeches.[23]

As the election result would prove, Menzies had no need to worry. Labor won what is probably the largest victory, still, in Australian political history – a landslide indeed. The UAP also lost its majority in the Senate, with Labor winning all nineteen seats contested under a system of voting that would be changed to a proportional system at the 1949 election. Disunity, and longevity at the helm, had all but ended the UAP as a political force. Australians were no longer feeling the pangs of unemployment, war spending had improved the economy, and the sense of pulling together as a nation behind a united and strong government was very appealing. Writing to Ken, Menzies noted how more and more Australians owed their comfortable lives and opportunity to government positions or, as Menzies put it, 'employment under the government – which is now the lot of a substantial proportion of Australians – having appeared to be financially advantageous, there will be a good deal of disposition to think that some socialist system is the right one for Australia'.[24]

Starting from scratch

While the emergence of a new non-Labor party after the 1943 federal election might have seemed inevitable to outsiders, it was no easy transition within the UAP ranks. Nor was it a smooth move for Robert Menzies as he mulled over his options in the aftermath of the 1943 election. He would accept the leadership of the UAP again but continue to equivocate in private as to his career prospects.

By the time of the 1943 election, the UAP had seen a number of breakaway political groups stand as separate parties – albeit without success in gaining seats and further damaging the non-Labor results at the polls. In New South Wales, where Menzies had never been popular with party officials, the UAP competed with two groups for non-Labor votes – the One Parliament for Australia and the Liberal Democrats. Undaunted, Menzies immediately looked to the future, and his place in it. Writing to Ken, he noted how his NSW rivals had done particularly poorly at the election, with his worst NSW critics losing their seats:

> On the personal side, it seems probable in the new parliament
> we will be without Spooner, Marr and McCall (a prospect
> which naturally does not depress me) … this the defeat of my
> bitterest critics [while] Hughes, Fadden and Page, each of
> whom can now be credited with at least one poisonous attack
> upon me in public, are just staggering home in seats which
> were thought to be overwhelmingly safe.[25]

With no small amount of ego, Menzies then commented that, overall, 'I am not so sure that the election isn't in a personal sense favourable to me'. Continuing, he outlined to Ken his feelings about renewal – something that had been a part of Menzies' thinking for more than a year. The battle now was at home:

In the next week or two there will be at least two questions
to be decided: The first is whether the UAP (which will, I
hope, reconstruct itself and get a better name) will claim
the leadership of the Opposition. It is entitled to it as the
majority Opposition party, and I can hardly believe that after
the experience of this election very many of its members will
have any faith in Fadden. The second question is who will
lead the UAP. Unless the party decides to claim the leadership
of the Opposition I will not be a candidate for the UAP
leadership, because after my recent experiences I have decided
that it is time the worm turned; and I will therefore not
serve as deputy to Fadden … Whoever becomes leader must
promptly set about the task of creating a fighting spirit and
building a real organisation all over Australia.[26]

Post-mortems on the UAP's election campaign and general
demise in 1943 were devastating, as Menzies' biographer Allan
Martin has documented, but with the loss of so many of Menzies' critics and opponents, and the general feeling that he stood
above the pack as a presence, the outcome of the party meeting to
elect a new leader saw Menzies emerge as not only the new UAP
leader but also the new opposition leader.

Spender's assessment of Menzies' ability to time his moves
and strategise is an acute one in any evaluation of the political figure Menzies became in the year or so after his resignation
as party leader and prime minister in 1941. Writing to Ken on
13 October 1943, Menzies described moments during the party
meeting that re-elected him leader by prefacing his descriptions
with, 'You would have been delighted if you could have been
hidden under a table in the Party Room the day the leadership
was determined'.[27] The tone of the letter is one of contentment
and not a little triumph. Menzies' sense of the ridiculous, and
his amusement at occasional high-minded naivety, such as the

suggestion to merge with the Country Party, is on full display:

> One of my supporters (at least I think he was!) then offered to
> move an amendment of a highly sentimental kind, favouring
> an approach to the CP for the purpose of bringing about a
> complete merger. This unreal but dazzling prospect of unity
> appealed at once to some of the elder brethren, the result
> being that within half an hour there were before the Chair
> the original motion and at least three amendments, with most
> speakers clutching at the idea that the issue of leadership
> might be evaded or postponed by opening up the indicated
> agrarian discussions. You'll of course agree with me that the
> most popular device in politics is postponement … Billy
> [Hughes], in the Chair was incredible. His grasp of procedure
> has never been very great, and the task of determining in
> what order and how you put to a meeting of reasonably
> talkative men a motion, an amendment, an amendment on
> the amendment, and an amendment on the amendment to the
> amendment to the motion proved entirely beyond him. For
> once I was sensible (as your mother would say) and did nothing
> to extract him from the tangle, having a vague idea in my mind
> that his claims to lead an outnumbered party in the hurly burly
> of parliamentary debate were rapidly fading

Menzies eventually took the lead at the meeting by announcing
he would vote against all motions before the chair and put his
own motion to propose that the UAP should lead the opposition
and that the new UAP leader should work to establish 'combined
opposition forces'. As he put it to Ken, 'they promptly threw out
their own amendments and motion with gusto, and unanimously
passed mine'.

Menzies was back at the helm of a ravaged UAP. It was a mission not entirely clear in his mind. Pattie Menzies, in an interview

with Gerard Henderson for his book *Menzies' Child*,[28] opined that for years her husband's great ambition had been the job of chief justice of Victoria. Shortly after his return as party leader, a chance to achieve this long-awaited prize seemed to come Menzies' way, when Victorian Chief Justice Sir Frederick Mann decided suddenly to retire. In 1958, former Victorian premier Sir John McDonald, who had been part of the UAP/Country Party ministry in 1944, told historian John Paul that when the position of chief justice became vacant in January 1944, Robert Menzies had allowed his name to go forward for the job.[29] Menzies was not chosen, not least because the Victorian Country Party premier at the time was Albert Dunstan, whose uneasy relations, over years, with the UAP did not work in Menzies' favour.

So Robert Menzies continued his career in politics, fate once more determining his path. While not alone in his belief in the need for a reborn non-Labor grouping, Menzies thus began the process of developing a new political party under his leadership.

Accounts of the founding of the Australian Liberal Party are numerous – most notably in Gerard Henderson's *Menzies' Child: The Liberal Party of Australia*, Allan Martin's *Robert Menzies: A Life*, volume 2, 1944–1978, and Ian Hancock's *The Liberals: The NSW Division 1945–2000* and entry on the Liberal Party of Australia in *The Oxford Companion to Australian History*. It is Hancock's argument that Menzies has been all too often given most of the credit for the foundation of the Liberal Party, 'bringing some 19 non-Labor parties and groups together' to make a national and permanent organisation. This overlooks the fact, he says, that 'many men and women were involved in the drawn-out process … animated by the post-war idealism of ex-service personnel, a deep-seated fear of socialism, and a commitment to free enterprise balanced by an acceptance of government involvement in the economy'.[30] To this Gerard Henderson counters that, without Bob Menzies' leadership, the work to hold on to the unity among such diverse groups would not have been successful, or even attempted.[31]

Menzies' opportunity to take such a lead began with the Powers Referendum in August 1944. This was the attempt by Labor to extend its wartime powers over the states for a further five years beyond the end of the war – including powers over employment and prices – as a policy move for postwar reconstruction. The referendum met with strong resistance. At the heart of the problem with the referendum was the complicated list of powers the government was asking voters to agree to – so much so, historian Paul Hasluck summarised that 'a vote for "No" did not entirely reject the need for constitutional reform; it merely indicated that the voter did not like all the present proposals for reform'.[32] The campaign, more importantly on the non-Labor side, gave Menzies some welcome airtime, as he took up his chance to work the states for the 'No' case. This activity engaged tens of thousands across the nation, bringing the disparate political groups of non-Labor activists together, a chance for renewed unity that Menzies himself noted in a statement on 16 June.[33]

The Powers Referendum, conducted with a sick prime minister at the helm and delayed news of the June Normandy landings belatedly bursting across newspaper headlines, was lost decisively – only South Australia and Western Australia voted yes and all but two of the electorates that had swung to Labor at the 1943 election voted no, while in Queensland and Tasmania all electorates voted no. Overall, out of seventy-four electorates just twenty-two had said yes or gone with the government they had so overwhelmingly elected just a year before.[34] Boosted by the results, within weeks Menzies had written to the leaders of all non-Labor parties and groups loosely aligned with the UAP to invite them to a conference in Canberra from Friday 13 October to Monday 16 October, with Sunday a free day.

Gerard Henderson has observed of this decision that in 'a reflection of the Protestant allegiance ... it was decided to give preference to keeping holy the Sabbath over the immediate need to establish a nationwide non-Labor organisation in Caesar's realm'.[35]

For all that (or as a reflection of that), the seventy-seven delegates met in Canberra's Masonic Hall. Menzies would oversee a second conference two months later, this time at Albury near the border of Australia's two most populous states, from 14 to 16 December. At this second conference, the Liberal Party of Australia was proclaimed with 'a quality and political understanding ... not exhibited by any non-Labor leader in the 1930s or 1940s'.[36] The organisational wing of this new party began well and would incorporate, by amalgamation, Elizabeth (May) Couchman's Australian Women's National League, whereby thousands of active women, mostly in Victoria, laid the foundations for the Liberal Party's branch structure. Even before the conference at Albury, Menzies was delighted at progress being made towards a new national non-Labor party. Writing to Ken on 6 December as he prepared for Albury, he was almost jubilant at what was in the making after so many decades: 'It does seem fantastic that for all these years we have gone along without any federal organisation at all'. Yet his letter also noted many of the hurdles still to be encountered, especially in New South Wales, where he described a 'bitter internecine war between the Democratic Party and the Liberal Democrats'.

Bedding down this new federal organisation was not achieved easily. In New South Wales, as Ian Hancock has analysed, the friction and divisiveness that had bedevilled Menzies as UAP leader the first time continued for some years – or, as Hancock put it, 'What seemed straightforward in Albury became convoluted in Sydney'.[37] In New South Wales it was the efforts of, among others, NSW state president Bill Spooner (brother of Eric), Tom

Ritchie, Reg Weaver, Neville Harding and Edith Shortland's Women's Central Committee that helped resist the disrupting presence of Ernest White from the Liberal Democratic Party. At the inaugural NSW State Council meeting on 28 June 1945, delegate John Cramer, representing Goulburn, accused White from the floor of 'acting in the interests of the Labor Party and the Communist Party',[38] but it took the presence of Menzies to pack the punch that shamed the floor. Addressing the delegates at a crucial point, Menzies commented that some state divisions of the Liberal Party were 'peaceable' and others 'warlike', adding that no executive chairman 'had a task so difficult and half so responsible as ... Mr Spooner'.[39] The poor showing of the Liberal Party at the 1946 federal election owed much to this lack of unity and open division in New South Wales, along with the party's tottering financial condition and its inability to achieve a partnership with the Country Party. Only after February 1948, with newly appointed general secretary John Carrick, did the real administrative work begin of building in a steady and unified way the strong NSW Division it would become.

The bigger picture

In Menzies' letters to his son Ken over the almost two years between the Albury conference and the 1946 election, there is a mood of optimism in Menzies that his new political party could well be on track to win government. Convinced of the economic unsoundness in Labor's promises for postwar spending, expanded social services and employment through public investment in major government projects, Menzies thought the Australian public would regard with suspicion any move to a more 'socialist program'.

By 26 March 1945, he believed the 'floating vote' (today's swinging vote) among small businesspeople and white-collar workers was moving away from Labor. While telling Ken that there had been 'difficulties, differences of opinion on executives and some jockeying for position here and there by representatives of older organisations' and that, in particular, he had needed to spend most of his time in Sydney 'where such difficulties have been most acute', Menzies could also report that the 'anti-Menzies tide of which one hears so much from the grumblers in Pitt Street and Castlereagh Street [Sydney headquarters] has turned in the suburbs'.[40] He based his feelings on his 'uncommon experience of being received with great personal enthusiasm'. In fact, he regarded his reception in Sydney as 'quite astonishing', adding that at 'six suburban meetings I had a total of 5000 people' and of these he estimated that some 3000 had become financial members. He was even attracting support from the *Sydney Morning Herald*, which now reported his speeches in longer passages than he had ever known.

Menzies, however, had allowed his personal triumph to colour his judgment. The popular success he faced at meeting after meeting was coming not from the general public across party boundaries but reunited non-Labor followers. As he witnessed the success of so many disparate non-Labor groups coming together into one national Liberal Party, Menzies told his son,

> I feel no doubt the government will lose ground at the next
> election … As you know, whenever the political pendulum
> swings, nobody can tell how far it is going to swing. It is
> therefore quite possible for a non-Labor victory to occur in
> 1946 as great as the Labor victory of 1943.[41]

Menzies' only qualification was that the government could still buy votes with added spending. As he put it, 'There is plenty of money in circulation and plenty of people will bless the government for it'. But there was another factor.

John Curtin's death in July 1945 had seen Ben Chifley take over as the Labor prime minister. Chifley was a fresh face for the postwar years, his safe hand guiding an expanded social program. The Labor caucus revitalised under Chifley as he began to push through reforming legislation. The Chifley style evoked hope of a new deal for labour and investment, the worker and wages, and for a postwar age to usher in an expanded role for government in the distribution of services to taxpayers. Gavin Souter has described Chifley as more suited to the job of prime minister than Curtin, and better at leading: '"Chif" was tougher than Curtin, and better at handling people'. He successfully managed firebrands Evatt and Ward, duchessing Evatt with such phrases as 'my learned friend' and 'the Doc', and charming Ward so that he was 'fairly eating out of his hand'.[42] All of that had an impact. Labor looked more united than it had been in years, and with a fresh prime minister at the helm the nation had steadied into peace and a new outlook. At the 1946 election, Labor lost six House of Representatives seats and the Liberal/Country Party coalition won seven, while Labor retained a large majority in the Senate with the Liberal Party left holding only three seats. Labor looked set for an easy run, and Menzies said little then or later about the result.

Menzies had come quite a way from the party disunity and enmity in 1940–41 but his feelings of elation had been engendered by the sudden warmth around him of colleagues and followers – something he had never really enjoyed in his years as an MP. He had known respect but little affection. In his battles outside his party with Labor opponents and their followers, nothing had changed. As he campaigned for the 1946 election, his legacy as the aloof 'pig-iron Bob' who had no time for the lower orders, did not suffer fools gladly and opposed socialism, met with organised resistance from hardened and unionised Labor supporters, many of them Communist Party operatives, who came along to disrupt his meetings. The old tag 'You can't win with Menzies' continued to haunt his reputation, as uproar engulfed audiences and election day drew closer.

At a Liberal campaign meeting in an industrial suburb of Geelong on 13 September 1946, *The Argus* reported that 'the audience included more Labor than Liberal supporters'.[43] All speakers were heckled, including the mayor of Geelong West, who did the introductions, and Menzies found himself forced to attack the propaganda of anti-Menzies flyers and pamphlets rather than advocate his party's policies, at one point saying, 'You Communists are desperately concerned with Russia but the Liberal party is desperately concerned with Australia and the Empire'. It was all high drama but counterproductive. At a subsequent meeting in Sydney's Darlinghurst on 16 September, there was a near riot, and twenty to thirty interjectors were removed after fights between groups of men and women and the police. Menzies even had trouble getting into the hall, with one wit calling out, 'How do you expect to get into power when you can't get into the Maccabean Hall?'[44] Bits of scrap iron in bags adorned with swastikas were thrown at him on the stage, just missing some in the audience, with a number of women reported as having to be dragged to safety. Microphones were damaged, wires cut. In general, the whole gathering became a rabble and fifteen men were under arrest by the end of proceedings.

Not surprisingly, on the eve of the election, in spite of maintaining optimism, Menzies noted that 'six weeks of incessant and nerve-racking travelling and speaking was almost unendurable'.[45] Election day 1946 was the Menzies couple's twenty-sixth wedding anniversary – but the election results when the tally came in did not encourage champagne. By the following Monday, the press was reporting Menzies' reaction: 'The result is profoundly disappointing ... My own campaign of the last three years would be unreal if I did not feel that a disastrous popular decision has been made'.[46] But politics is often full of surprises and miscalculations on all sides. It would be a disastrous and unpopular decision by Labor prime minister Ben Chifley and his Cabinet, in less than a year, that would tip the political tables in just one term, a turnaround that was unimaginable as the Liberal Party's Victorian Division placed advertisements in the press on 15 October 1946 for candidates to stand at the November 1947 state election – an election that would herald Menzies' ultimate rebirth from the ashes.

10

Winning with Menzies

About himself he said that he knew that he was the subject of
dislike & hostility throughout the community & thought that
perhaps his party cd not win under his leadership: he disliked
political atmosphere and surroundings: he wd be happy at the
bar & (in answer to my direct question) felt loss of limelight
a mre [sic] of indifference. He agreed that his party might
become an irrelevancy because the conflict might become
one betw communism and traditional labour. He sd Chifley
was decent and not stupid but had no ideas outside currency
stability and improved conditions of employt. All else (foreign
affairs, education, imperial connexion etc) he called high
fallutin.

– Owen Dixon, 28 January 1947[1]

A showdown between labour and capital had been coming for
some two decades. How this would play out in Australia through
the late 1940s and 1950s was not to be imagined. In January
1947, when Robert Menzies opened up to his good friend and a
justice of the High Court Owen Dixon, about his unhappiness in
politics, the lines of political battle were already being drawn, but
the extent of Australians' repugnance at any government lurch
to the extreme left was not yet in sight. With the bitter result

of his 1946 election defeat, Menzies could only feel that Labor seemed to hold the middle ground while the far left, the Communist Party of Australia, was becoming a more and more strident opposition to good government.

It was a measure of his despondency over the outcome of the 1946 election that Menzies thought this way. His chat with Owen Dixon, one of the few friends to whom he could be completely frank, offers a tiny window into Menzies' dejection – or what Menzies' biographer Allan Martin saw as 'a mood of self-questioning, even of doubt about the worthwhileness of the political life'.[2] Pattie Menzies, on the other hand, confided to Dixon days later that Menzies saw the law as a 'very small world' and he also needed to remember those who 'placed their faith in him'.[3] Elected unopposed to remain Liberal Party leader, Menzies was hanging on. Among party ranks, however, disquiet over his personality and unpopularity had begun to resurface, and the arguments about needing a leader with a more winnable style were gaining traction.

One of Menzies' critics was Tom Ritchie, a self-made Melbourne businessman who had relocated to Sydney and believed his contacts with party branches and factories left him more in touch with ordinary Australians.[4] When, in early 1947, a handful of leading members of the NSW Chamber of Manufacturers approached economist Douglas Copland – then Australian minister to China – suggesting he should express an interest in standing as a Liberal Party candidate at the 1949 elections with a view to becoming a Liberal leader, Ritchie gave his approval.[5] Copland considered this option for some months, albeit rejecting Menzies' suggestion he stand for a Tasmanian Senate seat. When, in the first half of 1947, the state elections for New South Wales and Queensland reinstated Labor governments, NSW Chamber of Manufacturers secretary Cecil Hall and Ritchie made further moves to enlist Copland, Ritchie expressing the view as late as

August 1947 that 'the future Liberal Prime Minister of Australia would be someone with political nous and ability, with the esteem of the electors',[6] an obvious dig at Menzies. Soon after, however, Copland accepted an offer to become vice-chancellor of the Australian National University.

With such behind-the-scenes mutterings about Menzies as leader, and heeding advice from the Liberal Party's federal director Don Cleland, Menzies resigned at a party meeting in Melbourne on 1 September 1947 to be re-elected unopposed as leader. The reason given publicly was that the party wanted Menzies' leadership approved by all parliamentary members[7] and the new Liberal senators had only taken their seats on 1 July. In fact, the move was designed to put an end to the rumblings about whether Menzies was the party's best hope for leader. Ironically, the vote turned out to be perfect timing for Menzies to have put himself forward once more – in a few months, facing industrial disputes, strikes and an unsavoury number of wage agreements in the unions' favour, the government had kicked a huge own goal over banking legislation.

Menzies had soldiered on for most of 1947, in spite of the rumours against his leadership. His modus operandi continued to be a campaign against the industrial disorder growing daily around union stoppages and disruption to commercial activity amid the general need for transport and other services. A renewed union industrial campaign had begun immediately following the federal election – within a week, the *Sydney Morning Herald* was reporting headlines of '50,000 involved in disputes'.[8] In the midst of such stoppages and stand-downs, on 13 October the temperature in Sydney soared to an unseasonable 35 degrees Celsius. Four days later, the *Sydney Morning Herald* editorial ran with the headline 'Sabotage of prosperity'.

Menzies had gone in hard over the influence of communists in the unions and on labour operatives at the 1946 election, but it did not resonate with the electorate. Jobs were easy to find and, after the upheaval of war, peacetime had its own rewards. Moreover, the Chifley Government had the confidence of voters, with its centralised management of the emerging peace economy, expanding government projects and guaranteed jobs for returned servicemen. Chifley was also successfully handling the ongoing repayment of the massive war debts, in particular by eventually coaxing Labor, in February 1947, to accept Australia's ratification of the Bretton Woods Agreement, which installed the International Monetary Fund.[9] By managing the firebrands within Labor, Chifley governed for the country rather than any sectional interest of the party. It would take longer for the ongoing disruptions of continuing industrial stoppages to have an impact on daily life and business sufficiently to arouse the ire of the voting public. But the banking debate, with its central focus on a government that might be compared to that of the Soviet Union, suddenly brought notions of communism into a new and local perspective.

Chifley biographer LF (Fin) Crisp wrote that 'the stoppages of 1945–49 were frequent and severe. Much badly needed production was lost and a great deal of hardship visited on all sections of the community – and not least of all the workers and their families'. He added that Chifley's term as prime minister had 'corresponded in time broadly with communist achievement of control in a record number of major industrial unions'.[10] With higher costs to business in wages and disruption, and the subsequent threat of inflation, the Chifley Government had sought greater control over Australia's financial sector. Under its Banking Act of 1945, local authorities and state governments were banned from dealing with private banks. In May 1947, Chifley attempted to widen this order to additional authorities, a move that provoked the Melbourne City Council to challenge Section 48 of the Banking Act in the High Court. On Wednesday

13 August, the High Court found against the federal government. Chifley now faced the prospect of the private banks challenging the entire act.

The move by Labor to enact peacetime control of the banks began in late 1944 – in other words, before the war ended. When a threat to their independence became obvious to the trading banks, the National Bank of Australasia's (NBA's) chief executive, Leslie J McConnan, whom historian Geoffrey Blainey has described as 'interested least in banking and most in public affairs',[11] attempted a united bank protest at any extension of wartime control of the banks. But there was a more cautious reaction from most other trading banks, which feared government reprisals. What resistance the NBA might muster, at that stage, failed to worry the Labor government.[12] Such was the lack of resonance in the community in relation to the government's move on the trading banks, at the 1946 election Menzies and Fadden made no issue over banking. But with the High Court's decision against Section 48 of the Chifley Government's Banking Act in August 1947, Menzies was offered a lifeline.

On Saturday 16 August, three days after the High Court decision and in a high-handed manner, Ben Chifley announced his government would prepare legislation to nationalise Australia's banking system. His statement, which came with no warning and consisted of just one sentence and a mere forty-two words, was described as set to 'explode his party's power' in the coming decade.[13] By 18 August, *The Argus* was flashing a page-one headline – '"Totalitarianism!" says banks' spokesman. Menzies declares: "To Russia for a parallel"'. McConnan, the political operator and bank manager, had the floor at last. Months of battle would follow, with the trading banks now united in a desperate bid to avoid extinction. On the day of the *Argus* headline warning of totalitarianism, the *Sydney Morning Herald* ran the page-one headline 'Bank decision staggers community. Millions involved'. Accusations of government secrecy and plotting to ambush the banks, suggestions that nationalisation would soon be extended to the insurance industry, notions that UK banks trading in Australia would close, reports that the government would compulsorily acquire shares in banks at a low price, criticism that the government had become 'dictatorial', and predictions that there would be large job losses in the banking industry as trading banks closed, were among the more compelling of the headlines that mushroomed. They also ensured that the outcries of protest came not just from bank employees but also bank customers and ordinary Australians.

Meanwhile, the banks began a coordinated advertising campaign, coupled with the collection of huge numbers of signatures on petitions. These mass appeals besieged both Parliament House and MPs' electoral offices, alongside mass protest meetings in cities and regional towns. A comprehensive account of how intense and widespread this campaign became is to be found in AL May's *The Battle for the Banks*.[14] Before the end of August, Menzies was addressing vast rallies of protesting bank employees and other interested individuals. The photos in newspapers showed crowds spilling out onto streets from major function centres, wide expanses of heads and hats, women and men. Menzies' middle class, invoked in his radio talks through 1942–43, was suddenly massed and angry. For all that, the Chifley Government ploughed on with its preparations for its banking legislation, indifferent to the clamour and blinded by the thought that there were two years to go before another federal election. This left it looking smug and indifferent to the plight of a significant section of voters.

This contempt for voters became evident on 11 September, at a meeting in the Ballarat Town Hall in Victoria, when Menzies read from a letter sent by the minister for commerce, Reg Pollard, to a bank officer who had written in protest at bank nationalisation. In his letter, Pollard accused the bank officer of only quoting from people who were 'under an obligation to your particular bank, and naturally would not desire to antagonise those to whom they are beholden'. After reading this out to the crowd, Menzies turned to his audience 'amid cheers' saying the statement was 'contemptible'.[15] The letter went on, further upbraiding the bank officer, Pollard writing, 'I owe nothing to you as far as my previous elections are concerned, as no doubt you were always anti-Labor'. Pollard had then proceeded to lecture the bank officer on the 'type of servitude' from which Labor had freed workers such as he.

The gloves were certainly off, but it was a strange government tactic to be quite so raw in a dispute with the public, or to exhibit personal acrimony towards a reasonable voter. It was manna from heaven for Menzies, and he jumped at the chance to address meeting after meeting over bank nationalisation, putting the boot into the government and his opponents generally. Then the Cain Labor Government of Victoria fell when the conservative Legislative Council refused supply over Labor's federal banking legislation. This brought on a Victorian state election campaign, during which local figure Menzies sallied forth alongside the Victorian Liberal leader, Tom Hollway, and the Victorian Country Party premier, John McDonald, making the case against bank nationalisation. Labor lost heavily on 8 November 1947. Commenting on the election campaign, historian David Day misses the point with his mock heroic claim that Menzies 'had a banner to flourish in his conservative crusade' and saw the chance to 'reinvent himself as the defender of everything decent in Australia'.[16] Menzies' strength in his campaign was his belief that bank nationalisation was economic suicide for Australia. The campaign was political tactics at their best, infused with passionate belief. The government had put a foot wrong and refused to sense its mistake, allowing its judgment to be clouded by ideology, as reflected in Labor MP Les Haylen's argument defending bank nationalisation that Labor had 'the guts to stand for the No. 1 plank of its platform', namely the socialisation of industry, production, distribution and exchange.[17] Labor's opponents had a clear run to the goalposts. Menzies was doing what any competent opposition leader is expected to do – take up the challenge and take on the government.

That other war

The Liberal Party campaign against the Chifley Government's bank nationalisation legislation was couched in war terms from the outset. Speaking at a rally of more than 6000, organised by the Liberal Party and held in the Sydney Town Hall on 25 August 1947, Menzies threw down the gauntlet by reference to the war against Hitler's National Socialists:

> Almost eight years ago I stood at this microphone as Prime Minister of this country and in the name of the free people of Australia declared war upon Germany and upon the German Fascist leaders … Today I stand here in the name of the same free people to declare war on the Fascists in Australia. (Applause) This is a new war … the weapons will not be bombs or rifles. They will be public opinion, speech and writings, and above all, the conviction of honest minds. Although it is a different kind of war the penalty of defeat will be no less than the loss of our liberties; no less than if Hitler had marched through London and the Swastika had flown over this Town Hall. (Cheers) The importance of this issue cannot be exaggerated. This is a proposal for a bank monopoly … [and] penetrates into the whole structure of life and liberty in Australia … an enormous step towards the creation of a State in which the government will tell you how to live and what you are to spend.[18]

The speech captured the emotion, fears, paranoia and, to a large extent, the reality of a government that had allowed ideological baggage from the bank crisis of 1930–31 to catch up with it. Labor having split in 1931, the Scullin Government fell after only two years, amidst an outpouring of popular rage that led tens of thousands to enlist in citizen groups. Such groups were held together and ballooned around a belief that Labor was unable to manage the economy following the stock market crash of October 1929 and subsequent credit crisis and depression of 1930–31. Within Labor, factions had formed over banking and financial policy, the most extreme proponents being Frank Anstey and Jack Lang, who sounded off at 'Money Power', a scenario couched in anti-Semitic phrases that blamed the financial crisis on a conspiracy by the banks to bleed honest workers. The uproar in Labor between populist extremists who supported NSW premier Jack Lang, financial expansionists such as John Curtin and Ted Theodore, and those wanting financial moderation such as Joe Lyons, eventually brought about a separate Lang Labor Party. Then, in March 1931, Lyons and a handful of Labor MPs walked from the caucus by voting against the expansionary legislation driven by Treasurer Ted Theodore. In May that year, the Scullin Government was forced to retreat from Theodore's inflationary drive and back a Premiers' Plan favouring reductions in government spending and balanced budgets. By then it was all too late; Labor would remain divided and splintered – and out of office – for more than a decade. In 1947, Eddie Ward would use the same 1930–31 arguments against Chifley when opposing ratification of the UN's Bretton Woods agreement on financial management.[19]

During Labor's wilderness years of the 1930s, the party for the workers had endorsed bank nationalisation. In his opening speech opposing Chifley's banking legislation, on 23 October 1947, Menzies reminded the House of Representatives that the first steps for this policy had begun in June 1931 at a conference of 'federal members of the ALP and trades unions [, which] appointed a special committee to devise ways and means of bringing about "the socialisation of industry, production, distribution and exchange"'.[20] In March 1931, Chifley had not joined Lyons but was certainly one of the moderates in caucus. By 1947, however, Chifley was sounding more like Jack Lang.

Chifley's fit of pique at the High Court's decision against Section 48 of his 1945 Banking Act was to provoke a year and more of public clamour. Australia had seen nothing like it since those mass meetings of the citizens groups that carried Joe Lyons and the UAP to power in December 1931, a movement in which Robert Menzies had been a central figure. As the Chifley Banking Bill made its way through parliament in late October and early November 1947, out on the hustings Menzies and his supporters sensed a return of the mood of 1931. So much so that, in campaigning during the 1947 Victorian state election at a large rally in Albert Park, Menzies in 'top form' referred to those 'old-style' rallies or what reporters referred to as just 'like old times'.[21]

Addressing the House of Representatives on Thursday 23 October, and opening the debate for the second reading of the Banking Bill, Menzies spoke of his 'heavy sense of responsibility'. He went on to outline, in graphic terms, the onslaught against ordinary Australians' savings and investments that bank nationalisation (a bank monopoly) would bring. In fact, the opposition's case was nothing less, he said, than a 'second battle for Australia, a battle in which victory will go to those who are not only brave, but alert and vigilant'. It was, he said, the war against a government that had chosen to install the methods of the fascists of the Soviet Union, Italy and Argentina[22] – none of which made any difference to the government's determination to bring the trading banks to their knees. Secure in its power, with strong majorities in both houses and only a little shaken by the Victorian election result two weeks later, the Chifley ministry remained unmoved. Three days after the Cain Government fell on 8 November, Chifley gave his MPs a pep talk and the minister for information, Arthur Calwell, responded to yet another Menzies attack in the House by saying, 'Imagine plunging Australia into a civil war over a few lousy pence … No matter how many millions the banks spend in this campaign, they cannot withstand the tide of progress. They are finished'.[23]

Unfortunately for the Chifley Government, Menzies' second battle for Australia would not be over by Christmas. On 19 November, as the Banking Bill passed the House of Representatives, Britons prepared excitedly for celebrations around the wedding of Princess Elizabeth and Prince Philip the next day. Within a week, the Banking Bill had made it through the Senate to become the Banking Act, only to be challenged in the High Court, within twenty-four hours, by the states of Victoria and South Australia and the banks.

The final battle

Just as Labor's policy to price and tax carbon in response to climate change would become the Achilles heel of the Rudd–Gillard governments sixty years later, so efforts to nationalise Australia's banks would undermine the Labor government of Ben Chifley. Australian electors are a pragmatic collective. Even Australia's White Australia Policy was based on a sense of material benefit – on the protection of jobs and a view of how best to maintain an Anglo standard of life. It did not take a great deal of persuasion to convince a fairly large slab of the Australian electorate that their healthy standard of living and economic prosperity could be undermined by Chifley's banking legislation and its attack on competition.

That the Communist Party of Australia was one of the strongest supporters of bank nationalisation hardly helped Labor either – in the Victorian election the Communist Party stood a minimum number of candidates, preferring to support Labor candidates openly.[24] Along the way, proponents and opponents of the legislation had even roped in support from some leaders of the Catholic hierarchy. Archbishop Beovich of Adelaide gave qualified support to the legislation, as did (eventually) Cardinal Gilroy in Sydney. But Archbishop Duhig of Brisbane opposed the bill from the outset as 'revolutionary' and only legitimate if supported by a referendum, while Archbishop Mannix of Melbourne gave a characteristically Mannix response that he would 'hold his peace and hope for the best', adding that he was sure 'the Communists will be delighted if the bill is passed'.[25]

Although Chifley's grand plan to nationalise the banks in Australia would never see daylight, this was not known in February 1948, when the High Court began hearing the challenge by the opponents of the Banking Act. Nor was it envisaged that the process to overturn the legislation would last until successful in appeals to the High Court of Australia and the Privy Council in London on 26 July 1949. Throughout the hearings – both in the High Court of Australia and in London before the Privy Council – Labor's attorney-general and minister for External Affairs, Bert Evatt appeared for the government and Garfield Barwick for the banks. As Gavin Souter, among others, has observed, Evatt 'was not the uniquely equipped defender that he imagined himself to be'.[26]

The case in the High Court was the longest in its history and ran from 8 February to 15 April in Melbourne and Sydney. Evatt had been a temperamental member of the High Court before entering parliament at the 1940 election, and his tendency to irritate the justices both when on the bench and appearing before it did not help. He spoke for eighteen days while Barwick spoke for only seven. Evatt's aggressive manner was on display even before the formal hearing of the case began, when he called for the disqualification of two of the judges on grounds of personal interests by way of bank shares held by Justice Hayden Starke's wife and Justice Dudley Williams' joint holding of shares in two banks. Overruled by the chief justice, John Latham, Evatt was left with some ground to make up. Instead, he plunged into prickly overkill. On 11 August 1948, the court handed down its majority decision in favour of the banks and the states, ruling important sections of the act invalid. Within two days of the High Court's decision, the Labor caucus endorsed the government's next move – an appeal to the Privy Council. This was a step heavily sponsored by Bert Evatt, who went on to lead a team of four Australian and three English barristers in London.

In spite of the Australian Government's wish to expedite the London hearing, the appeal to the Privy Council over the Australian Banking Act of 1947 broke records. After opening in mid-March 1949, it heard thirty-six days of addresses by various counsel. Evatt spoke for twenty-two days. Two participating justices, Lord Uthwatt and Lord du Parcq, died before it had finished. Nonetheless, the appeal was lost. By then, the federal election was just months away and the outcome was not looking promising for the Chifley Government after eighteen months of legal minefields and intensifying industrial disputes. In addition to all this, the government had lost in all states its referendum on 29 May 1948 to control rents and prices – which it had seen as a means to combat climbing inflation. In his biography of Chifley, David Day has commented that, in view of the anti–bank nationalisation campaign waged by Menzies and the opposition, 'the adverse vote was … a rejection of further socialisation and a poll on Chifley's plans for bank nationalisation'.[27] The Privy Council decision cemented the view that bank nationalisation was not for Australia. It left the Chifley

Government holding a smelly dead cat as it prepared for the polls.

The banking campaign was organised, well funded, strategic, and continued through 1949 and beyond. It also helped crystallise in the public's imagination a genuine worry that the Labor government had deliberate plans to 'socialise' Australia under an extreme left-wing, even communist, model. Gerard Henderson has argued that this view is to some extent unfair, if understandable.[28] The unions, heavily influenced by Communist Party (CPA) activists, were certainly part of the Labor network, but the Chifley Government also took on the communist-controlled Miners' Union in July 1949, when miners refused to mine coal – eventually sending in the army on 27 July. What's more, the unions controlled by the CPA had much to do with Labor's loss of government in December 1949. The CPA was no ally of the Labor government. Moreover, the activists who stood up to the left-wing–controlled unions were themselves Labor Party members – otherwise known as the Industrial Groups. That said, however, the Labor Party failed to offer leadership against the communist activists and, under pressure from its left-wing unions, once again broke into divided camps, with fractures that would continue and resurface in another party split for Labor during the 1950s. In 1949, only the Liberal/Country Party side of politics appeared consistently anti-communist.

From this, Menzies emerged as the leading opponent of the CPA and the communist-influenced unions. His views only hardened as union disruptions continued to batter away at industry through 1948–49. Heading to Europe with his wife Pattie and daughter Heather in June 1948 aboard a merchant ship, Menzies wrote to Ken of his antipathy to union activity in reaction to an autocratic and surly chief steward, whom he supposed to be a 'prominent official of the Norwegian Seamen's Union'. He concluded eventually that 'the more active a man is in union affairs the less competent he is in the affairs of his employer'.[29] That lengthy trip, from June to November 1948 – taken as much for Menzies' health[30] as for a need to make contact with Europe and America after the war – strengthened Menzies' resolve that socialisation needed to be resisted. From what he saw, he believed that the Attlee Government, with its nationalisation and social-welfare program, had not served the nation well. Writing to Ken from London, Menzies made a 'short observation' that included the comment:

> underneath a somewhat busy surface the true position of this country is rather alarming ... There is very little realisation among the mass of the people that the living standards and the social security and the Socialist experiments are being to a considerable extent financed by American loans [and] if the Americans were to cut off supplies there would be acute economic crisis ... the constant movement for greater and greater leisure is completely inconsistent with a real national attack upon a desperately serious economic problem.[31]

Country Party leader Artie Fadden recalled in his memoirs that 'On his return from overseas at the time of the Berlin blockade, when a war with Russia was feared, Menzies admitted that he saw Australian Communists as a fifth-column and he agreed that action should be taken to destroy the party'.[32]

After opting for no more than a forceful but reasoned opposition to the CPA's activities in 1946 and early in 1947, in December 1948 Menzies announced that the CPA could no longer be tolerated and that the Liberal Party would thenceforth advocate 'a complete ban upon the Communist Party and all other organisations which are Communist in aim and method'.[33] This decision, Gerard Henderson has argued, 'was a useful adjunct to Menzies' attack on the Chifley Government's attraction to socialism and regulation'.[34] Here was a renewed Menzies, but not only in personality. He had certainly matured as a leader and party administrator, even if he was still not a popular one. But more than this, the Robert Menzies who stood before Australians as the nation moved towards the federal election in 1949 was a leader fixed on a comprehensive platform. The Menzies vision certainly embraced the raw outlines of his 1942–43 radio lectures, but it also combined a contemporary view of liberalism that opposed a socialist program incorporating nationalisation and a welfare state. The Menzies vision would not impose a nanny state, but would offer moderate social benefits alongside a belief in individual merit.

Something of this developing commitment became clear in Menzies' articles sent back for publication during his trips abroad. He was away for many months, missing all the parliamentary sittings from September to December, including the budget sittings. With his lack of popular appeal, and the government's increasing woes on the industrial and banking fronts, Menzies' absence had no ill effect on the opposition's presence. And the Menzies' articles kept trickling in for ordinary news-gatherers at their offices and homes to register his continuing political campaigns against socialisation and disloyalty to the Empire and to the West in general, as the Cold War started to have a profound impact, with the Soviet advance across eastern and central Europe.

In a piece for the Melbourne *Herald*, Menzies argued for the British non-Labor parties to rethink their divisions and allow their unity to reshape British politics:

> the effect of a coming together of a non-socialist party would be tremendous. There would be a casting up of ideas, an invigorated policy, some new faces at least, new workers, a feeling that the burdens of the past had been thrown off and that the future was being attacked.[35]

This was a particularly Australian perspective. Menzies and the Liberals had refashioned Australia's non-Labor groups around new themes, still resonant in contemporary times. Sectional interests had combined – except for the rural Country Party, which would be a strong ally at the coming elections nonetheless – in a party platform endorsing the aspirations of individuals alongside moderate social benefits for the needy. In Britain, however, the Conservatives still represented and symbolised a landed minority with a legacy of indifference to social needs. The British Liberals, on the other hand, offered a middle way – one that Menzies recognised as bringing to the Conservatives something of his own Liberal Party of Australia. But without preferential voting, the non-Labor parts of British politics competed against each other. And this, for Menzies, was tantamount to allowing nationalisation and socialism take control of Britain:

> Many thousands of non-socialists who voted socialist at the last election 'for a change' will do so again rather than restore the Conservative Party. This is a dangerous state of affairs for all of us, for the nationalisation of iron and steel will doubtless be only the first of a series of production disasters.

Increasingly, Menzies' argument was couched in language opposed to socialism in all its aspects. Addressing the American Australian Association in New York in October 1948, Menzies urged a strengthening of the US–British Empire relationship in the light of a worsening scenario in Europe with parallels to 1938–39, as the 'Kremlin' imposed what Menzies called 'unlawful power'. Menzies urged Americans to stay with 'the enlightened self-interest of the Marshall Plan', adding that 'a permanently impoverished Britain would leave America facing a world pregnant with war'. 'You are vital to us', he told his American audience, 'and we are vital to you'.[36]

The postwar world was rapidly taking on new boundaries – the British Empire had begun to disintegrate with indigenous independence movements, while the Cold War had realigned former war allegiances. The schism between controlled economies and market-driven economies was widening. In Australia, a sense of unease over government control of industry and finance was also now resonating with ordinary households. The Chifley Government had captured many with expanded social benefits and wage increases, but inflation was eating at incomes and strikes had begun to threaten employment security – it has been calculated that more than a million working days were lost in New South Wales between 1945 and 1949 due to strikes.[37] Across Australia, working days lost on the waterfront more than doubled between 1944 and 1945 – from 35 178 to 77 969.[38] Meanwhile, with wartime insecurities abating, government control of so many aspects of life was no longer so welcome. Petrol rationing had become a huge issue.

It was indeed the right moment for the non-Labor side of politics to take a lead, but more was needed. Menzies' cautionary article on the need for greater cooperation between the British Conservatives and UK Liberals held lessons for his own side at home. The Liberal and Country Party candidates at elections drained the message by competing with each other rather than offering an all-out effort to defeat Labor. It was time for the Liberal Party in New South Wales and Victoria to work more closely with its Country Party allies.

Dick Casey, as Liberal Party federal president, floated this aim at the NSW State Council meeting in August 1948 but was told by the NSW state president, Bill Spooner, that his division would not be negotiating with the Country Party – the territorial mindset seemed set in stone. In the Country Party's annual report for 1948, its general secretary commented that the party had been 'the subject of an amalgamation blitz by the Liberal

Party in the year under review'.[39] In February 1949, Menzies wrote to Bill Spooner, who was under pressure in the Federal Executive over NSW intransigence regarding the Country Party. Menzies was very clear, saying, 'It would in our view be unfortunate if we approached the election in a state of open conflict with the Country Party. It would be equally unfortunate if there should be unresolved but acute differences of opinion between the parliamentary members and the organisation'.[40] The Country Party was ready to negotiate, meeting Spooner on 18 February and reaching an agreement: 'there would be just three triangular contests, a four-member joint Senate ticket for three winnable positions with the Liberals taking the first, second and fourth places, and a standing committee consisting of three representatives from each side to facilitate co-operation during the federal campaign'.[41] It would be the start not only of a professional and united election campaign for non-Labor but also a formal coalition that would stand the test of time over the coming six decades and beyond.

A perfect landing

For the non-Labor side of Australian politics, the federal election campaign of November–December 1949 was merely the last weeks of a campaign that had been ongoing since 1947 and the introduction of Chifley's Banking Bill. By the time of the election, the divisions between the Liberal and Country parties had been sorted out and the organisation of the new Liberal Party structure was well under way. This had meant an exhausting few years for party leaders and officials. At the end of 1947, Menzies had been warned of health problems and recovered only by taking off on a sea voyage to spend months in Europe and North America, using earnings from articles written for newspapers and journals to help fund the trip.[42] Within two weeks of the election campaign opening in November, newspapers were reporting that Menzies had lost his voice on the election trail in Brisbane and had to cancel two speeches he was to make in Sydney.[43]

But the tide was flowing the coalition's way. Menzies opened the Coalition campaign in Melbourne on 10 November, promising to fight socialism and all its works and pomps, dissolve the CPA, amend the constitution so that nationalisation of industry and finance would never be possible in Australia, end petrol rationing, give child endowment to the first child, build up coal reserves and offer incentives to miners to boost the coal industry. In stark contrast, Chifley opened his campaign a few days later making no significant promises and simply asking the electorate to judge Labor on its record and its ability so it could continue to build Australia. To the swinging voter, that Labor record was not so good. A Gallup poll of voters taken during the campaign indicated that 8 per cent were planning to switch from voting Labor in 1946 to Liberal in 1949. Of these, two-thirds gave bank nationalisation as a reason.[44] Menzies continued to address spill-over meetings far and wide, the crowds outside as big as those inside.

Polling day was Saturday 10 December. The following Monday, newspaper headlines across Australia gave the election to the Liberal/Country Party coalition of Bob Menzies in a landslide. An electoral redistribution of seats between 1946 and 1949 meant that in the 1949 House of Representatives election there were forty-seven new seats to be won. When all the votes had been counted, Labor would hold forty-seven seats in the new House of Representatives, the Liberals fifty-five seats and the Country Party nineteen seats. The increase in the number of Liberal Party MPs was significant. Just seventeen Liberals had sat in the House of Representatives after the 1946 election. In the Senate, the Liberal/Country Party coalition improved its numbers substantially, owing to the introduction of proportional representation and the added new seats. Yet Labor retained control of the Senate, owing to its vast majority of fifteen to three elected in 1946 under the old Senate voting system. With only half the Senate up for election, Labor had the advantage in spite of the swing against it. The Senate numbers after the 1949 election were thirty-four for Labor and twenty-six for the Liberal/Country Party coalition – a situation that would lead within a little over a year to a double dissolution over the failure to pass legislation to overturn the Banking Act of 1945.

It was a sublime moment for Menzies as he absorbed the victory of 1949, at the head of a new political party and a new political coalition with the Country Party (on a footing of mutual respect but where the Liberal Party would never again play second fiddle), and with a House majority big enough to gamble on a dissolution of the two houses if the Labor's Senate majority proved unworkable. Yet the triumph took a day to sink in properly with the exhausted leader. Interviewed for the front page of the Melbourne *Argus* on 12 December by Dulcie Foard, Menzies cut the weary figure of a man who may just have emerged from the battlefield a hero, but was still sobered by the shock of too much action.

The Argus ran three photos above the small piece by Foard, all taken at a press conference the day before. They featured three profile shots of Menzies looking down in different moments, his face drawn, his eyes closed and his chin propped on a hand, exhausted. No smiles there – just the strain of past years. The cliché 'So happy; So tired!' headed the article. 'I'm in a bit of a coma today', said Menzies:

> I'm only mildly excited yet. I should be home in bed. After a
> night's sleep I'll probably begin to take in what's happened –
> about halfway through tomorrow. I didn't get to bed until 3am,
> after struggling with figures. And I'm not ashamed to confess

that I stayed in bed all the morning – and let the world
go by …

Then he had got up and spent the rest of the day taking telephone calls, being photographed and speaking to his electorate
committee to thank them for helping him win Kooyong with an
even greater majority after his record win in 1946.

On Tuesday 13 December, Ben Chifley handed his resignation to the governor-general, William McKell. Two days later,
Robert Menzies, the leader so many for so long had said would
never lead his team into government again, presented himself at
Government House to receive his commission as Australia's new
prime minister. Menzies had promised and, like all new prime
ministers, must now deliver. But what no one could have imagined, as Menzies took the oath of office and returned to Melbourne to settle his Cabinet, was that not only had he won but
he would go on winning for another sixteen years and retire at
a time of his own choosing, undefeated. The 'bleeding' Robert
Menzies had spoken of in August 1941 had lasted less than a
decade and was not to return.

Conclusion
The long peace

In his inaugural RG Menzies Lecture in 1970, former Menzies colleague and occasional critic Percy Spender reflected on the nature of 'Liberalism' as the governing force of the party and governments established under Robert Menzies. 'The people's choice of government is not just a question of political performance of the party in power', Spender said. 'More critically, it is a choice between the kind of political and economic society they presently know – perhaps take for granted – and the kind of society under which they will live if the party out of power gains the reins of government'.[1]

Menzies retook the reins of government in December 1949 and retired as prime minister on Australia Day in 1966. By the time he retired – a rarity for any Australian prime minister – he had outlasted many rivals and, metaphorically speaking, buried quite a few opponents. He had seen off Labor leader Bert Evatt and all but ended the Labor leadership of Arthur Calwell. Among colleagues from his 1949 Cabinet, just Harold Holt and Jack McEwen remained in the parliament. Prime Minister Menzies Mark 2 had lived to overcome many of the failings of Prime Minister Menzies Mark 1, yet this was not all that contributed to such longevity at the national helm. The play of politics from 1949 to 1955 had a lot to do with the success of the second Menzies era.

As it turned out, Labor contributed greatly to Robert Menzies' success. Percy Spender had accurately suggested, in his

RG Menzies Lecture, that electors choose according to their economic and political best interests. Since Federation, Australia's political collectives had only gradually evolved. Splits and splinterings in political groupings meant that diverse party organisations often fielded candidates at elections. The major non-Labor party would find success, eventually, in a coalition with the Country Party. In bringing together the fractured remnants of the UAP in the mid-1940s and its breakaway political groupings, Menzies and his team had also created a blueprint for a majority conservative alliance that would stand the test of time.

On the side of Labor, the party created so early to serve the worker, a struggle would ensue over decades to contain or control influences from outside the party. In its earliest years, Labor banned its members from belonging to outside organisations with any sort of political association, but it would be the growing influence of the CPA, tolerated within sections of the union movement, that would deliver a killer blow to Labor in the 1950s. And it was a battle anyone could have seen coming, well before the stable Labor years of the Chifley Government.

Hal GP Colebatch has documented, in *Australia's Secret War: How Unionists Sabotaged Our Troops in World War II*, how a dogged belief among a majority of waterside unionists that the war effort was just another capitalist enterprise to be attacked (even after the end of the Nazi–Soviet Pact in June 1941) developed from a CPA influence unchecked on the docks for more than a decade. The war between capital and labour had morphed into an international vendetta to undermine democratic and Western governments.

Between 1939 and the late 1940s, the governments of Menzies, Curtin and Chifley had baulked at tackling union blackmail on the wharves. Each leader was in fear of the unionists offering worse if they did. Such action was out of control by 1942 – with sabotage of military operations and damage to equipment on the docks. Hal GP Colebatch has recorded witness after witness who related how groups of wharfies damaged vital supplies, delayed repair work on vessels or deliberately upset operations – in some cases costing the lives of Australian servicemen. Milne Bay is but one example:

> As Japanese forces attacked Milne Bay in 1942, and Australia and America tried to rush reinforcements to the aid of the troops holding on there, Townsville watersiders went on strike to prevent munitions being loaded ... A small group of US Army personnel ... eventually threw the watersiders off the wharf and loaded the guns themselves. By that time the rest of the convoy had sailed. The guns reached Milne Bay too late.[2]

Other waterside strikes were found to have left aircraft gun barrels for Milne Bay without mountings while watersiders in Townsville sabotaged radio sets. Such incidents became routine on wharves around Australia throughout the war years, leaving ordinary Australians at war not only abroad, but also at home.

In many industries, militant trade unionism continued to erode the authority of state and federal governments. It was on the back of the huge number of working days lost to strikes that Menzies eventually made his push for government in 1948–49. Ben Chifley had finally called in the military to break a long-running communist-led coalminers strike in July 1949, but only as a federal election loomed and his prospects of winning were rapidly declining. After his election win in December, Menzies would invoke the Crimes Act in 1950 after unions returned to their corrosive round of strike action against his government.

In all of this, the one side of politics that stood rock solid against the emerging cold war of hard-left unions against 'capitalist' Australia was the Liberal and Country parties. Within the

Labor Party, by the late 1940s, anti-communist members and unionists had begun to organise opposition to the efforts of their militant and communist-influenced colleagues. Led by figures such as Victorians John Mullens and Stan Keon (both Catholics and federal MPs), and union leaders such as the (non-Catholic) Federated Ironworkers' Laurie Short, these 'Groupers' had limited but significant success.[3] What they lacked, however, was open support from the Labor leadership.

Bert Evatt was elected to the Labor leadership after Chifley's death in June 1951. While he was believed, more than other Labor leaders, to sympathise in part with Labor's anti-communist groups, Evatt saw his finest hour as leading the 1951 campaign to defeat Menzies' referendum on giving the federal government powers to deal with the CPA. This led to open criticism from the opponents of communists within the party. Before long, Evatt was hastily trying to patch his differences with Labor's anti-communists, and duchessing Archbishop Mannix's man, BA Santamaria, at a private meeting in Melbourne's Hotel Windsor, where Evatt elaborated on what he would do on becoming prime minister after the election.[4] There were other meetings, and a phone call during which Evatt asked Santamaria to write his 1954 election speech.

Labor would, however, narrowly lose the 1954 election. The Menzies Government had easily won its double-dissolution election in 1951 but had subsequently lost ground after Evatt was installed as Labor leader and the referendum on control of the CPA was defeated. Then the economy began to improve, while the intensifying Korean War refocused people's attention on the dangers of communism. The drama surrounding the defection of Soviet couple Vladimir and Evdokia Petrov in April 1954 added to the feeling of communism's menace, especially as pictures of Mrs Petrov being manhandled onto a plane by Soviet agents at Sydney's Mascot airport were splashed across newspapers. Evatt also found himself being asked during the election campaign where the money was coming from for a pensions policy he could not fund. And then there was the royal tour of Australia by the new young Queen Elizabeth II and her husband Prince Philip, which lasted fifty-eight days from 3 February 1954. The celebrations that accompanied the couple's visits to all states and territories added to the warm feelings of good times around the nation. It was estimated that around 75 per cent of Australians caught sight of or watched ceremonies with the royal couple as they toured.

In the political climate that followed Labor's loss at the 1954 election, the division in Labor could only get worse. At its apex was a leader whose vanity and erratic behaviour made him a most unsuitable personality to deal with a party about to implode. Paul Hasluck worked closely with Evatt when recruited to the staff of the Department of External Affairs in 1941. Hasluck took Evatt's measure shrewdly at the time, summing him up in an interview long after as a politician who 'could have been on whichever side gave him the opportunity'.[5] As such, in his efforts to become prime minister in 1954, Evatt had played both sides within Labor only to lose the prize. Soon after, looking for a scapegoat, he blamed anti-communist Labor figures for the 1954 election loss, along with the outside influence of BA Santamaria, Melbourne's Archbishop Mannix and their Catholic Social Studies Movement. The outside influence of the CPA, meanwhile, was left unmentioned. Evatt had come to embody something of what Labor would itself soon seem to be: caught between rather than able to reconcile two ideologically motivated groups. In fact, it was Evatt's extraordinary use in parliament of information given to him by the Soviet foreign minister, Vyacheslav Molotov, while arguing his case against the government over the Petrov Royal Commission in late 1954, that sealed his fate with Labor's anti-communists.

The Labor split of the mid-1950s would begin in Victoria after eleven anti-communist Labor MPs crossed the floor of the Legislative Assembly to vote with the opposition on 19 April 1955. Their action would lead to the defeat of the Cain Labor Government at the election that followed. Soon after the Victorian defection, seven Labor MPs crossed the floor in the House of Representatives. The ripple effect saw the formation in 1957 of a new national Labor party, to be called the Democratic Labor Party (DLP). For nearly two decades, the DLP would attract a significant slab of Australian voters who, in a disciplined way, would preference the Coalition ahead of Labor at forthcoming elections. In this way, the DLP delivered Robert Menzies a comfortable term in the Lodge and almost certainly saved him from defeat in 1961.

Robert Menzies' resignation as prime minister in 1941 had much to do with the machinations of Labor's Bert Evatt, who had spurred the party on to 'play politics' at a time of national crisis. More than a decade later, however, it would be a case of tables turned. This left Robert Menzies as victor not only in his personal war to retain and then regain the prime ministership over the decade from 1939 to 1949, but also over his long-time foe Bert Evatt, whose demise brought down Labor. From this, Menzies would emerge, unchallenged as a national leader, at peace with himself, his party and his nation.

Appendix

Menzies' account of his 1941 resignation

<u>MOST SECRET</u>

1st September 1941

It cannot be frequently that one has the experience of resigning the Prime Ministership of one's country, and in order that I shall have some record of the circumstances I am setting them down while they are fresh in the memory.

The position of the Government has been very precarious; 36 all on the floor of the House, with the majority depending upon Wilson.

Hutchinson, McCall and Marr have been bitterly hostile, and with a Budget in the offing there has been every possibility of a fatal attack by Labour [sic].

The newspapers, notably the 'Sydney Morning Herald' and the Murdoch group, have been extremely hostile to me, the former blatantly and crudely, the latter with a little more subtlety, praising me and killing me in the same breath, the technique being that of the skilled slaughterman who calls attention to the beauties of the beast just as he strikes it down.

On 21st August we had a Cabinet meeting at Canberra. The aggressive wing of the Labour Party had become more active, partly as a result of newspaper encouragement, but primarily because of increasing hostilities and disloyalties on the Government side.

I informed my colleagues that my own view was that only one course was feasible, and that was for me to tender my resignation to the Governor-General and advise him to send for Mr. Curtin.

I pointed out that it was better to have Labour in without an election and under circumstances which enabled us to control them from the Opposition benches than after an election at which they would probably have a sweeping majority and go back for a three years' term.

This view, involving as it did, the sacrifice of Ministerial office, was received with horror, and I have no doubt that it was at this moment that the determination to remove me became crystallised.

Spooner then raised once more the question of making an offer of a National Government.

Page supported this strongly, saying that he felt that the thing of greatest urgency was for me to be sent to London to put urgent pressure on the British Government to send Capital ships to Singapore; and that the formation of a National Government would give a foundation for such an expedition which nothing else could provide.

I said that I was prepared to serve the country abroad if political stability could be secured, but that in my opinion the only real foundation for political stability was agreement between the Parties. I said that I would draft a letter to Curtin, making the offer, which is in fact set out in that letter.

This was unanimously approved and indeed described as most generous.

I then drafted the letter, took it into a joint meeting of the Government parties, where it was received with universal enthusiasm, Marr leaping to his feet and expressing his desire to propose a vote of approval and of confidence – which I said was unnecessary having regard to the obvious approval in the room. (A few days later, when my offer had been rejected, Marr had the effrontery in a joint Party meeting to describe my offer as 'a great mistake'.)

The letter went to Curtin on 22nd August, and to the press. The reactions which followed were curious. I think that most private citizens felt impressed by the fact that the Government, which still commanded more support in both Houses than the Opposition, should offer the Opposition half the seats in Cabinet, including the Prime Ministership.

But the majority of newspapers, addicted by this time to a miserable and ungenerous habit of mind, made little of the offer and directed their scribes at Canberra to write of it as if it were merely a new move in a somewhat tortuous party game.

On Monday, August 25th, Fadden rang me and said that as the Labour Party was meeting on the following day at Canberra to consider my offer he thought Ministers should be there to deal promptly with anything arising out of the reply.

Accordingly, I got in touch with all Ministers, suggesting that as many as could conveniently do so should be in Canberra for Tuesday afternoon. The notice was so short that McLeay, Abbott, McDonald and Eric Harrison (whose wife was then seriously ill; she died later in the week) were not able to be present.

The Labour Party's meeting was called for 3 p.m. Their executive had met in the morning and had drafted a reply for approval by the Party.

I met my Ministers at 2.30 p.m.

The proceedings began by me saying that as we would no doubt get the Labour reply that evening, we should endeavour to clarify our minds as to what we were to do in the event of the reply being unfavourable.

The first two Ministers to speak were Holt and Foll. Holt said that he thought the circumstances required candour and that, greatly as he admired my work, he felt bound to say that the prospects of Government success would be enhanced if there were a new Prime Minister. He suggested that Fadden would fill this office appropriately.

Foll, who had just returned from the Netherlands East Indies, said that my unpopularity in New South Wales and Queensland was such as to be a fatal handicap to the Government should an election come.

He criticised the newspapers for causing much of the difficulty and said that unhappily politics were proving too strong for statesmanship; he made it clear that so far as he was concerned a change in leadership was the only course.

At this stage – at about 3.35 p.m. – Curtin's reply to me arrived. It had been apparently promptly accepted without debate in the Labour Caucus.

We then resumed our own discussion. I wanted to get at the truth and explained at once to my colleagues that I desired complete frankness and that I was not going to give way to any personal feelings on a matter which seemed to me to call for completely objective treatment.

Thereupon, Page expressed the view that the right course was for another leader to take over the Government and for me to be sent to England as a Minister of State.

McEwen, with expression of personal regret, plumped unhesitatingly for a change of leadership, as did Collins and Anthony.

Spender took the same view, though he had the grace to say that nothing was more unpleasant for him because he owed the whole of his own political advancement to me.

At this stage Holt interrupted and said that he felt the same embarrassment because personally he owed everything in his political life to me.

I reassured them by saying that I was not taking anything that was being said as a personal attack, but that all I wanted to get at was the truth of their political view.

Spooner said that he favoured a change of leadership, as did Hughes, who had been somewhat quieter than usual, but whose desire to get rid of me was as clearly indicated as usual.

McBride, Collett, Leckie and Stewart stood firm, and strongly countered the suggestion that a change of this kind would serve any purpose. Leckie put it crudely but effectively when he told the others that what they were proposing to do was to try to placate their political enemies by cutting off their head and grovelling on their stomach.

I knew that when the absent Ministers arrived, Abbott would favour the Country Party view while I felt that I could rely on the complete loyalty of McLeay, Harrison and McDonald.

Fadden, throughout these discussions, said very little but renewed and reiterated his affirmation of loyalty to myself.

At about 5 p.m. I adjourned the Cabinet until 8.30 p.m., saying that I wanted to consider my position and that as I was still the principal actor in the drama, I must pay some attention to my lines, even though they appeared to fall in the 5th act of the play.

I then went back to the Lodge and went for a long walk with my wife. We unhesitatingly agreed that as my political leadership clearly rested upon nothing better than quicksands, I should resign. Leckie, who came for dinner, agreed. I rang up my father in Melbourne and left him at the other end of the telephone breathing threatenings and slaughter. He, in fact, at once convened one of our famous family conferences, which reached conclusions similar to my own.

At 8.30 the Cabinet met. I said – 'the discussion this afternoon has shown that I have forfeited the confidence of a majority of my colleagues'. Holt at once interrupted to say that he thought that was an unfair way of putting it. I replied: 'I am not talking about personal confidence but about political confidence, and surely it is clear that a Prime Minister whose colleagues feel he should cease to be Prime Minister because somebody else can more effectively lead has lost the political confidence of those serving under him.'

I then went on to say that the normal procedure in such a case would be for me to take the resignation of all those Ministers who had declared themselves against me.

At this point I paused for 15 or 20 seconds – and the effect was almost ludicrous. However, I went on to say that while such a course would be the correct one in time of peace, I did not propose to adopt it in time of war, because clearly it would completely split the Ministerial parties and ensure a Labour administration for a long time.

I said that I was not prepared to contribute to such a result because, while I had high regard for Curtin, I felt that many of his followers – and those the most active – were very dubiously British; were half-hearted about the war, and would lack the moral stamina to see it through. I said therefore that I thought that the lesser of two evils was for me to drop out of the picture. Therefore –

1   I would resign the Prime Ministership
2   I would go right out of the Cabinet, believing that the unpopu-
     larity attaching to me would continue to pursue any Govern-
     ment in which I was a leading member, and
3   I would certainly not go to London under existing circum-
     stances because I felt that the worst possible ambassador for
     Australia abroad would be a Prime Minister who had just lost
     the confidence of his own Government and Parliament.

I added that the new leader should not be nominated in the Cabinet itself but should be chosen by the joint Ministerial Parties and be promised unanimous support.

This pronouncement caused a sensation.

Spender, Holt and Collins felt that if I were not to go to London the whole position should be reconsidered.

I did not agree to this. I had heard their true views in the afternoon and it was absurd to think that I should forget them and carry on as if nothing had happened.

I assured the Cabinet that they would suffer no embarrassment from the manner in which I would handle the matter.

Discussion then arose as to whether the change should take place before the meeting of the House on the Wednesday.

McEwen and Anthony felt very strongly that it should, but most of us were clear that to change the leadership in the middle of the Supply Debate was merely to invite the Labour Party to attack, and that under these circumstances the new leader might well enjoy a record short term of office as Prime Minister.

On the morning of Wednesday the 27th, we met in Cabinet at 10 a.m. and it was agreed that my move should not be taken until after Parliament had disposed of the business in hand, i.e., the Supply Bill and the Adjournment.

At a joint Party meeting held at 11 a.m. it was agreed after some discussion that everybody should stand behind the Government the next day or two and that any of our troubles should be thrashed out thereafter.

Hutchinson and Marr indicated they wanted to raise the question of leadership.

McCall said that he would decline to support any government of which I was Prime Minister and offered the pleasing sentiment that he would select his own time at which and ground on which to bring the Government down.

The Supply Debate went on for the rest of the day and evening, and the House adjourned until Thursday at 2.30 p.m.

On Thursday morning the Labour Party had a Caucus at which there was fierce debate about launching an immediate attack.

Personally I hoped that they would, for such an attack would have clarified the political atmosphere and would, I thought, have put us in a better tactical position than a postponement of the attack until after the Budget.

But shrewd counsels prevailed in the Labour Party and the move to attack me was rejected.

As soon as Parliament adjourned in the late afternoon I called the Cabinet together and reiterated my former statement of my intentions, omitting, however, my previous statement regarding not serving in the new Cabinet.

There was a good deal of disturbance of mind, several Ministers feeling very sick about the position they had got into.

Their feelings were not improved by hearing the voice of Eric Harrison, who had specially driven up from Sydney, and Allan McDonald. Eric's speech was the best I ever heard him make. It was full of genuine feeling. There were no superfluous words in it.

He literally trounced disloyalty and fear and passionately urged me to fight the matter in the Party room and with the people.

I acknowledged his great support but pointed out that while a fight would be personally satisfactory to myself it could not possibly do the Government any good and could only contribute to a sweeping Labour victory.

We met again after dinner when I said that after much reflection I had reached the conclusion that if my resignation was to have any National value I must set an example of service by offering to serve in the new Government, though I realised all the difficulties associated with it.

I pointed out to my Country Party colleagues that as I owed the Prime Ministership to the fact that I was the leader of the U.A.P. I must first inform my own Party of my position and that we could then have a joint Party meeting.

Accordingly the U.A.P. met at 9.30 p.m. and I announced my intended resignation. At the same time I asked for and obtained an assurance that all members would be willing to support loyally a new leader chosen by a joint meeting.

Several Members spoke in terms of strong regret about the developments.

Arthur Coles, who up to 24 hours before had been among my most acid critics, suddenly became so warm a supporter that he swept out of the room, announcing his resignation from the Party.

On the motion of [William] Jolly, a resolution thanking me for my services, was carried. Many members of the Party were plainly stunned and upset by what was happening but there was no real attempt to discourage me from the indicated course.

The Country Party Members were then sent for, and on their arrival, nominations being called for, Hutchinson and Marr nominated Fadden. There were no other nominations and so Fadden was unanimously elected.

I then issued a statement to the press, and went home.

The statement was as follows: –

'In my recent offer to the Opposition I indicated that, to secure an all-Party administration, I was prepared to vacate the Prime Ministership. The offer was rejected.

'It follows that the next task was to get the greatest possible stability and cohesion on the Government side of the House.

'A frank discussion with my colleagues in the Cabinet has shown that while they have personal goodwill towards me, many of them feel that I am unpopular with large sections of the press and the people, that this unpopularity handicaps the effectiveness of the Government by giving rise to misrepresentation and misunderstanding of its activities, and that there are divisions of opinion in the Government parties themselves which would not or might not exist under another leader.

'It is not for me to be the judge of these matters, except to this extent: that I do believe that my relinquishing of the leadership will offer a real prospect of unity in the ranks of the Government parties. Under these circumstances, and having regard to the great emergencies of war, my own feelings must be set aside.

'I therefore invited the two parties to select another leader. They have unanimously chosen Mr. Fadden. Accordingly tomorrow I shall resign the Prime Ministership, and advise His Excellency to commission Mr. Fadden.

'The only stipulation made was this: that every man in both Parties must be prepared to give his wholehearted support, as I shall, to the new leader. This was accepted with one accord. But for it, my own resignation would have been futile and the vital interests of our country would not have been faithfully served. I am prepared to set an example in this matter of loyal service by accepting Cabinet office under Mr. Fadden if he so desires.

'I earnestly hope that my present action may help to enable government to be carried on without discord at a time when the nation urgently needs harmony in its own ranks.

'I lay down the Prime Ministership with natural regret. For years I have given of my best to the service of the country, and especially during the two years of war foundations have been laid and a national effort achieved in which I hope I shall be permitted to take proper pride.'

On the following morning, Friday the 29th August, I resigned, and recommended that Fadden be sent for.

Melbourne.
1/9/41.

Notes

Abbreviations

AGPS   Australian Government Printing Service
AWM   Australian War Memorial
CAC   Commonwealth Aircraft Corporation
CPD   *Commonwealth Parliamentary Debates*
H of R   House of Representatives
LAC   Library and Archives Canada
NAA   National Archives of Australia
NLA   National Library of Australia

Introduction: The Menzies history wars

1   Hasluck, Paul, *The Government and the People, 1939–1941*, AWM, Canberra, 1952, pp. 558–65.
2   Hasluck, *The Government and the People, 1939–1941*, p. 564
3   Day, David, *Menzies and Churchill at War: A Controversial New Account of the 1941 Struggle for Power*, Angus & Robertson, Sydney, 1986.
4   Steve Jodrell (director & writer), John Moore (producer & lead writer), Mick Cummins (writer), *Menzies and Churchill at War*, Screen Australia & 360 Degree Films, 2008, see 360degreefilms.com.au/productions/menzies-and-churchill-at-war.
5   This thesis has caught the imagination over time, even being repeated in John Charmley's biography of Churchill, *Churchill: The End of Glory* (Hodder & Stoughton, London, 1993, p. 444), using David Day's book as its sole supporting evidence.
6   Interview of Lord Carrington by Anne Henderson, House of Lords, 23 January 2013.
7   There is a different spelling for the surname Carington (one 'r') and the title Lord Carrington (two 'r's).
8   Henderson, Heather, *A Smile for My Parents*, Allen & Unwin, Sydney, 2013, pp. 115–16.
9   Menzies, Robert Gordon, *Afternoon Light: Some Memoirs of Men and Events*, Cassell, Melbourne, 1967, p. 56.
10   Brett, Judith, *Robert Menzies' Forgotten People*, Pan Macmillan, Sydney 1992.
11   'Allan Martin on Judith Brett and psychological history', *Sydney Institute Quarterly*, no. 32, March 2008, p. 27.
12   Heather Henderson edited a collection of her father's letters for publication in 2011, titled *Letters to My Daughter: Robert Menzies, Letters, 1955–1975* (Murdoch Books, Sydney, 2011).
13   Macintyre, Stuart, *A Concise History of Australia*, 3rd edn, Cambridge University Press, Melbourne, 2009, p. 215.
14   Research by Peter Hruby for *The Courier-Mail*, quoted in a letter from Peter

Kelly published in *The Australian*, 29 January 2013.

15 Aarons, Mark, *The Family File*, Black Inc., Melbourne, 2010, p. 94.
16 Carr, Bob, 'Communism and the labour movement', *Sydney Papers Online*, no. 12, 24 May 2011, www.thesydneyinstitute.com.au/publications/the-sydney-papers-online/page/13.

1   Nadir
1 Menzies, Robert Gordon, 'To the men of Ulster', *To the People of Britain at War from the Prime Minister of Australia: Speeches Delivered in Great Britain in 1941*, Longmans, London, p. 67.
2 'Most Secret – 1st September 1941', Papers of Sir Robert Menzies, NLA, MS 4936, Box 582, Folder 4.
3 Cable, Robert Menzies to Winston Churchill, 8 September 1941, Papers of Sir Robert Menzies, NLA, MS 4936, Box 581, Folder 20.
4 'Resignation of Mr Robert Menzies as Prime Minister; and possibility of his standing for Parliament in the United Kingdom', UK National Archives, PREM DO 121/50.
5 Interview of Geoffrey Blainey by Anne Henderson, Melbourne, 2 March 2013.
6 *The Road to El Alamein: Churchill's Desert Campaign* (television documentary), BBC TWO, aired 5 November 2012, see www.bbc.co.uk/programmes/b01nts8p.
7 Cable, Menzies to Churchill, 8 August 1941, Papers of Sir Robert Menzies, NLA, MS 4936 Box 581, Folder 28.
8 Cable, Menzies to Churchill, 8 August 1941.
9 Hasluck, *The Government and the People, 1939–1941*, pp. 532–33.
10 'Resignation of Mr Robert Menzies as Prime Minister'.
11 'Resignation of Mr Robert Menzies as Prime Minister'.
12 'Resignation of Mr Robert Menzies as Prime Minister'.
13 'Resignation of Mr Robert Menzies as Prime Minister'.
14 Menzies, *Afternoon Light*, p. 57.
15 Menzies, *Afternoon Light*, p. 61.

2   The clan and its legacy
1 Henderson, Heather, *A Smile for My Parents*, p. 1.
2 Blainey, Geoffrey, *Gold and Paper: A History of the National Bank of Australasia Limited*, Georgian House, Melbourne, 1958, p. 177.
3 Menzies, *Afternoon Light*, p. 7
4 Menzies, *Afternoon Light*, p. 8.
5 Menzies, *Afternoon Light*, p. 8.
6 Brett, *Robert Menzies' Forgotten People*, p. 205.
7 Martin, AW, 'Menzies the man', in Scott Prasser, JR Nethercote & John Warhurst (eds), *The Menzies Era: A Reappraisal of Government, Politics and Policy*, Hale & Iremonger, Sydney, 1995, p. 21.
8 Henderson, Heather, *A Smile for My Parents*, p. 6.
9 Perkins, Kevin, *Menzies: Last of the Queen's Men*, Rigby, Adelaide, 1968, p. 134.
10 Q&A section, speech by Heather Henderson, Sydney Institute, 23 October 2013, www.thesydneyinstitute.com.au/podcast/remembering-sir-robert-and-dame-pattie-mezies.
11 This episode is extensively covered in Henderson, Anne, *Joseph Lyons: The People's Prime Minister*, NewSouth Publishing, Sydney, 2011.
12 Brett, *Robert Menzies' Forgotten People*, p. 173.
13 Brett, *Robert Menzies' Forgotten People*, p. 175.

14 Dawes, Allan, 'Typescripts relating to Robert Menzies', NLA, MS 8792.
15 Notes by Paul Hasluck for a review of Kevin Perkins' *Menzies: Last of the Queen's Men*, sent to Allan Martin by Nicholas Hasluck, AW Martin Collection, NLA, MS 9802, Box 7.
16 Notes by Paul Hasluck.
17 Notes by Paul Hasluck.
18 Martin, AW, *Robert Menzies: A Life*, vol. 1, 1894–1943, Melbourne University Press, Melbourne, 1993, pp. 33–35.
19 Joske, Percy, *Sir Robert Menzies 1894–1978: A New, Informal Memoir*, Angus & Robertson, Sydney, 1978, p. 26.
20 Interview of Professor Geoffrey Blainey by Anne Henderson, Melbourne, 2 March 2013.
21 Joske, *Sir Robert Menzies 1894–1978*, p. 7.
22 Menzies, 'To the men of Ulster', p. 65.
23 Martin, *Robert Menzies*, vol. 1, p. 14.
24 Joske, *Sir Robert Menzies 1894–1978*, p. 5.
25 Martin, *Robert Menzies*, vol. 1, p. 30.
26 *CPD*, H of R, vol. 159, p. 19.
27 Seth, Ronald, *R.G. Menzies*, Cassell, London, 1960, p. 60.
28 Letter, Robert Menzies to Ken Menzies, 18 February 1943, supplied by Heather Henderson from the Menzies family collection.
29 Letter, Robert Menzies to Ken Menzies, 5 June 1945, Menzies family collection.
30 Letter, Frank Menzies to Robert Menzies, 5 May 1942, Menzies family collection.
31 Seth, *R.G. Menzies*, p. 57.
32 Letter, Robert Menzies to Ken Menzies, 2 September 1943, Menzies family collection.

3 Last days of appeasement

1   Blake, Robert, 'How Churchill became prime minister', in Robert Blake & William Roger Louis (eds), *Churchill: A Major New Assessment of His Life in Peace and War*, WW Norton & Co., New York, 1993, p. 258.
2   Langmore, Diane, *Glittering Surfaces: A Life of Maie Casey*, Allen & Unwin, Sydney, 1997, p. 59.
3   *The Argus*, 19 April 1939, p. 1.
4   Martin, *Robert Menzies*, vol. 1, p. 270.
5   Earle Page gives a personal account of his moves against Menzies in his memoir *Truant Surgeon: The Inside Story of Forty Years of Australian Political Life*, edited by Anne Mozley, Angus & Robertson, Sydney, 1963, pp. 270–78.
6   Notes by Paul Hasluck, sent to AW Martin by Nicholas Hasluck, Papers of Allan Martin, NLA, MS 9802, Box 7.
7   Lyons, Enid, *Among the Carrion Crows*, Rigby, Australia, 1972, p. 65; Henderson, Anne, *Joseph Lyons*, pp. 424–25.
8   Page, *Truant Surgeon*, pp. 275–78.
9   *CPD*, H of R, vol. 159, p. 20.
10 Souter, Gavin, *Acts of Parliament: A Narrative History of the Senate and House of Representatives, Commonwealth of Australia*, Melbourne University Press, Melbourne, 1988, p. 319.
11 *CPD*, H of R, vol. 159, p. 15.
12 Letter, Helen Page to Ken Menzies, 1979, Menzies family collection.
13 Tink, Andrew, *Air Disaster Canberra: The Plane Crash that Destroyed a*

Government, NewSouth Publishing, Sydney, 2013, p. 76.

14 Davey, Paul, *The Nationals: The Progressive, Country and National Party in New South Wales 1919 to 2006*, Federation Press, Sydney, 2006, pp. 129–30.

15 Menzies, *Afternoon Light*, pp. 13–14.

16 Cited in Hasluck, *The Government and the People, 1939–1941*, p. 88.

17 *CPD*, H of R, vol. 159, p. 193.

18 Dilks, David (ed.), *The Diaries of Sir Alexander Cadogan, OM, 1938–1945*, Cassell, London, 1971, p. 119.

19 Kershaw, Ian, *Making Friends with Hitler: Lord Londonderry and Britain's Road to War*, Allen Lane, London, 2004, p. 27.

20 Kershaw, *Making Friends with Hitler*, p. 27

21 *CPD*, H of R, vol. 159, p. 201.

22 Martin, *Robert Menzies*, vol. 1, pp. 233–36; *CPD*, H of R, vol. 159, p. 201.

23 *CPD*, H of R, vol. 159, pp. 201–202.

24 Hasluck, *The Government and the People, 1939–1941*, p. 108.

25 *CPD*, H of R, vol. 159, p. 199.

26 *CPD*, H of R, vol. 159, p. 203.

27 *CPD*, H of R, vol. 159, p. 209.

28 *CPD*, H of R, vol. 160, p. 1381.

29 *CPD*, H of R, vol. 159, p. 225.

30 *CPD*, H of R, vol. 159, p. 233.

31 *Sydney Morning Herald*, 25 May 1939, p. 11.

32 *Sydney Morning Herald*, 1 June 1939, p. 13.

33 'Lord Keynes', 'The Great Depression in Europe: real GDP data for 22 nations' and 'The Great Depression in Western offshoots: real GDP Data for 4 nations', Social democracy for the 21st century: a post Keynesian perspective (blog), socialdemocracy21stcentury.blogspot.com.au/2013/07/the-great-depression-in-europe-real-gdp.html and socialdemocracy21stcentury.blogspot.com.au/2013/03/the-great-depression-in-western.html.

34 *CPD*, H of R, vol. 159, p. 232.

35 Roberts, Andrew, *The Holy Fox: The Life of Lord Halifax*, Phoenix, London, 1991, p. 163.

36 Dilks (ed.), *The Diaries of Sir Alexander Cadogan, OM, 1938–1945*, p. 188.

37 *Sydney Morning Herald*, 11 July 1939, p. 11.

38 *Sydney Morning Herald*, 12 July 1939 p. 14.

39 Hasluck, *The Government and the People, 1939–1941*, p. 58.

40 Hasluck, *The Government and the People, 1939–1941*, p. 60.

41 *Canberra Times*, 27 June 1939, p. 1.

42 Ross, AT, *Armed and Ready: The Industrial Development and Defence of Australia, 1900–1945*, Turton & Armstrong, Sydney, 1995, pp. 285–93.

43 Ross, *Armed and Ready*, p. 127.

44 *The Argus*, 29 May 1939, p. 1.

45 *The Argus*, 29 May 1939, p. 1.

46 Neale, RG (ed.), *Documents on Australian Foreign Policy, 1937–49*, vol. 2, 1939, AGPS, Canberra, 1976, p. 173.

47 Aarons, *The Family File*, p. 94.

48 *The Age*, 29 August 1939, p. 8.

49 Dilks (ed.), *The Diaries of Sir Alexander Cadogan, OM, 1938–1945*, pp. 212–13.

50 *The Argus*, 26 August 1939, p. 1.

51 *Sydney Morning Herald*, 4 September 1939, p. 11.

52 *CPD*, H of R, vol. 161, p. 40.

53 *The Argus*, 26 September 1939, p. 3.
54 Letter, Robert Menzies to Ken Menzies, 6 December 1939, Menzies family collection.

4 Collective insecurity
1 Shedden, Frederick, Preface, 'Book 3: The notable war record of the Menzies government, 1939–1941', Shedden Collection, NAA, A5954/765/2.
2 Macintyre, *A Concise History of Australia*, p. 191.
3 Macintyre, *A Concise History of Australia*, p. 192.
4 Henderson, Anne, *Joseph Lyons*, pp. vii–x.
5 Henderson, Anne, *Joseph Lyons*, pp. 392–93.
6 Shedden, Frederick, Introduction, 'Book 3: The notable war record of the Menzies government, 1939–1941', Shedden Collection, NAA, A5954/765/3.
7 Edwards, Peter, *Prime Ministers and Diplomats: The Making of Australian Foreign Policy, 1901–1949*, Oxford University Press in association with the Australian Institute of International Affairs, Melbourne, 1983, p. 130.
8 Horner, David, *Inside the War Cabinet: Directing Australia's War Effort, 1939–1945*, Allen & Unwin, Sydney, 1996, pp. 2–3.
9 *The Argus*, 2 January 1940, p. 5.
10 Martin, *Robert Menzies*, vol. 1, p. 293.
11 Menzies to Archie Cameron, 20 October 1939, NLA, MS 4936, Box 582, Folder 31.
12 Cameron to Menzies, 19 October 1939, NLA, MS 4936, Box 582, Folder 31.
13 Cameron to Menzies, 29 January 1940, NLA, MS 4936, Box 582, Folder 31.
14 Cameron to Menzies, 5 February 1940, NLA, MS 4936, Box 582, Folder 31.
15 Henzell, Ted, *Australian Agriculture: Its History and Challenges*, CSIRO Publishing, Melbourne, 2007, p. 18.
16 Quoted in Golding, Peter, *Black Jack McEwen: Political Gladiator*, Melbourne University Press, Melbourne, 1996, p. 78.
17 Horner, *Inside the War Cabinet*, p. 12.
18 Neale (ed.), *Documents on Australian Foreign Policy 1937–49*, vol. 2, 1939, p. 441.
19 Horner, *Inside the War Cabinet*, p. 14.
20 Menzies to Cameron, 5 February 1940.
21 *Sydney Morning Herald*, 8 March 1940, p. 9.
22 *Sydney Morning Herald*, 7 March 1940, pp. 9–10.
23 *The Argus*, 15 March 1940, p. 1.
24 *Sydney Morning Herald*, 7 March 1940, p. 10.
25 Spender, Percy, *Liberalism: Some Thoughts on the Past, Some Thoughts on the Future*, RG Menzies Lecture Trust, Brisbane, 1970, p. 4.
26 Ross, Lloyd, *John Curtin: A Biography*, Macmillan, Melbourne, 1977, p. 194.
27 *Canberra Times*, 20 April 1940, p. 2; *The Argus*, 20 April 1940, p. 5.
28 Hasluck, *The Government and the People, 1939–1941*, p. 179.
29 Lovell, David W & Windle, Kevin, *Our Unswerving Loyalty: A Documentary Survey of Relations between the Communist Party of Australia and Moscow, 1920–1940*, ANU E Press, Canberra, 2008, p. 50.
30 Lovell & Windle, *Our Unswerving Loyalty*, p. 586.
31 *Sydney Morning Herald*, 3 April 1940, p. 13.
32 Lovell & Windle, *Our Unswerving Loyalty*, p. 588.
33 Colebatch, Hal GP, 'Treachery: the Communist Party and the Labor Party', *National Observer*, no. 59, summer 2004, www.nationalobserver.net/2004_summer_112.htm.

34 *Sydney Morning Herald*, 1 January 1940, p. 7.
35 Spratt, Elwyn, *Eddie Ward: Firebrand of East Sydney*, Rigby, Adelaide, 1965, p. 67.
36 Colebatch, 'Treachery'.
37 *Canberra Times*, 20 April 1940, p. 1.
38 *Sydney Morning Herald*, 11 April 1940, p. 9.
39 *The Argus*, 20 April 1940, p. 1.
40 *Canberra Times*, 17 June 1940, p. 2.
41 Blake, 'How Churchill became prime minister', pp. 262–63.
42 Halifax, The Earl of, *Fulness of Days*, Collins, London, 1957, p. 219.
43 Olson, Lynne, *Troublesome Young Men: The Rebels Who Brought Churchill to Power and Helped Save England*, Farrar, Straus and Giroux, New York, 2007, p. 312.
44 Minutes, Australian War Cabinet, Canberra, 8 May 1940, NAA, A5954/46.
45 Neale (ed.), *Documents on Australian Foreign Policy 1937–49*, vol. 3, 1940, Document 215, p. 272.
46 Neale (ed.), *Documents on Australian Foreign Policy 1937–49*, vol. 3, 1940, Document 215, p. 273.
47 Neale (ed.), *Documents on Australian Foreign Policy 1937–49*, vol. 3, 1940, Document 400, p. 454.
48 Neale (ed.), *Documents on Australian Foreign Policy 1937–49*, vol. 3, 1940, Document 420, p. 475.
49 Edwards, *Prime Ministers and Diplomats*, p. 124.
50 *The Courier-Mail*, 29 June 1940, p. 1.
51 Spender, Percy, *Politics and a Man*, Collins, Sydney, 1972, p. 64.
52 Spender, *Politics and a Man*, p. 65.
53 *Sydney Morning Herald*, 10 August 1940, p. 12.

5   War on all fronts

1   Letter, Robert Menzies to Richard Casey, 8 December 1940, Papers of Sir Robert Menzies, NLA, MS 4936, Box 581, Folder 23.
2   Letter, Menzies to Casey, 8 December 1940.
3   Blainey, Geoffrey, *The Steel Master: A Life of Essington Lewis*, Melbourne University Press, Melbourne, 1995, pp. 148–49.
4   Ross, *Armed and Ready*, p. 292. In chapter 10, 'The disorganisation of the aircraft production industry 1939–41', Andrew Ross gives a comprehensive account of the establishment of the Beaufort bomber scheme and its dispute with the CAC, the roles of Harold Clapp and Lawrence Wackett in the dispute, and the internal problems of British involvement in Australian aircraft manufacture in the 1930s and 1940s.
5   *The Argus*, 26 September 1939, p. 3.
6   Souter, Gavin, *Company of Heralds: A Century and a Half of Australian Publishing by John Fairfax Limited and Its Predecessors, 1831–1981*, Melbourne University Press, Melbourne, 1981, p. 185.
7   Souter, *Company of Heralds*, p. 188.
8   Lawson, Valerie, 'Norton, Ezra (1897–1967)', *Australian Dictionary of Biography*, National Centre of Biography, Australian National University, adb.anu.edu.au/biography/norton-ezra-11260/text20085.
9   Letter, Warwick Fairfax to Robert Menzies, 17 July 1941, Papers of Sir Robert Menzies, NLA, MS 4936, Box 582, Folder 39.
10 Letter, Fairfax to Menzies, 29 July 1941, Papers of Sir Robert Menzies, NLA, MS 4936, Box 582, Folder 39.

11 Letter, Robert Menzies to Hugh McClure-Smith, 21 August 1940, Papers of Sir Robert Menzies, NLA, MS 4936, Box 581, Folder 25.

12 'Notes of an interview held on the evening of Monday 27 May 1940, at the office of Mr Kingsley Henderson, between Messrs KA Henderson, JB Aitken and Staniforth Ricketson', Papers of Sir Robert Menzies, NLA, MS 4936, Box 581, Folder 22.

13 Perkins, *Menzies*, p. 50.

14 Letter, Menzies to McClure-Smith, 21 August 1940, Papers of Sir Robert Menzies, NLA, MS 4936, Box 581, Folder 25.

15 *CPD*, H of R, vol. 163, p. 1366.

16 Hasluck, *The Government and the People, 1939–1941*, p. 236.

17 Hasluck, *The Government and the People, 1939–1941*, p. 237.

18 'Notes relative to lobbying preceding conference, May 25th, 1940', Papers of Sir Robert Menzies, NLA, MS 4936, Box 581, Folder 26.

19 Spender, *Politics and a Man*, p. 52.

20 Letter, Percy Spender to Robert Menzies, 12 June 1941, Papers of Sir Percy Spender, NLA, MS 4875, Box 1 'Correspondence'.

21 Spender, *Politics and a Man*, p. 52.

22 *The Argus*, 3 August 1940, p. 1.

23 *The Argus*, 8 August 1940, p. 1.

24 *The Argus*, 30 July 1940, p. 2.

25 *Sydney Morning Herald*, 9 August 1940, p. 6.

26 *Sydney Morning Herald*, 17 August 1940, p. 14.

27 Souter, *Acts of Parliament*, p. 328.

28 Tink, *Air Disaster Canberra*, pp. 172–73.

29 Menzies, *Afternoon Light*, p. 18.

30 Telegram, Bert Evatt to John Latham, Chief Justice, High Court, Melbourne, 2 September 1941, Papers of Sir Robert Menzies, NLA, MS 4936, Box 581, Folder 25.

31 *The Argus*, 14 September 1940, p. 5.

32 Day, David, *John Curtin: A Life*, HarperCollins, Sydney, 1999, p. 384.

33 Letter, Menzies to Casey, 8 December 1940.

34 Letter, Menzies to Casey, 8 December 1940.

35 Letter, Menzies to Casey, 8 December 1940.

6 War at a distance

1 Interview of Geoffrey Blainey by Anne Henderson, Melbourne, 2 March 2013.

2 Olson, *Troublesome Young Men*, p. 258.

3 Olson, *Troublesome Young Men*, p. 257.

4 Neale (ed.), *Documents on Australian Foreign Policy 1937–49*, vol. 4, July 1940 – June 1941, Cablegram 14, p. 325.

5 Wahlert, Glenn, *The Western Desert Campaign 1940–41*, Army History Unit, Canberra, 2006, p. 64.

6 Martin, AW & Hardy, Patsy (eds), *Dark and Hurrying Days: Menzies' 1941 Diary*, NLA Publishing, Canberra, 1993, p. 60.

7 Menzies diary entry, 1 February 1941, *Dark and Hurrying Days*, p. 27.

8 Brett, *Robert Menzies' Forgotten People*, pp. 150–52.

9 Henderson, Anne, *Joseph Lyons*, p. 420; *CPD*, H of R, vol. 157, p. 49.

10 Manchester, William & Reid, Paul, *The Last Lion: Winston Spencer Churchill Defender of the Realm, 1940–1965*, Little, Brown, New York, 2012, p. 423.

11 Quoted in Martin, *Robert Menzies*, vol. 1, p. 316.

12 Neale (ed.), *Documents on Australian Foreign Policy 1937–49*, vol. 4, July 1940 – June 1941, Cablegram 627, p. 285.

13 *The Age*, 30 November 1940, p. 3.

14 Neale (ed.), *Documents on Australian Foreign Policy 1937–49*, vol. 4, July 1940 – June 1941, Document 52, p. 196

15 Gilbert, Martin, *Finest Hour: Winston S. Churchill 1939–1941*, Heinemann, London, 1983, pp. 821–22.

16 Gilbert, *Finest Hour*, p. 822.

17 *Canberra Times*, 21 December 1940, p. 2.

18 Menzies diary entry, 24 January 1941, *Dark and Hurrying Days*, p. 17.

19 Menzies diary entry, 27 January 1941, *Dark and Hurrying Days*, p. 20.

20 Menzies diary entry, 29 January 1941, *Dark and Hurrying Days*, p. 23.

21 Menzies diary entry, 29 January 1941, *Dark and Hurrying Days*, p. 24.

22 Roberts, Andrew, *Eminent Churchillians*, Phoenix, London, 1995, p. 170.

23 Churchill, Winston S, *The Second World War*, vol. 3, *The Grand Alliance*, Cassell, London, 1950, p. 365.

24 Menzies, *Afternoon Light*, p. 64.

25 War Cabinet Conclusions, 24 February 1941, UK National Archives, CAB 65/17/20, p. 102.

26 Day, *John Curtin*, p. 47.

27 Day, *John Curtin*, p. 47.

28 Menzies diary entry, 26 April 1941, *Dark and Hurrying Days*, p. 119.

29 Young, Kenneth (ed.), *The Diaries of Sir Robert Bruce Lockhart*, vol. 1, 1939–1965, Macmillan, London, 1980, p. 93.

30 Charmley, *Churchill*, p. 449.

31 Menzies diary entry, 26 April 1941, *Dark and Hurrying Days*, p. 119

32 Menzies diary entry, 22 April 1941, *Dark and Hurrying Days*, p. 116.

33 Colville, John, *Footprints in Time: Memories*, Collins, London, 1976, p. 129.

34 James, Robert Rhodes (ed.), *Chips: The Diaries of Sir Henry Channon*, Weidenfeld & Nicolson, London, 1967, p. 293.

35 James (ed.), *Chips*, p. 292.

36 Pimlott, Ben (ed.), *The Second World War Diary of Hugh Dalton 1940–45*, Jonathan Cape, London, 1985, p. 163.

37 Day, *John Curtin*, p. 150.

38 Olson, *Troublesome Young Men*, p. 324.

39 Young (ed.), *The Diaries of Sir Robert Bruce Lockhart*, vol. 1, p. 20.

40 Young (ed.), *The Diaries of Sir Robert Bruce Lockhart*, vol. 1, p. 20.

41 Young (ed.), *The Diaries of Sir Robert Bruce Lockhart*, vol. 1, p. 69.

42 Olson, *Troublesome Young Men*, p. 331.

43 Young, Kenneth, *Churchill and Beaverbrook: A Study in Friendship and Politics*, Eyre & Spottiswoode, London, 1966, p. 173.

44 Young, *Churchill and Beaverbrook*, p. 175.

45 Olson, *Troublesome Young Men*, p. 330.

46 War Cabinet Conclusions, 24 February 1941, UK National Archives, CAB 65/21/8, p. 2.

47 War Cabinet Conclusions, 24 February 1941, p. 3.

48 War Cabinet Conclusions, 27 February 1941, UK National Archives UK, CAB 65/21/9, pp. 1–3.

49 Martin, *Robert Menzies*, vol. 1, pp. 325–29.

50 *The Times* (London), 22 April 1941, p. 4

51 Martin, *Robert Menzies*, vol. 1, p. 331.

52 Churchill, *The Grand Alliance*, p. 90.
53 Martin, *Robert Menzies*, vol. 1, p. 329.
54 Menzies diary entry, 21 February 1941, *Dark and Hurrying Days*, p. 62.
55 Wills, Clair, *That Neutral Island: A Cultural History of Ireland During the Second World War*, Faber & Faber, London, 2007, pp. 39–41.
56 Barnard, Ellsworth, *Wendell Willkie: Fighter for Freedom*, Northern Michigan University Press, Marquette, Michigan, 1966, p. 278.
57 War Cabinet Memorandum, 'The Australian war effort', 10 March 1941, UK National Archives, CAB 66/15/28, p. 5.
58 Dilks (ed.), *The Diaries of Alexander Cadogan, OM, 1938–1945*, p. 359.
59 'Note of conversation between AVA [AV Alexander], RG Menzies, et al.', 8 March 1941, Churchill Archives Centre, Cambridge, AVAR 5/5/13.
60 War Cabinet Conclusions, 31 March 1941, UK National Archives, CAB 65/18/12, p. 177.
61 Menzies diary entry, 9 March 1941, *Dark and Hurrying Days*, p. 85.
62 War Cabinet Conclusions, 24 March 1941, UK National Archives, CAB 65/18/10, p. 166.
63 Wills, *That Neutral Island*, pp. 5–6.
64 'Mr Menzies, Australian premier: visit to Ireland', National Archives of Ireland, PRES/1/P 1963.
65 'Mr Menzies, Australian premier: visit to Ireland'.
66 War Cabinet Memorandum, 'Ireland: report of a visit by the Prime Minister of the Commonwealth of Australia', UK National Archives, CAB 66/16/5.
67 Menzies diary entry, 10 April 1941, *Dark and Hurrying Days*, p. 110.
68 Churchill, *The Grand Alliance*, p. 641.

7   Menzies' dark and hurrying day

1   Nicolson, Harold, *The War Years 1939–1945*, Atheneum, New York, 1967, pp. 155.
2   Soames, Mary, *A Daughter's Tale: The Memoir of Winston Churchill's Youngest Child*, Black Swan, London, 2012, pp. 243–44.
3   Sherwood, Robert E, *The White House Papers of Harry L Hopkins*, Eyre & Spottiswoode, London, 1948, p. 239.
4   Menzies diary entry, 21 April 1941, *Dark and Hurrying Days*, p. 116.
5   Menzies diary entries, 3, 4 and 26 March 1941, *Dark and Hurrying Days*, pp. 72, 81, 96.
6   O'Neill, Robert, 'Japan and British security in the Pacific', in Blake & Louis (eds), *Churchill*, p. 282.
7   O'Neill, 'Japan and British security in the Pacific', p. 283.
8   Soames, *A Daughter's Tale*, p. 246.
9   Sherwood, *The White House Papers of Harry L. Hopkins*, pp. 255–56.
10 Nicolson, *The War Years 1939–1945*, p. 154.
11 Colville, John, *The Fringes of Power: Downing Street Diaries 1939–1955*, Weidenfeld & Nicolson, London, 2004, pp. 296–97.
12 Menzies diary entry, 14 April 1941, *Dark and Hurrying Days*, p. 112.
13 Colville, *The Fringes of Power*, p. 293.
14 James (ed.), *Chips*, p. 290.
15 Menzies diary entry, 5 February 1941, *Dark and Hurrying Days*, p. 33.
16 James (ed.), *Chips*, p. 293.
17 James (ed.), *Chips*, p. 298.
18 Pimlott (ed.), *The Second World War Diary of Hugh Dalton 1940–1945*, p. 169.

19 Pimlott (ed.), *The Second World War Diary of Hugh Dalton 1940–1945*, p. 169.

20 Colville, *The Fringes of Power*, p. 313.

21 Day, *Menzies and Churchill at War*, p. 36.

22 Horner, *Inside the War Cabinet*, p. 58.

23 Menzies diary entries, 1–2 March and 31 March 1941, *Dark and Hurrying Days*, pp. 70–71, 99.

24 Hasluck, *The Government and the People, 1939–1941*, pp. 315–17.

25 Day, *Menzies and Churchill at War*, p. 47.

26 Pickersgill, JW, *The Mackenzie King Record*, vol. 1, 1939–1944, University of Chicago Press, Chicago, 1960, pp. 213–14; Diaries of William Lyon Mackenzie King, LAC, www.collectionscanada.gc.ca/databases/king.

27 Menzies diary entry, 11 March 1941, *Dark and Hurrying Days*, p. 87

28 Day, *Menzies and Churchill at War*, p. 91.

29 Menzies diary entry, 11 March 1941, *Dark and Hurrying Days*, p. 87.

30 Fort, Adrian, *Nancy: The Story of Lady Astor*, Jonathan Cape, London, 2012, p. 278.

31 Menzies diary entry, 21 March 1941 *Dark and Hurrying Days*, p. 93.

32 Diaries of William Lyon Mackenzie King, 7 May 1941, LAC, www.collectionscanada.gc.ca/databases/king/001059-119.02-e.php?&page_id_nbr=22654&interval=20£&PHPSESSID=43sa4lv343999vb6hpcn1859o3.

33 Menzies diary entry, 6 April 1941, *Dark and Hurrying Days*, p. 113.

34 Menzies diary entry, 30 April 1941, *Dark and Hurrying Days*, p. 121.

35 Roskill, Stephen, *Hankey, Man of Secrets*, vol. 3, 1931–1963, Collins, London, 1974, p. 501.

36 Martin & Hardy (eds), 'Appendix III: Appraising Churchill', *Dark and Hurrying Days*, p. 159.

37 Eden, Anthony, *Full Circle: The Memoirs of Anthony Eden*, Cassell, London, 1960, p. 447.

38 Menzies diary entry, 28 April 1941, *Dark and Hurrying Days*, p. 120.

39 Day, *Menzies and Churchill at War*, p. 104.

40 Day, *Menzies and Churchill at War*, p. 133.

41 '1941 Diary (Visit to London)', Shedden Collection, NAA, A5954, 16/1. Shedden's sentence in parentheses that a dominion prime minister might lead the Empire in a time of war was omitted from a subsequent draft entitled 'Chapter 30: An appraisal of Prime Minister Menzies in 1941'.

42 Letter, Maurice Hankey to Samuel Hoare, 11 September 1941, 'Correspondence – General', Archives of Lord Hankey of the Chart (Maurice Hankey), Churchill Archives Centre, Cambridge, HNKY 4/33.

43 Letter, Lord Halifax to Maurice Hankey, 25 May 1941, 'Correspondence – Special', Archives of Lord Hankey of the Chart (Maurice Hankey), Churchill Archives Centre, Cambridge, HNKY 5/4.

44 Diaries of William Lyon Mackenzie King, 7 May 1941, LAC, www.collectionscanada.gc.ca/databases/king/001059-119.02-e.php?&page_id_nbr=22654&interval=20£&PHPSESSID=43sa4lv343999vb6hpcn1859o3.

45 Diaries of William Lyon Mackenzie King, 8 May 1941, LAC, www.collectionscanada.gc.ca/databases/king/001059-119.02-e.php?&page_id_nbr=22658&interval=20£PHPSESSID=enallahtf1a62kmrr5tt41ppg1.

46 Henderson, Gerard, 'Menzies and Churchill at war – as told by Aunty', *Sydney Institute Quarterly*, no. 35, June 2009, p. 13.

47 Diaries of William Lyon Mackenzie King, 15 May 1941, LAC, www.collectionscanada.gc.ca/databases/king./001059-119.02-e.php?&page_id_

nbr=22671&interval=20££&PHPSESSID=8vqrgeu7prdn4gm5blp29e2qv0.
48 Young (ed.), *The Diaries of Sir Robert Bruce Lockhart*, pp. 69–70.

8 The enemy within
1 Owen Dixon, Personal Diary, 1941, Papers of Sir Owen Dixon, NLA, MS Acc09.166, Box 9.
2 *Sydney Morning Herald*, 26 May 1941, p. 9.
3 *Sydney Morning Herald*, 26 May 1941, p. 8.
4 *Sydney Morning Herald*, 26 May 1941, p. 8.
5 *The Argus*, 26 May 1941, p. 1.
6 Martin, *Robert Menzies*, vol. 1, p. 365.
7 Spender, *Politics and a Man*, p. 158.
8 Cable, Menzies to Bruce, 13 August 1941, Papers of Sir Robert Menzies, NLA, MS 4936, Box 582, Folder 29.
9 *The Argus*, 26 April 1941, p. 1.
10 D'Cruz, V, 'Menzies' foreign policy, 1939–41: preserving the good life', *Australian Quarterly*, vol. 39, no. 3, September 1967, p. 43.
11 Hasluck, *The Government and the People, 1939–1941*, p. 567.
12 Blainey, *Gold and Paper*, p. 349.
13 Hasluck, *The Government and the People, 1939–1941*, p. 566.
14 *The Argus*, 26 April 1941, p. 1.
15 Menzies diary entry, 7 May 1941, *Dark and Hurrying Days*, p. 124.
16 Hasluck, *The Government and the People, 1939–1941*, p. 429.
17 *CPD*, H of R, vol. 167, p. 17.
18 Hasluck, *The Government and the People, 1939–1941*, p. 495.
19 *CPD*, H of R, vol. 167, pp. 80–81.
20 Hasluck, *The Government and the People, 1939–1941*, p. 280.
21 Hasluck, *The Government and the People, 1939–1941*, p. 492.
22 Henderson, Anne, *Joseph Lyons*, p. 290.
23 *CPD*, H for R, vol. 167 p. 74.
24 Notes by Paul Hasluck for a review of Kevin Perkins' *Menzies: Last of the Queen's Men*, sent to Allan Martin by Nicholas Hasluck, AW Martin Collection, NLA, MS 9802, Box 7.
25 'Most secret 1st September 1941', Papers of Sir Robert Menzies, NLA, MS 4936 Box 583, Folder 44.
26 Spender, *Politics and a Man*, p. 164.
27 Joske, *Sir Robert Menzies 1894–1978*, p. 123.
28 Joske, *Sir Robert Menzies 1894–1978*, p. 122.
29 Hasluck, *The Government and the People, 1939–1941*, p. 533.
30 Hasluck, *The Government and the People, 1939–1941*, p. 533.
31 Interview of Geoffrey Blainey by Anne Henderson, Melbourne, 2 March 2013.
32 Spender, *Politics and a Man*, p. 154.
33 'Notes of an interview held on the evening of Monday 27 May 1940, at the office of Mr Kingsley Henderson, between Messrs KA Henderson, JB Aitken and Staniforth Ricketson', Papers of Sir Robert Menzies, NLA, MS 4936, Box 581, Folder 22.
34 Souter, *Company of Heralds*, pp. 195–99.
35 Hasluck, *The Government and the People, 1939–1941*, p. 528.
36 Pickersgill, *The Mackenzie King Record*, vol. 1, 1939–1944, pp. 216–17.
37 Pickersgill, *The Mackenzie King Record*, vol. 1, 1939–1944, p. 233.
38 Diaries of William Lyon Mackenzie King, 1 August 1941, LAC,

www.collectionscanada.gc.ca/databases/king/001059-119.02-e.php?&page_id_
nbr=23003&interval=20&PHPSESSID=qhp31sq1hhmdeskbcnnvnd5973.

39 Martin, *Robert Menzies*, vol. 1, p. 373.
40 *The Mercury*, 18 July 1941, p. 1.
41 Souter, *Acts of Parliament*, p. 340.

9 On the wings of a phoenix
1 Hasluck, *The Government and the People, 1939–1941*, p. 273.
2 Quoted in Henderson, Heather, *A Smile for My Parents*, p. 65.
3 Quoted in Henderson, Heather, *A Smile for My Parents*, p. 68.
4 Fitzhardinge, LF, *The Little Digger 1914–1952: William Morris Hughes, a Political Biography*, vol. 2, Angus & Robertson, Sydney, 1979, p. 656.
5 Fitzhardinge, *The Little Digger 1914–1952*, vol. 2, p. 655.
6 *Sunday Telegraph*, 31 August 1941 (photo), p. 1.
7 *Canberra Times*, 5 September 1941, p. 4.
8 Letter, Ken Menzies to Robert Menzies, 15 May 1942, Menzies family collection.
9 Henderson, Heather, *A Smile for My Parents*, p. 141.
10 Martin, *Robert Menzies*, vol. 1, p. 399.
11 Henderson, Anne, *Enid Lyons: Leading Lady to a Nation*, Pluto Press, Melbourne, 2008, p. 264.
12 Shlaes, Amity, *The Forgotten Man: A New History of the Great Depression*, HarperCollins, New York, 2007, p. 111.
13 Brett, *Robert Menzies' Forgotten People*, p. 41.
14 Spender, *Politics and a Man*, p. 190.
15 Letter, Robert Menzies to Ken Menzies, 18 February 1943, Menzies family collection.
16 Spender, *Politics and a Man*, p. 200.
17 Fitzhardinge, *The Little Digger 1914–1952*, p. 661.
18 *The Advocate* (Burnie), 7 April 1943, p. 5.
19 *Sydney Morning Herald*, 19 August 1942, p. 7.
20 Reid, Alan, 'Menzies & Curtin reach a parting of the ways', *The Sun* (Sydney), 27 August 1941, p. 5.
21 Hasluck, Paul, *The Government and the People, 1942–1945*, AWM, Canberra, 1970, p. 362.
22 Hasluck, *The Government and the People, 1942–1945*, p. 365.
23 Letter, Robert Menzies to Ken Menzies, 30 June 1943, Menzies family collection.
24 Letter, Robert Menzies to Ken Menzies, 2 September 1943, Menzies family collection.
25 Letter, Robert Menzies to Ken Menzies, 2 September 1943.
26 Letter, Robert Menzies to Ken Menzies, 2 September 1943.
27 Letter, Robert Menzies to Ken Menzies, 13 October 1943, Menzies family collection.
28 Interview of Dame Pattie Menzies by Gerard Henderson, 7 August 1989.
29 Interview of John Paul by Anne Henderson, 6 March 2014.
30 Hancock, Ian, 'Liberal Party of Australia', in Graeme Davison, John Hirst & Stuart Macintyre (eds), *The Oxford Companion to Australian History*, revised edn, Oxford University Press, Melbourne, 2001, p. 390.
31 Henderson, Gerard, *Menzies' Child: The Liberal Party of Australia, 1944–1994*, Allen & Unwin, Sydney, 1994, p. 87.
32 Hasluck, *The Government and the People, 1942–1945*, p. 539.
33 Martin, AW, *Robert Menzies: A Life*, vol. 2, 1944–1978, Melbourne University

Press, Melbourne, 1999, p. 7.

34 Hasluck, *The Government and the People, 1942–1945*, p. 539.

35 Henderson, Gerard, *Menzies' Child*, p. 75.

36 Henderson, Gerard, *Menzies' Child*, p. 85.

37 Hancock, Ian, *The Liberals: The NSW Division of the Liberal Party of Australia, 1945–2000*, Federation Press, Sydney, 2007, p. 53.

38 Hancock, *The Liberals*, p. 57.

39 Hancock, *The Liberals*, p. 58.

40 Letter, Robert Menzies to Ken Menzies, 26 March 1945, Menzies family collection.

41 Letter, Robert Menzies to Ken Menzies, 26 March 1945.

42 Souter, *Acts of Parliament*, p. 376.

43 *The Argus*, 14 September 1946, p. 1.

44 *The Argus*, 17 September 1946, p. 1.

45 *The Argus*, 27 September 1946, p. 1.

46 *Sydney Morning Herald*, 30 September 1946, p. 1.

10 Winning with Menzies

1   Owen Dixon diary entry, 28 January 1947, quoted in Ayres, Philip, *Owen Dixon*, Miegunyah Press, Melbourne, 2003, p. 183.

2   Martin, *Robert Menzies*, vol. 2, p. 61.

3   Quoted in Owen Dixon diary entry, 8 February 1947, quoted in Martin, *Robert Menzies*, vol. 2, p. 62.

4   Hancock, IR, 'Ritchie, Sir Thomas Malcolm (1894–1971)', *Australian Dictionary of Biography*, National Centre of Biography, Australian National University, adb.anu.edu.au/biography/ritchie-sir-thomas-malcolm-11532/text20573.

5   Harper, Marjorie, *Douglas Copland: Scholar, Economist, Diplomat*, Miegunyah Press, Melbourne, 2013, p. 301.

6   Harper, *Douglas Copland*, p. 303.

7   *The Argus*, 2 September 1947, p. 1.

8   *Sydney Morning Herald*, 9 October 1946, p. 1.

9   Crisp, LF, *Ben Chifley: A Biography*, Longmans, Melbourne, 1961, pp. 205–11.

10 Crisp, *Ben Chifley*, pp. 345–47.

11 Blainey, *Gold and Paper*, p. 370.

12 Blainey, *Gold and Paper*, p. 361.

13 Blainey, *Gold and Paper*, p. 365.

14 May, AL, *The Battle for the Banks*, Sydney University Press, Sydney, 1968, pp. 26–29.

15 *The Argus*, 12 September 1947, p. 1.

16 Day, David, *Chifley*, HarperCollins, Sydney, 2001, p. 459.

17 Haylen, Leslie, *Twenty Years' Hard Labor*, Macmillan, Melbourne, 1969, pp. 31–32.

18 *Sydney Morning Herald*, 26 August 1947, p. 5.

19 Crisp, *Ben Chifley*, p. 209.

20 *The Argus*, 24 October 1947, p. 1.

21 *The Argus*, 28 October 1947, p. 1.

22 *The Argus*, 24 October 1947, p. 1.

23 *Sydney Morning Herald*, 13 November 1947, p. 1.

24 *The Argus*, 27 October 1947, p. 1.

25 May, *The Battle for the Banks*, pp. 54–55.

26 Souter, *Acts of Parliament*, p. 388.

27 Day, *Chifley*, p. 468.

28 Henderson, Gerard, *Menzies' Child*, pp. 106–107.
29 Letter, Robert Menzies to Ken and Ian Menzies, 28 June 1948, Menzies family collection.
30 Martin, *Robert Menzies*, vol. 2, pp. 85–86.
31 Letter, Robert Menzies to Ken Menzies, 9 September 1948, Menzies family collection.
32 Fadden, Arthur, *They Called Me Artie: The Memoirs of Sir Arthur Fadden*, Jacaranda Press, Brisbane, 1969, pp. 99–100.
33 Holt, Edgar, *Politics Is People: The Men of Menzies' Era*, Angus & Robertson, Sydney, 1969, p. 95.
34 Henderson, Gerard, *Menzies' Child*, p. 107.
35 *The Herald* (Melbourne), 7 October 1948, p. 4.
36 *The Herald* (Melbourne), 8 October 1948, p. 2.
37 Davey, *The Nationals*, p. 152.
38 Colebatch, Hal GP, *Australia's Secret War: How Unionists Sabotaged Our Troops in World War II*, Quadrant Books, Sydney, 2013, p. 258.
39 Davey, *The Nationals*, p. 157.
40 Hancock, *The Liberals*, p. 75.
41 Hancock, *The Liberals*, pp. 75–76.
42 Martin, *Robert Menzies*, vol. 2, pp. 84–85.
43 *Sydney Morning Herald*, 18 November 1949, p. 1.
44 May, *The Battle for the Banks*, p. 126.

Conclusion: The long peace

1 Spender, *Liberalism*, p. 10.
2 Colebatch, *Australia's Secret War*, pp. 2–3.
3 There are several comprehensive accounts of the Groupers' struggle against the CPA-dominated unions in the 1940s and 1950s. The best is Robert Murray's *The Split: Australian Labor in the Fifties* (Cheshire, Melbourne, 1970).
4 Murray, *The Split*, pp. 145–47.
5 Hasluck, Nicholas, *Paul Hasluck: The War Years*, video and transcript, Papers of Nicholas Hasluck, NLA, nla.ms-vid001155 (MS 8328/9/1).

Bibliography

Letters and primary documents

Menzies family collection
Letters kindly supplied by Heather Henderson.

National Library of Australia
Papers of Sir Richard Casey, NLA, MS 5335.
Papers of Sir Owen Dixon, NLA, MS Acc09/166.
Papers of Nicholas Hasluck, NLA, MS 8328.
Papers of Sir Paul Hasluck, NLA, MS 5274.
Papers of Joseph Aloysius Lyons, NLA, MS 4851.
Papers of Allan Martin, NLA, MS 9802.
Papers of Sir Robert Menzies, NLA, MS 4936.
Papers of Sir Earle Page, NLA, MS 1633.
Papers of Sir Percy Spender, NLA, MS 4875.

National Archives of Australia
Shedden Collection, NAA, A5954.

The University of Melbourne Archives
Papers of William Sydney Robinson, 2001.0070.

Churchill Archives Centre, Cambridge
Papers of AV Alexander, AVAR.
Papers of Sir Alexander George Montagu Cadogan, ACAD.
Diaries/memoirs of Lord Caldecote, INKP.
Papers of Alfred Duff Cooper (1st Viscount Norwich), DUFC.
Diaries/memoirs of Sir Walter Crocker, CRKR.
Papers of Admiral Sir Andrew Brown Cunningham, CUNN.
Diaries/memoirs of Admiral Sir William Davis, WDVS.
Papers of Lord Halifax, HLFX.
Papers of Maurice Hankey, HNKY.
Papers of Sir Horace Seymour, SEYR.

Cambridge University Library
Diary and papers of Viscount Templewood.

London School of Economics
Papers of Hugh Dalton.

Library and Archives Canada
Diaries of William Lyon Mackenzie King, www.collectionscanada.gc.ca/databases/
king.

UK National Archives (Public Records Office)
'1941–1942 Australia, Resignation of Mr Menzies as Prime Minister; and possibility
of standing for Parliament in the United Kingdom', DO 121/50.
War Cabinet Conclusions, CAB 65.
War Cabinet Memoranda, CAB 66.

National Archives of Ireland
'Mr Menzies, Australian premier: visit to Ireland', National Archives of Ireland,
PRES/1/P 1963.

Books

Aarons, Mark, *The Family File*, Black Inc., Melbourne, 2010.
Ayres, Philip, *Owen Dixon*, Miegunyah Press, Melbourne, 2003.
Barker, Elisabeth, *Churchill and Eden at War*, Macmillan, London, 1978.
Barnard, Ellsworth, *Wendell Willkie: Fighter for Freedom*, Northern Michigan
University Press, Marquette, Michigan, 1966.
Beale, Howard, *This Inch of Time: Memoirs of Politics and Diplomacy*, Melbourne
University Press, Melbourne, 1977.
Beaverbrook, Lord, *The Decline and Fall of Lloyd George*, Collins, London, 1963.
Blainey, Geoffrey, *The Steel Master: A Life of Essington Lewis*, Melbourne University
Press, Melbourne, 1995.
—— *Gold and Paper: A History of the National Bank of Australasia Limited*, Georgian
House, Melbourne, 1958.
Blake, Robert & Louis, William Roger (eds), *Churchill: A Major New Assessment of
His Life in Peace and War*, WW Norton & Co., New York, 1993.
Brett, Judith, *Robert Menzies' Forgotten People*, Pan Macmillan, Sydney, 1992.
Bunting, Sir John, *R.G. Menzies: A Portrait*, Allen & Unwin, Sydney, 1988.
Carington, Peter Baron, *Reflect on Things Past: The Memoirs of Lord Carrington*,
Collins, London, 1988.
Carlyon, Norman D, *I Remember Blamey*, Sun Papermac, Melbourne, 1981.
Casey, Lord, *Personal Experience 1939–1946*, Constable & Co., London, 1962.
Charmley, John, *Churchill: The End of Glory*, Hodder & Stoughton, London, 1993.
Churchill, Winston S, *The Second World War*, vol. 3, *The Grand Alliance*, Cassell,
London, 1950.
Colebatch, Hal GP, *Australia's Secret War: How Unionists Sabotaged Our Troops in
World War II*, Quadrant Books, Sydney, 2013.
Collier, Richard, *1941: Armageddon*, Hamish Hamilton, London, 1981.
Colville, John, *The Fringes of Power: Downing Street Diaries 1939–1955*, Weidenfeld
& Nicolson, London, 2004.
—— *The Churchillians*, Weidenfeld & Nicolson, London, 1981.
—— *Footprints in Time: Memories*, Collins, London, 1976.
Crisp, LF, *Ben Chifley: A Biography*, Longmans, Melbourne, 1961.
Crowe, Catriona, Fanning, Ronan, Kennedy, Michael, Keogh, Dermot & O'Halpin,

Eunan (eds), *Documents on Irish Foreign Policy*, vol. VI, *1939–1941*, National Archives, Dublin, 2008.

Cumpston, IM, *Lord Bruce of Melbourne*, Longman Cheshire, Melbourne, 1989.

Davey, Paul, *The Nationals: The Progressive, Country and National Party in New South Wales 1919 to 2006*, Federation Press, Sydney, 2006.

Davison, Graeme, Hirst, John & Macintyre, Stuart (eds), *The Oxford Companion to Australian History*, Oxford University Press, Melbourne, 1998.

Day, David, *Chifley*, HarperCollins, Sydney, 2001.

—— *John Curtin: A Life*, HarperCollins, Sydney, 1999.

—— *Menzies and Churchill at War: A Controversial New Account of the 1941 Struggle for Power*, Angus & Robertson, Sydney, 1986.

——*The Politics of War*, HarperCollins, Sydney, 2003

Dilks, David (ed.), *The Diaries of Sir Alexander Cadogan, OM, 1938–1945*, Cassell, London, 1971.

Downer, Alexander, *Six Prime Ministers*, Hill of Content, Melbourne, 1982.

Dowsing, Irene, *Curtin of Australia*, Acacia Press, Melbourne, 1968.

Eden, Anthony, *Full Circle: The Memoirs of Anthony Eden*, Cassell, London, 1960.

Edwards, Peter, *Prime Ministers and Diplomats: The Making of Australian Foreign Policy, 1901–1949*, Oxford University Press in association with the Australian Institute of International Affairs, Melbourne, 1983.

Ellis, Ulrich, *A History of the Australian Country Party*, Melbourne University Press, Melbourne, 1963.

Fadden, Arthur, *They Called Me Artie: The Memoirs of Sir Arthur Fadden*, Jacaranda Press, Brisbane, 1969.

Fitzhardinge, LF, *The Little Digger 1914–1952: William Morris Hughes, a Political Biography*, vol. 2, Angus & Robertson, Sydney, 1979.

Fort, Adrian, *Nancy: The Story of Lady Astor*, Jonathan Cape, London, 2012.

Frame, Tom, *The Life and Death of Harold Holt*, Allen & Unwin, Sydney, 2005.

Freudenberg, Graham, *Churchill and Australia*, Macmillan, Sydney, 2008.

Gilbert, Martin, *Finest Hour: Winston S. Churchill 1939–1941*, Heinemann, London, 1989.

Golding, Peter, *Black Jack McEwen: Political Gladiator*, Melbourne University Press, Melbourne, 1996.

Halifax, The Earl of, *Fulness of Days*, Collins, London, 1957.

Hancock, Ian, *The Liberals: The NSW Division of the Liberal Party of Australia, 1945–2000*, Federation Press, Sydney, 2007.

Harper, Marjorie, *Douglas Copland: Scholar, Economist, Diplomat*, Miegunyah Press, Melbourne, 2013.

Hasluck, Paul, *The Chance of Politics*, Text, Melbourne, 1997.

—— *The Government and the People, 1942–1945*, AWM, Canberra, 1970.

—— *The Government and the People, 1939–1941*, AWM, Canberra, 1952.

Haylen, Leslie, *Twenty Years' Hard Labor*, Macmillan, Melbourne, 1969.

Hazlehurst, Cameron, Menzies Observed, George Allen & Unwin, Sydney, 1979.

Henderson, Anne, *Joseph Lyons: The People's Prime Minister*, NewSouth Publishing, Sydney, 2011.

—— *Enid Lyons: Leading Lady to a Nation*, Pluto Press, Melbourne, 2008.

Henderson, Gerard, *Menzies' Child: The Liberal Party of Australia, 1944–1994*, Allen & Unwin, Sydney, 1994.

Henderson, Heather, *A Smile for My Parents*, Allen & Unwin, Sydney, 2013.

—— (ed.), *Letters to My Daughter: Robert Menzies, Letters, 1955–1975*, Murdoch Books, Sydney, 2011.

Henzell, Ted, *Australian Agriculture: Its History and Challenges*, CSIRO Publishing, Melbourne, 2007.

Holt, Edgar, *Politics Is People: The Men of Menzies' Era*, Angus & Robertson, Sydney, 1969.

Horner, David, *Defence Supremo: Sir Fredrick Shedden and the Making of Australian Defence Policy*, Allen & Unwin, Sydney, 2000.

—— *Inside the War Cabinet: Directing Australia's War Effort, 1939–1945*, Allen & Unwin, Sydney, 1996.

—— Hudson, W.J., *Casey*, Oxford University Press, Melbourne, 1986.

James, Robert Rhodes (ed.), *Chips: The Diaries of Sir Henry Channon*, Weidenfeld & Nicolson, London, 1967.

Joske, Percy, *Sir Robert Menzies 1894–1978: A New, Informal Memoir*, Angus & Robertson, Sydney, 1978.

Kershaw, Ian, *Making Friends with Hitler: Lord Londonderry and Britain's Road to War*, Allen Lane, London, 2004.

Langmore, Diane, *Glittering Surfaces: A Life of Maie Casey*, Allen & Unwin, Sydney, 1997.

Lee, David, *Stanley Melbourne Bruce: Australian Internationalist*, Continuum, London, 2010.

Long, Gavin, *Greece, Crete and Syria*, AWM, Canberra, 1953.

Lovell, David W & Windle, Kevin, *Our Unswerving Loyalty: A Documentary Survey of Relations between the Communist Party of Australia and Moscow, 1920–1940*, ANU E Press, Canberra, 2008.

Lukacs, Joh, *Five Days in London*, May 1940, Yale University Press, New Haven and London, 1999.

Lyons, Enid, *Among the Carrion Crows*, Rigby Limited, Adelaide, 1972.

Macintyre, Stuart, *A Concise History of Australia*, 3rd edn, Cambridge University Press, Melbourne, 2009.

Martin, Allan W, *Robert Menzies: A Life*, vol. 2, 1944–1978, Melbourne University Press, Melbourne, 1999.

—— *Robert Menzies: A Life*, vol. 1, 1894–1943, Melbourne University Press, Melbourne, 1993.

—— & Hardy, Patsy (eds), *Dark and Hurrying Days: Menzies' 1941 Diary*, NLA Publishing, Canberra, 1993.

May, AL, *The Battle for the Banks*, Sydney University Press, Sydney, 1968.

Menzies, Robert Gordon, *The Measure of the Years*, Cassell, London, 1970

—— *Afternoon Light: Some Memoirs of Men and Events*, Cassell, Melbourne, 1967.

—— *To the People of Britain at War from the Prime Minister of Australia: Speeches Delivered in Great Britain in 1941*, Longmans, London, 1941.

Murray, Robert, *The Split: Australian Labor in the Fifties*, Cheshire, Melbourne, 1970.

Nairn, Bede, *The 'Big Fella': Jack Lang and the Australian Labor Party 1891–1949*, Melbourne University Press, Melbourne, 1986.

Neale, RG (ed.), *Documents on Australian Foreign Policy, 1937–49*, vols 2–4, 1939 – June 1941, AGPS, Canberra, 1976–80.

Nicolson, Harold, *The War Years 1939–1945*, Atheneum, New York, 1967.

Olson, Lynne, *Troublesome Young Men: The Rebels Who Brought Churchill to Power and Helped Save England*, Farrar, Straus and Giroux, New York, 2007.

Page, Earle, *Truant Surgeon: The Inside Story of Forty Years of Australian Political Life*, edited by Anne Mozley, Angus & Robertson, Sydney, 1963.

Perkins, Kevin, *Menzies: Last of the Queen's Men*, Rigby, Adelaide, 1968.

Bibliography

Pickersgill, JW, *The Mackenzie King Record*, vol. 1, 1939–1944, University of Chicago Press, Chicago, 1960.

Pimlott, Ben (ed.), *The Second World War Diary of Hugh Dalton 1940–45*, Jonathan Cape, London, 1985.

Prasser, Scott, Nethercote, JR & Warhurst, John (eds), *The Menzies Era: A Reappraisal of Government, Politics and Policy*, Hale & Iremonger, Sydney, 1995.

Reid, Paul & Manchester, William, *The Last Lion: Winston Spencer Churchill, Defender of the Realm, 1940–1965*, Little, Brown, New York, 2012.

Roberts, Andrew, *Eminent Churchillians*, Phoenix, London, 1995.

—— *The Holy Fox: The Life of Lord Halifax*, Phoenix Giant, London, 1991.

Roskill, Stephen, *Hankey: Man of Secrets*, vol. 3, 1931–1963, Collins, London, 1974.

Ross, AT, *Armed and Ready: The Industrial Development and Defence of Australia, 1900–1945*, Turton & Armstrong, Sydney, 1995.

Ross, Lloyd, *John Curtin: A Biography*, Macmillan, Melbourne, 1977.

Sawer, Geoffrey, *Australian Federal Politics and Law, 1929–1949*, Melbourne University Press, Melbourne, 1963.

Seth, Ronald, *R.G. Menzies*, Cassell, London, 1960.

Sherwood, Robert E, *The White House Papers of Harry L. Hopkins*, vol. 1, September 1939 – January 1942, Eyre & Spottiswoode, London, 1948.

Shlaes, Amity, *The Forgotten Man: A New History of the Great Depression*, HarperCollins, New York 2007.

Soames, Mary, *A Daughter's Tale: The Memoir of Winston Churchill's Youngest Child*, Black Swan, London, 2012.

Sòuter, Gavin, *Acts of Parliament: A Narrative History of the Senate and House of Representatives, Commonwealth of Australia*, Melbourne University Press, Melbourne, 1988.

—— *Company of Heralds: A Century and a Half of Australian Publishing by John Fairfax Limited and Its Predecessors, 1831–1981*, Melbourne University Press, Melbourne, 1981.

—— *Heralds and Angels: The House of Fairfax 1841–1990*, Melbourne University Press, Melbourne, 1991.

Spender, Jean, *Ambassador's Wife*, Angus & Robertson, Sydney, 1968.

Spender, Percy, *Politics and a Man*, Collins, Sydney, 1972.

—— *Liberalism: Some Thoughts on the Past, Some Thoughts on the Future*, RG Menzies Lecture Trust, Brisbane, 1970.

Spratt, Elwyn, *Eddie Ward: Firebrand of East Sydney*, Rigby, Adelaide, 1978.

Starr, Graeme, *Carrick: Principles, Politics and Policy*, Connor Court, Ballan, Victoria, 2012.

Stewart, Andrew, *Empire Lost: Britain, the Dominions and the Second World War*, Continuum, London, 2008.

Taylor, A.J.P., *Beaverbrook: A Biography*, Simon & Schuster, New York, 1972.

Thorne, Christopher, *Allies of a Kind: The United States, Britain, and the War against Japan, 1941–1945*, Oxford University Press, New York, 1979.

Tink, Andrew, *Air Disaster Canberra: The Plane Crash that Destroyed a Government*, NewSouth Publishing, Sydney, 2013.

Wahlert, Glenn, *The Western Desert Campaign 1940–41*, Army History Unit, Canberra, 2006.

Waters, Christopher, *Australia and Appeasement: Imperial Foreign Policy and the Origins of World War II*, IB Taurus, London, 2012.

Wills, Clair, *That Neutral Island: A Cultural History of Ireland During the Second World War*, Faber & Faber, London, 2007.

Young, Kenneth, *Churchill and Beaverbrook: A Study in Friendship and Politics*, Eyre & Spottiswoode, London, 1966.

—— (ed.), *The Diaries of Sir Robert Bruce Lockhart*, vol. 1, 1939–1965, Macmillan, London, 1980.

Ziegler, Philip, *Diana Cooper*, Hamish Hamilton, London 1981.

Articles and papers

Carr, Bob, 'Communism and the labour movement', *Sydney Papers Online*, no. 12, 24 May 2011, www.thesydneyinstitute.com.au/publications/the-sydney-papers-online/page/13.

Colebatch, Hal GP, 'Treachery: the Communist Party and the Labor Party', *National Observer*, no. 59, summer 2004, pp. 52–66, www.nationalobserver.net/2004_summer_112.htm.

D'Cruz, V, 'Menzies' foreign policy, 1939–41: preserving the good life', *Australian Quarterly*, vol. 39, no. 3, September 1967, pp. 38–48.

The Round Table: A Quarterly Review of the Politics of the British Commonwealth, no. 125 (Ninth War Number), December 1941.

Spender, Sir Percy, 'Liberalism – Some Reflections on the Past, Some Thoughts on the Future', Inaugural R.G. Menzies Lecture, 1970.

Newspapers

The Advocate (Burnie)
The Age
The Argus
The Australian
Canberra Times
The Courier-Mail
Daily Telegraph (Sydney)
The Herald (Melbourne)
Irish Times
The Mercury (Hobart)
Sunday Telegraph (Sydney)
Sydney Morning Herald
The Times (London)

Acknowledgments

This book has been some time in progress – and follows on from the work I have done on 1930s Australia around the prime ministership of Joseph Lyons. The Menzies years, between 1939 and 1949, have a direct link to that era. I owe a debt to the published letters and memoirs of Heather (Menzies) Henderson relating to her father, Robert Menzies. In addition, Heather Henderson has given me access to her family collections, along with insights that have helped in a more factual analysis of Sir Robert as a political figure. This material has been invaluable.

Acting on a suggestion from Australia's high commissioner to the UK, Mike Rann, I interviewed Lord Carrington in the House of Lords in January 2013. Peter Carington supplied important perspectives on Robert Menzies in relation to his visit to London in early 1941.

Sydney lawyer Jeff Kildea was helpful in providing contact with Dermot Keogh in Ireland, with respect to Menzies' visit to Dublin in April 1941. Likewise, Professor Carl Bridge, director of the Menzies Centre for Australian Studies at King's College London, assisted regarding additional research at the UK Public Records Office – for which I am grateful to Eureka Henrich, who supplied additional documents.

There is already much published material on Australia in the 1940s. However, discussions with Nicholas Hasluck in relation to his father Paul Hasluck's writings on the period, along with Geoffrey Blainey's account of how the era might now be reassessed, gave me clearer and fresher perspectives. Sydney academic John Barrington Paul was not only an assiduous reader of the manuscript, but also provided a gem of new information on Menzies' state of mind, regarding politics, in early 1944.

In my research, the staff of the National Library of Australia, the National Archives of Australia, the University of Melbourne Archives, the Cambridge Churchill Archives Centre, Cambridge University Library, the London School of Economics, the UK National Archives and the National Archives of Ireland were at all times most helpful and generous.

In the production of this book, I am also extremely grateful for the sponsorship of the photographs and artwork by the Kooyong 200 Club, its chairman John Booth and the Hon. Josh Frydenberg MP, the Member for Kooyong.

As always, I could not have managed without the technical support of the Sydney Institute's Lalita Mathias, assisted by Hannah Kane, Anusha Rutnam, Michael Gemmell, Nathan Lenthen and Rubee King.

Behind the scenes, my husband Gerard Henderson not only read the final manuscript and commented (valuably), but also lent many volumes from his unique and extensive library of Australian politics and history – for which I am very appreciative. After more than forty years of collaboration, his input to my evaluations of Australia's twentieth-century political history is a support I cannot value highly enough.

At NewSouth Publishing, thanks to Phillipa McGuinness, Heather Cam and Nicola Young for their professional guidance as ever.

Index

Index page.

Advance praise for
Menzies at War

'At a personal level how fortunate I am to see this book. It throws light for me on a period in my father's public life of which I could not possibly have had any first-hand experience. At the national level, how fortunate we all are to have an important part of our nation's history recounted in such a professionally researched and objectively recorded way. We owe Anne Henderson a tremendous debt.'

— Heather Henderson, author and daughter of Sir Robert Menzies

---

'*Menzies at War* is a thoughtful contribution to our understanding of Australia's longest-serving prime minister.

A great deal has been written about Sir Robert Menzies's leadership during the post-war period, but little has been written about Menzies' first prime ministership in the midst of a world war.

The lessons that Menzies learned during 1939–41 laid the foundation for the formation of the Liberal Party and a period of leadership that might never have an equal.

On the 75th anniversary of the start of World War II, Anne Henderson's work is a significant addition to Australia's understanding of crucial period in our history and the contribution of our greatest national leader.'

— The Hon Tony Abbott MP, Prime Minister of Australia

'Anne Henderson reminds us of Menzies' many achievements as war leader, including his establishment of Australia's first diplomatic missions in the United States and Japan. A brilliant exposé of a Prime Minister who was an architect of Australia's postwar alliance with the United States, manager of a period of extraordinary economic growth, patron of federal involvement in education and a founding father of the Liberal Party of Australia.'

— The Hon Julie Bishop MP, Minister for Foreign Affairs and federal member for Curtin

———————————

'Anne Henderson has written a brilliant account of ten crucial years – 1939–49 – in the life of Robert Menzies, one of the greatest Australian leaders in the twentieth century. In that decade his political fortunes fell and rose; he helped the world defeat the horror of fascism; he created and led one of the most successful political parties of the period, the Australian Liberal Party; and then he steadfastly confronted the threat of international communism at home and abroad.

Henderson's diligent, original research convincingly debunks many of the myths propagated by psychobabble historians and other members of 'The Academy of the Left'. In particular, her work on Robert Menzies' historic 1941 visit to wartime Britain shows how absurd was the notion that he sought to overthrow and replace Winston Churchill. In the postwar period she demonstrates that Robert Menzies' fear of the Stalinist subversion of the Communist Party of Australia was not some Oedipal paranoia but well grounded in the realities of the time.

This is an important book which will help show how the fashionable scholars who have so long dominated political history writing in Australia – and nearly always sought to diminish if not denigrate Robert Menzies – were wrong, wrong, wrong. He was one of those titans who took part in the creation of the postwar world, and whose convictions and courage have advanced human freedom and prosperity more than at any other time in history. Anne Henderson analyses and describes this all wonderfully well.'

— William Shawcross CVO, author and broadcaster

'Anne Henderson has written a tour de force. With extensive research and penetrating insights *Menzies at War* brings to life the challenges and opportunities that confronted our longest-serving and arguably greatest prime minister Sir Robert Menzies during his first term in office. A must-read for all those interested in this fascinating and vital period in Australia's history.'

— The Hon Josh Frydenberg MP, Parliamentary Secretary to the Prime Minister and federal member for Kooyong